Airlines in
Transition

Airlines in Transition

Nawal K. Taneja
Massachusetts Institute of
Technology

LexingtonBooks
D.C. Heath and Company
Lexington, Massachusetts
Toronto

Library of Congress Cataloging in Publication Data

Taneja, Nawal K
    Airlines in transition.

    Bibliography: p.
    Includes index.
    1. Aeronautics, Commercial. 2. Air lines. I. Title.
HE9776.T36   387.7   80-8735
ISBN 0-669-04345-1

Copyright © 1981 by D.C. Heath and Company

Published simultaneously in Canada

Printed in the United States of America

International Standard Book Number: 0-669-04345-1

Library of Congress Catalog Card Number: 80-8735

Contents

List of Figures

List of Tables

Foreword

Watching the airline industry is not unlike observing Mt. St. Helens. The past few years have been the most turbulent in this industry's history. Record earnings in 1978 have been followed by record losses in 1980. Major realignments in route structures and managements continue. And while all hope for a return in time to a more stable situation, no one dares forecast how that stability will be achieved.

Displaying courage and a high order of analytical skill, Dr. Taneja has entered this stormy scene and produced a work that should be of major assistance to both airline executives and government officials. His treatment of international air-transport problems is particularly illuminating.

Of special note is the pervasive impact of deregulation and its implementation across the entire spectrum of airline management. While no one questions the principles of minimum regulation and maximum competition, one cannot view the current airline picture—national and international—without wondering whether a more thoughtful and perhaps more measured approach would have better served the traveling public. One must also wonder about the arrogance of power on the part of government officials.

The clock cannot, of course, be turned back. However, the new administration should examine the airline situation carefully to see if the process of deregulation can somehow proceed with less wear and tear on people, on relations between nations, and on the economic fiber of a vital industry.

Clifton F. von Kann
Major General, U.S. Army (Retired)
President, National Aeronautic Association

Preface and Acknowledgments

Since the publication of *The Commercial Airline Industry* less than five years ago, airlines have undergone dramatic changes, partly because of deregulation and partly because of rising costs. As a result, I have received numerous inquiries and encouragement from instructors and students about updating the material. *Airlines in Transition* complements rather than replaces *The Commercial Airline Industry*; it provides the reader with an understanding of the rapidly evolving structure of the airline industry. *Airlines in Transition* is primarily directed at advanced-undergraduate and first-year graduate students studying transportation and at airline-management-trainee programs.

Many individuals contributed to the development of this book. I wish to express my gratitude to George James, Lee Howard, and David Swierenga of ATA; Ed Pina and his staff at Boeing; John Feren, William Messecar, and Mark Schlansky of Douglas Aircraft; Denise Duffy and Don Pengelly at IATA; Chris Lyle at ICAO; George Sarames of Lockheed-California; and Harold Shenton at TWA. In addition, colleagues at the Flight Transportation Laboratory of M.I.T. and Flight Transportation Associates, Inc., particularly Stanley Heck, provided valuable comments, and Carolyn, my wife, provided needed encouragement. Ruth Erickson, with the help of Linda Martinez, did an excellent job of typing, editing, and retyping the manuscript; and the staff at Lexington Books saw the manuscript through production. I thank all of them for their assistance.

1 Introduction

The domestic and international commercial airline industries are moving through a transition period that is challenging and demanding. The legislated decrease in the economic regulation by the Civil Aeronautics Board (CAB), combined with escalating fuel prices, high inflation, and interest rates, up- and down-swings in the U.S. economy, and the declining value of the U.S. dollar, have all joined forces to create a new operating and marketing climate. The purpose of this book is to explore the impact these factors have had and will continue to have in shaping the airline industry as it enters the decade of the eighties.

Regulatory Environment

Although the Airline Deregulation Act was not passed until October 1978, the deregulation movement had gained sufficient momentum by 1974, when President Ford asked Congress to establish a commission to investigate the need, role, and impact of regulatory agencies to determine if some agencies might have increased the costs of products and services to the consumer. This request grew out of pressure from the academic community and the business community, both of which were critical of the inefficiencies and lack of innovation in the regulated industries. In these criticisms, the airline industry had been singled out for its lack of competition due to tight control over routes and rates. And the CAB was held responsible for high fares and rates resulting from the protection of inefficient carriers.

Reason for Deregulation

During this period, under the leadership of Senator Edward Kennedy, the subcommittee on Administrative Practice and Procedure of the Senate Judiciary Committee, held hearings on the airline industry and concluded the need for regulatory reform. This conclusion was seconded by an internal CAB study. Supported by Federal Express and Flying Tiger, the airfreight industry exerted strong pressure for deregulation. And P.L. 95-163 did remove virtually all CAB authority over the U.S. air-cargo and combination airfreight operations beginning November 1977.

Despite the introduction of various bills in the House and the Senate, Chairman Alfred E. Kahn could not wait for Congress to act and decided on his own to start reducing CAB control over entry, exit, and pricing in the

U.S. domestic passenger industry. The airlines, initially sceptical of the benefits of deregulation, challenged the theories of the deregulators. Deep discount fares were implemented to demonstrate to the CAB that lower fares could be introduced within a regulated industry. But, realizing the momentum achieved by the deregulation movement, a number of carriers changed positions and began to support deregulation. According to a former chairman of the CAB, the airlines "had to join the deregulators or perhaps go down trying to lick them."[1] The result was the enactment of the Airline Deregulation Act of 1978. According to the current schedule, entry controls and price regulation disappear from the law in 1982 and 1983; the CAB itself is expected to disappear in 1985. Management of the transition has been delegated by Congress to the CAB.

In the international market, the aviation community had been concerned for some time with numerous aspects of the regulatory systems due to a lack of internationally honored policies. These concerns had reached such a critical stage that the International Civil Aviation Organization convened its first Special Air Transport Conference in April 1977 to examine and formulate recommendations on these policy issues. During this two-week conference, attended by more than 450 participants from 110 delegations from around the world, numerous recommendations were made in four areas: tariff enforcement, policy concerning nonscheduled air transport, regulation of capacity in international air transport, and the machinery for the establishment of international air-transport fares and rates.

In the United States, when President Ford's committee was studying the necessary changes to U.S. aviation policy, the British gave notice of their intention to terminate the Bermuda One agreement effective June 1977. The primary reason for the denunciation of the thirty-year-old agreement was the imbalance in commercial activity between the two countries. Britain still favored protectionism while the United States pushed hard for freedom of the air. The subsequent agreement, Bermuda Two, signed on 23 July 1977, represented a compromise providing some protectionism and some liberalism.

The Bermuda Two agreement enabled Laker Airways to enter the North Atlantic market. And it was Laker's entry which, more than any other factor, brought pressure on the incumbent carriers to introduce deep discount fares. However, the Carter administration considered Bermuda Two excessively protectionist and began to formulate U.S. international aviation policy based on free-market competition with the object of achieving a wide variety of service and price options for the consumer. Seven specific policy goals were established to implement the administration's procompetitive policy. Using these policy guidelines, colloquially called "open skies," the United States began negotiating new bilateral agreements, starting with

Mexico (January 1978) and the Netherlands (March 1978). The majority of the international aviation community not only questioned the wisdom of the U.S. policy advocating free-for-all competition but violently objected to its "divide-and-conquer" implementation strategy. In some cases the United States used market leverage to convince recalcitrant countries to accept its policy; in other cases, new route opportunities were exchanged for low fares and multiple designation.

The international aviation community's criticism of U.S. international aviation policy took on new dimensions in June 1978 when the CAB initiated its Show-Cause proceeding which threatened at its outset to prevent multilateral airline tariff discussions. The CAB's case was based on the Sherman Antitrust Act of 1890 which stated that agreements restraining trade or commerce among the states or with foreign nations were illegal. Universal objection to the CAB's unilateral policy to disrupt the global air-transport network and the restructuring of IATA led the CAB to terminate, at least temporarily, its Show-Cause proceeding.

In the meantime, the United States continued to promote its pro-competitive policy in negotiating bilateral agreements and Congress began hearings on the proposed International Air Transportation Competition Act of 1979 to promote competition in the international marketplace. The primary goal of the act, passed in 1980, is to place maximum reliance on competitive market forces to achieve efficient service so that more people will be able to travel to more places at lower prices. In addition, the act contains language that will prevent foreign carriers and their governments from placing unreasonable restrictions on U.S. carriers, resulting in their inability to compete effectively.

Partly because of the sweeping changes introduced and implemented by the United States (ranging from free-capacity determination, liberal bilateral agreements, and partly because of the abortive attempt to dismantle the IATA traffic conference machinery) the international aviation community met once again, in February 1980, at the International Civil Aviation Organization's Second Air Transport Conference. Attendees attempted to find common approaches to resolve the problems affecting air transportation worldwide. Once again delegations from over 100 nations met for two weeks and made numerous recommendations to coordinate government policies on regulation of international air-transport services and the mechanisms for establishing and enforcing international tariffs.

Although the major regulatory changes have taken place either within the United States or with a dozen or so bilateral partners of the United States, other low-fare policies have been implemented over the last few years in a number of short-haul intra-European markets, and in a few long-haul markets between Europe and Africa, India, and Australia. Once again, the impetus for low fares was provided by the threat of Laker even though

British Airways had proposed the implementation of APEX fares long before the arrival of Laker. Using the APEX fare concept, the new Australian international civil-aviation policy has allowed the implementation of new deep discount fares that are competitive with charters or potential new entrants such as Laker. These new fares are negotiated on a bilateral basis with entry, frequency, and capacity limitations.

Both U.S. and Australian policy has created an environment in which low fares can be established outside of the multilateral forum. The international community must therefore decide if either of these two systems is adequate to meet future needs of governments, airlines, and consumers. However, not only must the international air transportation meet more conditions than the availability of low fares, but there is more than one way to achieve low fares. Given the differences in the philosophies, no single policy has worldwide application. In the case of Australia, the isolated geographic location with a tremendous concentration of long-haul routes and ethnic markets makes it possible for scheduled carriers to offer charter-type fares to develop markets. In the United States, an enormous domestic market with efficient airlines makes possible a relatively free market environment. Other countries, with markets limited in size, a large percentage of business traffic, and corporate objectives that go beyond maximization of profits, cannot implement either the U.S. or the Australian policy. The national airlines of the third world fall into this category. Consequently, the only effective and responsible solution for members of the international aviation community is one that is multilaterally based.

Economic Environment

The air-transport industry is influenced as much by the economic environment as by the regulatory environment. And in recent years, the economic environment has changed worldwide, partly as a result of the oil shortages and increasing fuel prices. Since one of the primary objectives of the liberalization of regulatory policies was to reduce fares and rates, it is questionable how much the fares and rates can be lowered at a time when all components of airlines' costs are escalating at a high rate. The proponents of liberalization and free-market philosophy point out that this is the ideal time to free the industry of regulatory controls so that management can decide on the optimal use of scarce resources. The opponents see this time as ideal for an exercise of regulatory constraints to improve airline efficiency and effectiveness. The new Australian international civil-aviation policy is an example of this view. It allows the introduction of low fares through an improvement in productivity, resulting from high load factors and utilization of aircraft. Although both policies are very controversial, proponents and opponents agree that the radically changed economic environment has had and will continue to have a significant impact on the airline industry.

Until the 1970s, and particularly until 1973, major industrialized countries had experienced significant economic prosperity. The OECD countries, for example, had recorded an annual average rate of 5 percent growth in gross national product (GNP) and almost 4 percent in personal disposable income from 1960 through 1973. This economic prosperity had a substantial influence on world trade and tourism, and, in turn, on the development and expansion of the air-transportation industry. Through increasing aircraft productivity (technological improvements) and relatively low operating costs (resulting from low inflation and interest rates, low user charges and low fuel prices), airlines were able to offer low fares and rates. The air-transportation industry went through an enormous expansion phase when benefits from strong economies and low fares and rates were realized.

Since 1973, however, the worldwide economic environment has changed. Between 1974 and 1979, the GNP of OECD nations increased at an annual average rate of about 3 percent. Between the same two periods, inflation increased at an annual average rate of over 9 percent (compared to about 4 percent between 1960 and 1973). The growth rate of disposable income per capita had declined between the two periods. Part of the increase in inflation rate during the 1974 to 1979 period was the result of the enormous increase in the price of aviation fuel. From 1959 through 1973, jet fuel cost was a mere 10 cents per gallon. Fuel price was therefore a relatively unimportant factor in the operation of aircraft. By the end of 1980, the same fuel cost has averaged $1 per gallon in the United States and even more in foreign markets.

Perhaps even more important than deregulation are changes in the world economies that are reshaping the air-transportation industry. High inflation rates in general and the price of fuel in particular have slowed the growth in real incomes and altered the buying habits of passengers and shippers. A large proportion of the discretionary travelers appear, for example, to be willing to accept much lower quality of service in return for lower fares. Such a trend will have a profound influence on future market-strategy planning. Consider also the impact of increased fuel prices on aircraft operations: high fuel prices have made about one-third of the U.S. trunk carriers' aircraft prematurely obsolete economically. And, in order to improve productivity, the industry is moving toward the hub-and-spoke type of network, and the existing carriers are dropping short-haul services some of which are being picked up by commuter carriers and some by new carriers such as Midway.

The slowed growth in the economies, high operating cost, and a change in the composition of U.S. travelers have produced a challenging economic environment for implementation of the new liberalized regulatory policies—

free-for-all competition and lower promotional fares. Since the majority of
nations view their airlines as instruments of foreign policy and integral parts
of their national economies, it is paramount that the international aviation
community establish regulatory policies on a multilateral basis; policies that
not only harmonize divergent national objectives but are consistent with the
changing economic environment.

On the domestic scene, slowdown in the U.S. economy and the continuing fuel price increases have had a significant impact on airline traffic,
capacity, yields, and costs. For the U.S. scheduled industry, 1980 represented
the worst year from the point of view of growth in annual traffic (minus 5
percent) and the third year since 1938 when the industry posted an operating
loss. For 1980 the operating loss is expected to be $200 million, representing
an operating profit margin of minus 0.5 percent. Such a financial performance is a disaster during a year when the industry spent $3.7 billion in new
plant and equipment. Current forecasts of operating profit for 1981 stand
at $750 million, an amount that represents only about one-third of the re-
quired minimum level to meet the capital needs of the industry. Given the
economic and regulatory environments it is time for airlines to reflect on
their present state and to contemplate what lies ahead.

Note

1. S.D. Browne, "The Stormy Air Ocean," in *Air Service in the
1980s—Setting the Stage* (Mexico City: Airport Operators Council International, 30 September 1980), p. 5.

2 Overview of the Industry

U.S. Operations

Classification of Carriers

Historically, there have been eleven different classes of air carriers operating in the United States. These classes were distinguished in general by the operating authority and included domestic trunk carriers, local-service carriers, international and territorial carriers, all-cargo carriers, Alaskan carriers, Hawaiian carriers, helicopter carriers, supplemental carriers, intrastate carriers, commuter carriers, and indirect air carriers. With new legislation, the exact boundaries in carrier classification have been arbitrary. Nevertheless, to provide some continuity during the transition state, the historical classification is maintained in this chapter.

The domestic trunk carriers transport the lion's share of the passenger and freight traffic (table 2-1) and operate primarily within and between the fifty states of the United States over routes serving primarily larger communities with medium and long-stage lengths. The share of traffic carried by the trunk carriers has, however, declined from 95.1 percent in 1960 to 86.5 percent in 1979 (see table 2-2). In 1979, the average length of a passenger trip on domestic trunk carriers was 854 miles, ranging from 1,870 miles for Pan American to 623 miles for Delta. Trunk carriers conduct

Table 2-1
Market Structure, All Services, 1979

	Revenue Ton-Miles (millions)	Percent
Domestic trunks	21,550	62.4
Local service	2,198	6.4
International trunks	7,553	21.9
Domestic all cargo	972	2.8
International all cargo	1,302	3.7
Intra-Alaskan	171	0.5
Intra-Hawaiian	135	0.4
Other	657	1.9
Total	34,538	100.0

Source: Air Transport Association, *Air Transport 1980* (Washington, D.C.: 15 June 1980).

7

Table 2-2
U.S. Domestic Scheduled Traffic History by Class of Carriers
(billions RPMs)

Year	Trunks	Locals[a]	Regional[b]	Intrastate[c]	Total
1960	30.8	1.1	0.3	0.2	32.4
1965	52.6	2.6	0.6	0.6	56.3
1970	95.9	7.4	0.9	1.9	106.1
1971	97.8	7.9	0.8	2.1	108.6
1972	108.2	8.9	1.0	2.2	120.3
1973	115.4	9.8	1.1	2.5	128.8
1974	117.6	10.8	1.3	2.7	132.4
1975	119.4	10.7	1.6	2.9	134.6
1976	131.4	12.1	1.7	3.2	148.4
1977	141.3	13.5	1.8	3.8	160.4
1978	164.2	16.5	2.0	4.6	187.3
1979	180.7	19.9	2.4	5.8	208.8

Source: Lockheed-California Company, "World Air Traffic Forecast 1980," Report no. FEA/2968 (Burbank, California: September 1980).

Note: Domestic includes all traffic within and between the fifty states; also U.S.-Canada transborder traffic. Traffic between mainland and U.S. Virgin Islands and Puerto Rico is classified as international.

[a]Local service carriers.

[b]Intra-Alaska, intra-Hawaii, other airlines not included elsewhere.

[c]Formerly intrastate carriers (until 1979) Air Florida, Air California, Pacific Southwest (PSA), and Southwest.

operations with large aircraft over routes that have relatively high traffic volumes. As of 1980, there are only ten trunk carriers following the merger between Pan American and National Airlines. A list of the domestic trunk carriers in order of revenue passenger enplanements in 1979 and average on-flight passenger trip length is shown in table 2-3. The passenger and stage-length numbers are for domestic operations only. The rank order was distorted in 1979 due to strikes at: United from 31 March 1979 to 27 May 1979; Hughes Air West from 10 September 1979 to 9 November 1979; and Ozark from 14 September 1979 to 4 November 1979.

Local-service carriers operate routes of lesser density between the smaller traffic centers and between those centers and principal centers. Some of these carriers receive subsidy (public-service revenue) for providing service to cities that do not produce sufficient revenue to cover the cost. The name "local-service carriers" is perhaps misleading since the geographic territory of many of these carriers (for example, USAir and Republic) is quite extensive. Due to short stage lengths (averaging about 385 miles) and low-density routes, small equipment is used. However, under deregulation these carriers have capitalized on their favorable fleet and relative strength in short-haul traffic to integrate their route structures, resulting in signifi-

Table 2-3
Domestic Carriers by Size, 1979

Domestic Trunk-line Carrier	Revenue Passenger Enplanements (000)	On-Flight Passenger Trip Length (miles)[a]
Eastern Airlines	42,724	635
Delta Air Lines	40,274	623
United Air Lines	35,373	1,041
American Airlines	31,009	1,040
Trans World Airlines	22,574	1,046
Braniff International	14,353	746
Western Airlines	11,952	823
Northwest Airlines	11,636	862
Continental Air Lines	9,874	917
Pan American World Airways	9,275	1,870
National Airlines	6,582	1,102
Local-Service Carrier		
USAir	14,060	359
Republic	12,031	306
Frontier Airlines	6,539	457
Piedmont Airlines	5,429	353
Hughes Air West	5,045	495
Texas International Airlines	4,441	492
Ozark Air Lines	4,034	385

Source: U.S. Civil Aeronautics Board, *Air Carrier Traffic Statistics* (Washington, D.C.: December 1979), and Air Transport Association, *Air Transport 1980* (Washington, D.C.: 15 June 1980).

[a]Scheduled services.

cant growth and profitability. Table 2-3 shows the current list (1979) of these carriers by size. In 1975 the board changed the status of Air New England from a commuter service to a local-service carrier and, subsequently, to a regional carrier. Since then a number of other regional carriers have initiated service, including: Air Midwest (operating out of Chicago's Midway Airport), Cochise (out of Tucson), and Sky West (out of St. George, Utah).

International and territorial carriers conduct operations between the United States and foreign countries as well as offer services to U.S. territories and possessions. With the exception of United, all domestic trunk-carriers listed in table 2-3 also provide some international and territorial service. With a long-average stage length of almost 2,200 miles, the international and territorial carriers use large aircraft to serve these markets. In recent years, a number of these existing trunk carriers, such as Braniff, Delta, and Northwest, have expanded their network significantly. In addition, scheduled international service is offered by former nonscheduled carriers such as Capitol and World and by former intrastate carriers, such as Air Florida and PSA.

All-cargo carriers are primarily engaged in the transportation of freight. At present there are three U.S. all-cargo carriers. All three, Airlift International, the Flying Tiger Line, and Seaboard World Airlines, are authorized to conduct both domestic and international operations. Recently, Seaboard World has been acquired by Flying Tiger, allowing the latter to offer U.S. domestic, transatlantic and transpacific service. The all-cargo carriers compete actively with the passenger carriers that carry cargo both in passenger aircraft as well as all-freighters. Table 2-1 shows the size of the all-cargo carriers relative to the passenger carriers. The domestic all-cargo carriers account for less than 3 percent of the total revenue ton-miles; international all-cargo carriers, less than 4 percent.

Alaskan air carriers operate completely within the state of Alaska using small- and medium-sized aircraft over medium stage lengths (687 miles average in 1979). At present there are five carriers with Alaska Airlines, which is the largest, having carried over a million passengers in 1979 with an average passenger length of haul of 815 miles. The other carriers are Wien Air Alaska, Kodiak-Western Alaska Airlines, Munz Northern Airways, and Reeve Aleutian Airways. Table 2-1 shows that of the total U.S. scheduled carriers, the Alaskan carriers accounted for about one-half of 1 percent of the total revenue ton-miles.

The Hawaiian carriers' operations are confined to the islands of the State of Hawaii and represent a very small fraction of the total certificated route air carriers. At present there are two carriers offering interisland service in Hawaii. Aloha Airlines and Hawaiian Airlines enplaned 2.97 and 3.80 million passengers in 1979, respectively, with an average passenger stage length of 130 miles.

Helicopter air carriers offer intracity, intra-airport, and city-airport service with extremely short stage lengths. At present, only New York Airways is in operation.

Supplemental air carriers, although initially authorized to conduct unlimited charter services, are now authorized to conduct scheduled operations. And a number of these carriers, such as World and Capitol, are taking full advantage of this newly acquired authority. At present there are eight supplemental carriers. Table 2-4 shows the relative size of each supplemental carrier in terms of revenue passenger-miles and freight ton-miles. Most of the supplemental carriers are fairly active in the transportation of military troops and supplies. For the supplemental industry, nonscheduled passenger operations for the armed forces account for about one-fourth of total activity. In freight, transportation for the military represents almost half of the total activity.

The operations of intrastate carriers in the past were restricted to an area within one state, and the group was not regulated by the board. Instead they were regulated by an agency in their own state. The largest intrastate

Table 2-4
Traffic Statistics of Individual Supplemental Air Carrier (Twelve Months Ending 31 December 1979)

	Nonscheduled Operations			Scheduled Operations		
	Domestic	International	Total	Domestic	International	Total
Capitol International[a]						
Passenger miles (000)	350,801	1,521,911	1,872,712	31,016	225,144	256,160
Freight ton-miles (000)	—	—	—	18	453	471
Evergreen International						
Passenger miles (000)	133,105	389,741	522,846	—	—	—
Freight ton-miles (000)	47,562	341	47,903	—	—	—
Rich International						
Passenger miles (000)	—	—	—	—	—	—
Freight ton-miles (000)	—	7,023	7,023	—	—	—
Transamerica[b]						
Passenger miles (000)	227,374	3,477,975	3,705,349	NA	NA	159,481
Freight ton-miles (000)	174,067	84,375	258,442	NA	NA	703
World[b]						
Passenger miles (000)	159,406	2,330,043	2,489,449	110,402	—	110,402
Freight ton-miles (000)	—	182	182	267	—	267
Zantop International						
Passenger miles (000)	—	—	—	—	—	—
Freight ton-miles (000)	17,831	—	17,831	—	—	—

Source: U.S Civil Aeronautics Board, *Air Carrier Traffic Statistics* (Washington, D.C.: December 1979).
[a]Scheduled domestic and international operations began 1 September 1979 and 1 May 1979, respectively.
[b]Scheduled operations began 1 May 1979.

carrier by far is Pacific Southwest Airlines (PSA) which until recently operated only within California. However, with deregulation, a number of intrastate carriers such as Air Florida and PSA have become interstate and even international carriers.

Over the years, a number of local-service carriers have abandoned the very low density and short-haul markets. Many of these markets have been taken over by commuter air carriers that conduct services according to a published schedule on specific routes. The commuter carriers were not regulated by the board as long as they operated with aircraft that had a gross takeoff weight less than 12,500 pounds. In 1972 the board changed this requirement to thirty seats or 7,500 pound payload unless the operations of larger aircraft were warranted to satisfy the needs of specific markets. And, in 1978, the limits were raised to sixty seats or a payload of 18,000 pounds. In 1979 there were 257 commuter carriers reporting traffic data to the board. Table 2-5 shows a summary of the traffic carried by the commuters during the last ten years.

The twelve months ending December 1970 made up the first year covered by the CAB Form 298-C report; total commuter scheduled passengers in that year were 4.3 million. The total for the twelve months ending on 31 December 1979 represents an average yearly growth rate of 11.1 percent. Scheduled cargo transported increased from 43.5 million pounds in 1970 to 401.6 million pounds in 1978, and decreased to 182.6 million pounds in 1979. Mail transported by commuters increased from 73.5 million pounds in 1970 to a high of 164.7 million pounds in 1975 and has decreased to 13.3 million pounds for 1979. The decrease in scheduled cargo is the result of commuters now reporting their all-cargo operations on Form 291 instead of Form 298-C. As a result, it is estimated that 293 million pounds of cargo was transported by commuters who went from 298 authority to 401 and

Table 2-5
Commuter Air Carrier Traffic Activity

Year	Passengers (000)	Cargo (000 lbs)	Mail (000 lbs)
1970	4,270	43,527	73,479
1971	4,698	51,203	100,683
1972	5,262	74,573	126,177
1973	5,688	92,963	147,796
1974	6,842	138,279	156,293
1975	6,666	169,203	164,682
1976	7,305	216,811	108,597
1977	8,505	271,242	71,395
1978	10,074	401,638	40,122
1979	11,054	182,613	13,341

Source: U.S. Civil Aeronautics Board, *Commuter Air Carrier Traffic Statistics* (Washington, D.C.: 1980).

418 authority.[1] The decline in mail carried reflects the large cutback by the Postal Service in the use of the commuters to carry mail.

In 1979, the commuter-carrier industry served 2,105 passenger city-pair markets; 1,610 of these generated less than ten passengers per day; 318 generated between 10 and 39, and 177 generated 40 or more passengers per day. About two-thirds of the domestic markets were intrastate. The total of 257 commuter air carriers served 824 airports representing 2,450 city-pairs. Of the 225 passenger-carrying commuters, 96 reported an annual volume of under 10,000 passengers, 97 reported between 10,000 and 100,000, and 32 reported more than 100,000 passengers per year. Two carriers in the group enplaned more than 500,000 passengers per year.

Until 1978, the commuter carriers were issued with a certificate of airworthiness complying with the specifications of part 23 (covering general aviation aircraft) of the Federal Aviation Regulations (FAR). However, the increased activity, a need for greater operating flexibility, and an increase in number and diversification of operations led the FAA to examine the need to have part 24 for the certification of commuter type aircraft. Part 24 regulations would have been less stringent than part 25. However, it appears that there were no significant cost savings from certifying an aircraft to part 24 compared to part 25. Therefore, the FAA is seriously considering dropping the adoption of part 24 regulations that would have applied to sixty-or-fewer seat aircraft. Under these circumstances, it is possible that the FAA could incorporate changes to part 25 to accommodate commuter type aircraft. There is a need, for example, to implement changes in regulations relating to aisle width, passenger evacuation, and all-power flight control system.

Historically, indirect air carriers have not actually transported the air freight but have acted as agents between the shipper and the air carrier. Airfreight forwarders are indirect air carriers that conduct business under the exemption authority of the board. An airfreight forwarder collects individual shipments, consolidates them into a large load, and hands it to an airline to fly to a specific city. With deregulation of the airfreight industry in 1977, a number of large airfreight forwarders have expanded to include aircraft operations. This movement started prior to deregulation since some forwarders, such as Emery Air Freight, were not satisfied with the quality and quantity of service provided by the airlines, particularly with freighters. Further discussion of this topic is in chapter 9.

Since deregulation, some new carriers (such as Air Midway) have entered the market while others (such as Air Florida and PSA) have expanded their operations considerably to include intercity transportation. Still others were either commuter carriers (such as Golden West) or supplemental carriers (such as Transamerica and World). All these carriers have so far been classified by the CAB in the "other" category. As of December

1979, the certificated route air carriers included: Air California, Air Florida, Air Midwest, Air Wisconsin, Altair Airlines, Apollo Airways, Aspen Airways, Big Sky Airlines, Colman Air Transport, Golden West Airlines, Mackay International, Mississippi Valley Airlines, New Haven Airways, Pacific Southwest Airlines, Southeast Airlines, Southwest Airlines, Swift Air Lines, Transamerica Airlines, and Wright Air Lines.

Effective 1981, the CAB has regrouped the carriers into four categories. The major trunks are combination carriers with annual revenue over $1 billion. This group consists of the existing trunk carriers and USAir. The second category is the nationals, divided into two classes, combination and specialized. Carriers in this group will have annual revenue between $75 million and $1 billion. The combination group consists of twelve carriers (Air California, Air Florida, Alaska, Aloha, Frontier, Hawaiian, Ozark, Piedmont, PSA, Southwest, Texas International, and Wien) and the specialized group consists of six carriers (Airlift, Capitol, Federal Express, Flying Tiger, Transamerica, and World). The third category is the large regionals with annual revenue between $10 and $75 million. This category has nine combination carriers (Air Midway, Air Wisconsin, Altair, ANE, ASPEN, Golden West, Midway, Reeve, and Swift Air) and six specialized carriers (Alaska International, Evergreen, Midwest, Rosenbaum, Summit, and Zantop). The fourth category consists of small regionals with annual revenue under $10 million. This group is further divided into three categories: combination, all cargo, and charter.

Composite Industry Data

U.S. domestic passenger traffic grew at an annual rate of 12.6 percent during the 1960s and at a rate of 7.8 percent during the 1970s, as a result of strong economic growth and decreasing real fares (table 2-6). The average annual growth during the last two decades was 10.4 percent. During 1980, however, U.S. domestic traffic is not expected to increase over the 1979 level due to a decline in real GNP and a substantial increase in average passenger yield. U.S. domestic passenger traffic accounts for about three-fourths of the total world domestic traffic and about one-third of total world scheduled and nonscheduled traffic (see table 2-6). The other important domestic markets are Far East and South Asia (10 percent), Europe (6 percent), Latin America (5 percent), and Canada (4 percent).

Although the U.S. airlines account for 84.6 percent of the passenger miles of the common carriers, their share of the U.S. passenger miles is only 13.6 percent when the private automobile is included in the total traffic. In terms of passenger travel between the United States and foreign countries, airlines carry well over 90 percent of the passengers. The U.S. international

Table 2-6
ICAO World Air Passenger Traffic 1960 to 1978

	Revenue Passenger Miles (Billions)			Average Annual Growth Rate (%)	
	1960	1970	1978	1960 to 1970	1970 to 1978
U.S. domestic[a]	32.4	106.1	208.8[e]	12.6	7.8[f]
Other domestic	10.9	31.4	74.9	11.2	11.5
Total domestic	43.2	137.4	262.1	12.3	8.4
North Atlantic[b]	6.9	30.0	65.0[e]	15.8	9.0[f]
Trans pacific[c]	1.8	10.0	26.5[e]	18.7	11.4[f]
Western hemisphere	4.2	17.6	31.7	15.3	7.6
Europe[d] Asia/Oceania	2.8	12.4	41.8	16.1[g]	16.4
Intra-Asia/Oceania	1.2	6.2	22.2	16.0	17.4
Intra-Europe[d]	6.7	21.5	53.2	12.4[g]	12.0
Other international	1.0	5.9	19.3	19.5[g]	15.9
Total international	24.7	103.2	244.9	15.4	11.4
Total scheduled	67.9	240.6	507.0	13.5	9.8
Nonscheduled	5.9	52.4	76.7	24.4	4.9
Total scheduled and nonscheduled	73.8	293.0	583.7	14.8	9.0

Source: Lockheed-California Company, "World Air Traffic Forecast 1980," Report no. FEA/2968 (Burbank, California: September 1980).

Note: ICAO world excludes domestic traffic of the USSR and East Germany, but includes Taiwan. Traffic is defined by on-flight origin and destination.

[a]Fifty state basis all years; includes all certificated carriers.
[b]Includes IATA and non-IATA carriers, includes Miami-Europe.
[c]North America-Far East, Oceania.
[d]Includes North Africa and Middle East as part of Europe.
[e]1979 traffic.
[f]1970 to 1979.
[g]Includes Aeroflot traffic 1970 and thereafter but not included in 1960.

trunk lines carry about 44 percent of these passengers. The rest is shared by all the foreign-flag carriers operating to and from the United States.

The average domestic air passenger yield in 1979 was 8.94 cents (11.34 cents for first class and 8.34 cents for coach). Real yield declined by 5.2 percent in 1979 but increased 14.8 percent during the first quarter of 1980 and 12.4 percent during the second quarter of 1980. For the domestic trunk carriers the actual yield increased 25.6 percent between August 1979 and August 1980.

Most of the passenger and cargo traffic is carried in the 2,542 aircraft in the carrier fleet in 1979, consisting of jet aircraft that were purchased in the last two decades, beginning with the Boeing 707/DC-8 type and followed by the smaller two- and three-engine DC-9, Boeing 737, and Boeing 727 types. The 1970s witnessed the introduction of wide-body jets, beginning with the Boeing 747 and followed by the DC-10, Lockheed 1011, and the Airbus. (Approximately one-half of the aircraft in service are more than ten years old (see figure 2-1).) The jet aircraft in the early 1960s reduced the unit operating costs and the wide-body aircraft continued the trend. Successive generations of jet aircraft provided lower operating costs (higher productivity), lower specific fuel consumption (figure 2-2), and lower noise levels (figure 2-3). These trends are expected to continue with the new generation aircraft such as the Boeing 767 and the proposed Douglas DC XX.

The U.S. scheduled airline industry employs over 340,000 persons. Approximately 29 percent of these employees represent aircraft traffic servicing personnel. Other major categories include: office employees (21 percent); mechanics (13 percent); cabin crew (15 percent); and pilots and copilots (9 percent). Labor costs represented, in 1979, 39.9 percent of the trunk and local carriers' operating expenses. In 1979, the average labor cost per employee was $30,033 compared to $11,700 in 1969.

Route Structure

Traditionally, the long-haul, high-density routes have been served by the trunk carriers and short-haul feeder routes by the local-service carriers. The former have always been in favor of dropping their short-haul routes and the latter in favor of picking up longer-haul routes. The process has intensified in the last two years. Since deregulation the local-service carriers have expanded their networks significantly relative to the trunk carriers, many of which have actually reduced their networks. During 1979, United, for example, eliminated a substantial portion of its flights of less than 200 miles, almost dismantled its operational base at Cleveland, and stopped serving major points such as Atlanta and New Orleans. The average passenger-trip length increased between first quarter 1979 and 1980: 1.8 percent for the trunk carriers and 12.3 percent for the local-service carriers. In addition to the change in average length of haul, the industry has increased its focus on the development of hub-and-spoke type networks.

In the United States, scheduled air service is offered in almost 60,000 city-pairs. However, the top 1,000 city-pairs account for about 70 percent of the passenger traffic. Table 2-7 shows the concentration of passenger traffic in the U.S. domestic city-pairs ranked in terms of passenger volume. Less than 2 percent of all city-pairs account for more than 70 percent of the passengers. The densest domestic route in terms of passenger volume is New York-Washington, D.C., which accounts for more than 6,200 passengers daily. These data should be used with caution since they do not contain intrastate traffic. When intrastate traffic is included, the San Francisco-Los Angeles route is probably the densest route in the United States, if not the

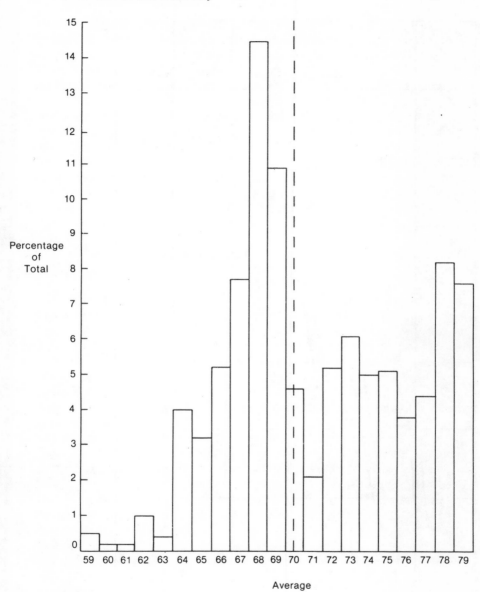

Source: Air Transport Association of America.
Figure 2-1. Percent of Aircraft Fleet by Date of Acquisition

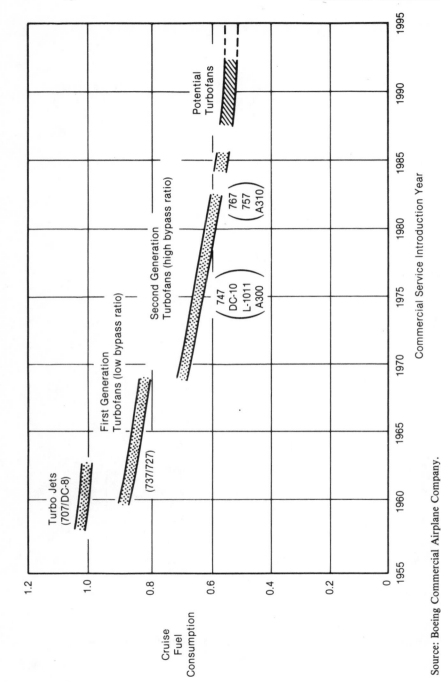

Figure 2-2. Fuel Consumption Improvements

Source: Boeing Commercial Airplane Company.

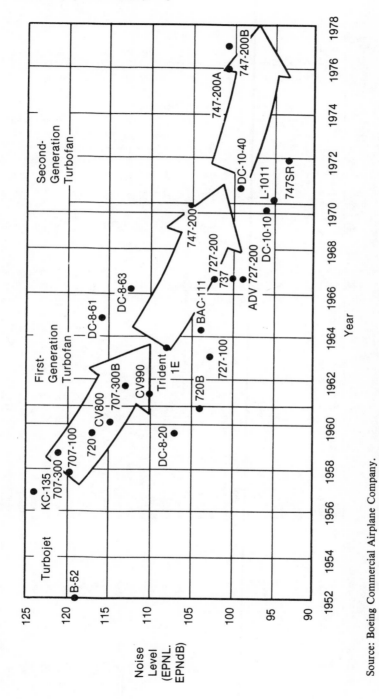

Figure 2-3. Progress in Noise Reduction

Source: Boeing Commercial Airplane Company.

Table 2-7
Concentration of Passenger Traffic in the U.S. Domestic City-Pairs (10 Percent Sample for Twelve Months Ending 30 September 1979)

Rank Passengers	Passenger Miles	City-Pair	Passengers (10 Percent Sample)	Cumulative Percent of Total
1	40	New York-Washington, D.C.	219,604	1.19
2	55	Boston-New York	210,567	2.32
3	1	Los Angeles-New York	207,863	3.45
4	7	Chicago-New York	207,352	4.57
5	3	Miami-New York	195,667	5.63
6	5	Fort Lauderdale-New York	173,200	6.56
7	38	Los Angeles-San Francisco	141,931	7.33
8	2	New York-San Francisco	135,357	8.06
9	4	Chicago-Los Angeles	107,150	8.64
10	327	Honolulu-Lihue, Hawaii	90,424	9.13
20	27	Los Angeles-Seattle	64,309	13.13
30	26	Dallas/Fort Worth-Los Angeles	51,309	16.24
40	71	San Francisco-Seattle	44,593	18.85
50	297	New York-Rochester, New York	39,896	21.09
60	639	Portland, Oregon-Seattle	36,224	23.12
70	472	Reno, Nevada-San Francisco	33,776	25.00
80	123	Dallas/Fort Worth-Denver	30,190	26.72
90	22	Los Angeles-Philadelphia	28,361	28.30
100	91	Fort Lauderdale-Philadelphia	26,187	29.77
200	630	Milwaukee-Minneapolis	15,788	40.44
300	149	New York-San Antonio	10,847	47.45
400	369	Baltimore-Fort Lauderdale	8,615	52.65
500	403	Kansas City, Missouri-Phoenix	7,080	56.85
600	1738	Greensborough, North Carolina-Washington, D.C.	5,761	60.34
700	253	Atlanta-Seattle	5,027	63.25
800	128	Chicago-Kahului, Hawaii	4,355	65.79
900	708	Boston-Jacksonville, Florida	3,821	68.00
1000	1751	Orange County, California-Tucson, Arizona	3,341	69.91

Source: U.S. Civil Aeronautics Board, *Origin-Destination Survey of Airline Passenger Traffic, Domestic*, vol. XI1-3-1, (Washington, D.C.: third quarter 1979), pp. 32-43.

world, in terms of passenger volume. Since deregulation, however, individual city-pair traffic density is changing, partly due to the increase in the hub-and-spoke activity and partly due to the fragmentation of passenger traffic.

Although the board has always encouraged competition, since deregulation the extent of this competition has increased significantly. Table 2-8 shows the extent of competition in the top twenty-five domestic city-pairs. While the total number of competitors in a market varies, the effective number of competitors generally ranges from two to four. In table 2-8, an effective carrier is defined as one that serves at least 10 percent of the total traffic carried by the largest carrier in that market. If this definition is relaxed slightly, then the effective number of carriers increases significantly in some markets. In the transcontinental market, there are more competitors

Table 2-8
Competition in the Top Twenty-Five U.S. Domestic City-Pairs (Twelve Months Ending 30 September 1979)

| | | Number of Competitors | | |
		Total	Effective	Airlines
1	New York-Washington	10	3	AA, BN, EA
2	Boston-New York	5	2	AA, EA
3	Los Angeles-New York	6	3	AA, TW, UA
4	Chicago-New York	6	3	AA, TW, UA
5	Miami-New York	6	3	DL, EA, NA
6	Fort Lauderdale-New York	3	3	DL, EA, NA
7	Los Angeles-San Francisco	8	4	DL, TW, UA, WA
8	New York-San Francisco	6	3	AA, TW, UA
9	Chicago-Los Angeles	4	4	AA, CO, TW, UA
10	Honolulu-Lihue	2	2	HA, TS
11	Detroit-New York	5	2	AA, NW
12	Atlanta-New York	3	2	DL, EA
13	Boston-Washington	6	3	AA, DL, EA
14	New York-Orlando	3	3	DL, EA, NA
15	Honolulu-Kahului	2	2	HA, TS
16	New York-Pittsburgh	4	3	AL, TW, UA
17	Las Vegas-Los Angeles	4	1	WA
18	Chicago-Minneapolis	5	3	NC, NW, UA
19	New York-Tampa	3	3	DL, EA, NA
20	Los Angeles-Seattle	6	3	NA, UA, WA
21	Chicago-Detroit	7	3	AA, NW, UA
22	Cleveland-New York	6	3	AA, TW, UA
23	Honolulu-Los Angeles	6	5	CO, NW, PA, UA, WA
24	Chicago-Washington	5	3	AA, TW, UA
25	Dallas and Fort Worth-New York	4	2	AA, BN

Source: U.S. Civil Aeronautics Board, *Origin-Destination Survey of Airline Passenger Traffic, Domestic*, vol. X11-3-2, (Washington, D.C.: third quarter 1979).
Note: Trunk, local service, and intra-Hawaiian carriers only are included.

than shown in table 2-8. This includes Capitol, Eastern, Pan American, and World. Moreover, TWA is a significant carrier in the Ft. Lauderdale/Miami-New York market, Republic in the Detroit-New York market, PSA in the Las Vegas-Los Angeles market, World in the Honolulu-Los Angeles market, and Air Midway in the Chicago-Washington market.

Economic and Financial Structure

As shown in table 2-1, the combination carriers account for 94 percent of the total revenue ton-miles. Although these carriers are authorized to transport both passengers and cargo, they have concentrated on passenger transportation during the last three decades. Table 2-9 shows that the U.S. domestic trunk carriers derive 88 percent of their revenue from passenger transportation. The corresponding figures for the local-service carriers and the U.S. international trunk carriers are 87.8 percent and 78.5 percent, respectively. Revenue derived from freight, express, and cargo is a very small fraction of the total revenue. For the all-cargo carriers, the largest component of revenue is freight: 92.7 percent for domestic operations and 58.9 percent for international operations. Other components of revenue for the all-cargo carriers are express, mail, and charter.

Since 1977, there has been a significant increase in the proportion of traffic carried at discount fares. For domestic trunk carriers the percentage of total coach traffic traveling on discount fares increased from less than 40 percent in January 1977 to 67 percent in August 1980. On the other hand, reduced fare yield as a percent of the full-fare coach yield has been decreasing since 1977. The combined effect of these two trends has been an increase in the reduced fare revenue as a percent of total coach revenue. For total scheduled operations in August 1980, 35 percent of the total full-fare traffic produced 49 percent of the total revenue while 65 percent of traffic traveling on reduced fares produced 51 percent of the total revenue. On the average the reduced fare passenger received a discount of 43.3 percent.

Table 2-9 also shows the breakdown of operating expenses. For all classes of carriers, the largest component of operating expense is flying operations (36.7 percent) followed by aircraft and traffic servicing (17.1 percent). An examination of the various cost categories shows that the largest increases have been in fuel costs. The domestic trunks paid about 10 cents for a gallon of fuel in 1973 compared to 39 cents in December 1978, 74 cents in December 1979, and 88 cents in July 1980.

Table 2-9 also shows the data on profitability for 1979. The industry posted a profit of $409 million, representing a profit margin on sales of 1.6 percent and rate of return on investment of 7.0 percent. The level of profit during 1979 was considerably lower than the level during 1978 when the

Table 2-9
Operating Revenues, Expenses, and Profit (1979)
($000)

	Total U.S. Scheduled	Domestic Trunk	Local Service	International Trunk	Intra-Alaskan	Intra-Hawaiian	All-Cargo Domestic	All-Cargo International	Other[b]
Operating revenues, total	27,257,195	17,466,701	2,805,391	5,191,457	204,811	179,218	315,552	383,132	690,932
Passenger	22,792,108	15,364,444	2,464,259	4,076,328	101,896	150,639	—	—	634,542
Freight	2,335,864	961,091	110,732	710,441	21,580	4,476	292,394	225,652	9,498
U.S. mail	460,694	267,444	34,775	106,905	21,451	1,237	3,531	23,696	1,655
Express	52,612	45,908	3,991	733	12	—	1,589	—	379
Charter	519,323	148,116	42,434	158,481	3,425	16,764	7,435	122,668	20,000
Public-service revenue	83,579	—	72,388	—	5,047	—	—	—	6,144
Other[a]	255,789	88,742	63,110	97,486	1,643	1,495	155	1,326	1,832
Operating expenses, total	27,041,780	17,550,553	2,674,952	5,105,028	203,325	177,571	306,751	402,911	620,888
Flying operations	9,925,242	6,508,479	954,494	1,795,279	73,388	56,075	129,833	166,610	241,084
Maintenance	3,024,896	1,964,963	323,931	520,806	25,022	23,349	35,997	50,746	84,082
General services and administration									
Passenger service	2,650,548	1,859,552	206,746	530,721	14,234	7,844	5	6,495	24,951
Aircraft and traffic servicing	4,618,589	2,889,541	575,573	819,550	42,942	33,957	83,084	102,481	71,461
Promotion and sales	3,463,810	2,093,203	464,011	765,125	17,079	30,327	16,539	25,521	52,005
Administrative	1,067,675	607,159	130,280	189,361	1,632	14,142	13,275	21,215	90,611
Total	11,800,622	7,449,457	1,376,612	2,319,077	75,888	86,272	112,904	155,713	239,028
Depreciation and amortization	1,678,295	1,084,440	138,334	354,144	9,770	9,426	20,412	25,428	35,565
Net operating income	215,215	(63,852)	130,439	86,429	1,486	1,647	8,801	(19,779)	70,044
Interest expense ($000)	618,822	340,216	90,419	116,605	8,008	7,448	14,946	17,490	23,690
Income taxes ($000)	(165,056)	(161,016)	24,621	(31,596)	1,809	(1,219)	(6,402)	(6,679)	15,426
Net profit or (loss) ($000)	409,246	143,891	95,261	100,757	2,518	2,010	11,224	11,550	62,458
Profit margin on sales (%)	1.6	0.8	3.4	1.9	1.2	1.1	3.6	3.0	8.9
Rate of return on investment (%)	7.0	5.4	12.1	7.9	8.5	11.2	10.6	8.6	n.a.

Source: Air Transport Association, *Air Transport 1980*, (Washington, D.C.: 15 June 1980).

[a]Includes excess baggage, foreign mail, miscellaneous operating revenues, and other transport.

[b]Does not include Apollo, Cochise, Coleman, Mackey, Mississippi Valley, and New Haven.

profit margin was 5.2 percent and return on investment, 13.0 percent. During 1979, the domestic trunks performed considerably worse than local-service carriers, a return on investment of 5.4 percent compared to 12.1 percent. During the first six months of 1980, the ten trunk carriers posted a net loss of $335 million but the seven local carriers plus Air Florida, PSA, and Southwest posted a net profit of $28 million.

Table 2-10 shows the important items in the balance sheet of the industry as well as the individual groups. In each case the largest component of the assets is represented by the flight and ground equipment. The cost value of flight and ground equipment (excluding depreciation) represents 90.6 percent of total assets for the scheduled industry. Long-term debt represented 23.7 percent of the total liabilities and equity for the industry. The high proportion of long-term debt is a major drain on the net operating income of the air carriers. For instance, in 1979, the U.S. scheduled airlines earned a net operating income of $215 million, while the interest on their debt amounted to $619 million. The debt to equity ratio for the trunk carriers had reached a value of around one during the 1977 to 1978 period but then began to increase again. For the local-service carriers, this ratio declined sharply between 1969 (from over six) and 1974 (about two) and has remained stable since then.

The board compensates certain classes of carriers for maintaining service on routes that are inherently unprofitable but nevertheless eligible to receive service under the public-interest concept. The board computes the level of subsidy by forecasting the amount of funds needed for break-even operation of the route, including a reasonable rate of return on investment and income taxes. In 1979, the board recommended payment of $72.4 million for the local-service carriers, $5.0 million for intra-Alaskan carriers, and $6.1 million for other carriers.

Worldwide Operations

Market Size

In 1979 all U.S. carriers combined accounted for 37.9 percent of the total world passenger traffic. Of the remaining 62.1 percent of traffic carried by non-U.S. carriers, the largest share is accounted for by the scheduled services of European carriers. Figure 2-4 shows the historical growth of various components of world passenger traffic. And table 2-11 shows the historical breakdown of world passenger traffic carried by non-U.S. carriers. The share of passenger traffic carried by scheduled operations of European carriers has declined from 37.8 percent in 1960 to 26.9 percent in 1979; and the share of Latin American, Caribbean, and Canadian opera-

Table 2-10
Balance Sheet (1979)
($000)

	Total U.S. Scheduled	Domestic Trunk	Local Service	Intra-Alaskan	Intra-Hawaiian	All Cargo	Other
Assets							
Current assets	6,563,691	5,424,175	700,606	45,891	50,113	209,021	133,885
Investments and special funds	1,194,218	1,051,449	59,463	2,623	1,287	54,798	24,598
Flight equipment	18,610,794	15,781,603	1,626,261	120,349	82,460	506,570	493,551
Ground property and equipment	3,579,164	3,143,664	216,059	44,073	13,583	98,216	63,569
Reserve for depreciation	(9,746,491)	(8,765,370)	(598,589)	(48,790)	(22,942)	(159,829)	(150,971)
Other property	4,410,720	3,506,405	408,763	16,316	41,024	284,234	153,978
Deferred charges	348,965	225,868	102,338	803	2,679	9,148	8,130
Total assets	24,961,063	20,367,795	2,514,901	181,265	168,204	1,002,158	726,740
Liabilities							
Current liabilities	7,070,942	5,931,864	663,426	55,326	55,271	218,789	146,266
Long-term debt	5,778,736	4,227,959	849,242	68,255	67,380	364,963	200,937
Other non-current liabilities	3,156,908	2,662,680	233,239	2,870	14,832	116,303	127,004
Deferred credit	1,459,873	1,342,829	36,979	4,303	4,369	37,136	34,257
Stockholders' equity net of treasury stock	7,494,584	6,202,463	732,015	50,511	26,352	264,967	218,276
Preferred stock	168,676	116,924	47,565	—	50	353	3,784
Common stock	283,109	180,946	28,002	9,697	8,347	37,376	18,741
Other paid-in capital	3,113,265	2,566,438	333,496	15,100	8,452	94,982	94,796
Retained earnings	3,934,664	3,342,268	323,337	26,231	9,511	132,255	101,062
Less: treasury stock	5,128	4,113	385	515	8	—	107
Total liabilities and equity	24,961,063	20,367,795	2,514,901	181,265	168,204	1,002,158	726,740

Source: Air Transport Association, *Air Transport 1980* (Washington, D.C.: 15 June 1980).

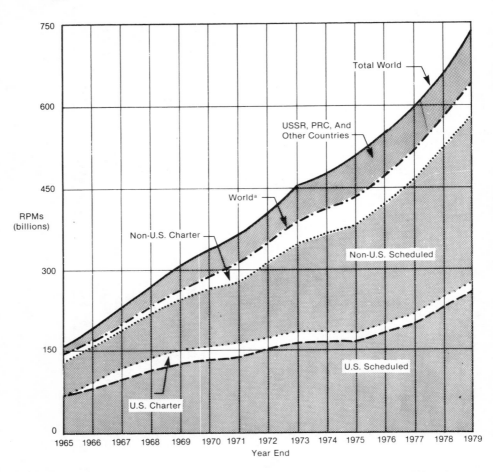

Source: Boeing Commercial Airplane Company, "Dimensions of Airline Growth" (March 1980), p. 18.

[a]Excludes USSR, PRC, and other countries, but includes Taiwan and all-charter carriers.

Figure 2-4. World Total Revenue Passenger Miles

tions decreased from 18.3 percent to 11.2 percent during the same period. Most of the gain in share was experienced by the carriers in Asia and the Pacific, charter operations, and scheduled carriers from the Middle East.

Table 2-12 shows the pertinent information on world air transport operations for the year 1979. The reader is cautioned on two points. First, the data shown in figure 2-4 may not correspond exactly to those shown in table 2-12, as they are derived from two different sources. Second, both sources state that the statistics are preliminary estimates. Given these two

Table 2-11
History of Non-U.S. Airlines' Passenger Traffic

	Revenue Passenger Miles (billions)									
	1960		1965		1970		1975		1979 (est)	
Category	Actual	Percent	Actual	Percent	Actual	Percent	Actual	Percent	Actual	Percent
Scheduled services										
Europe	14.9	37.8	28.3	32.8	53.4	30.0	84.6	26.4	122.6	26.9
Asia and Pacific	4.5	11.4	10.4	12.0	23.0	12.9	54.1	16.9	90.4	19.9
Latin America, Caribbean, and Canada	7.2	18.3	10.9	12.6	20.2	11.3	36.8	11.5	50.9	11.2
Africa	1.2	3.0	2.5	2.9	4.9	2.7	10.1	3.2	15.0	3.3
Middle East	0.9	2.3	2.2	2.5	4.3	2.4	9.3	2.9	20.8	4.6
Subtotal	28.7	72.8	54.3	62.8	105.7	59.3	194.9	60.9	299.6	65.9
Total charter services	3.0	7.7	8.2	9.5	22.5	12.6	48.3	15.0	60.3	13.2
Total non-U.S. carrier	31.7	80.5	62.5	72.3	128.2	71.9	243.1	75.9	359.9	79.1
USSR, People's Republic of China, and other misc. countries	7.7	19.5	23.9	27.7	50.0	28.1	77.1	24.1	94.9	20.9
Total world non-U.S. airlines	39.4	100.0	86.4	100.0	178.2	100.0	320.2	100.0	454.8	100.0

Source: Boeing Commercial Airplane Company, "Dimensions of Airline Growth" (March 1980), pp. 30-31.

Table 2-12
World Air Transport Operations (1979)

Activity	International	Domestic	Total
Passengers carried (000)	158,000	589,000	747,000
Freight tonnes carried (000)	4,185	7,015	11,200
Passenger kilometres (millions)	440,000	617,000	1,057,000
Available seat-kilometres (millions)	688,000	904,000	1,592,000
Passenger load factor (percent)	63.9	68.2	66.4
Tonne-kilometres performed:			
Passenger (millions)	39,860	55,250	95,110
Freight (millions)	18,660	9,150	27,810
Mail (millions)	1,410	2,020	3,430
Available tonne-kilometres (millions)	98,300	111,500	209,800
Weight load factor (percent)	61.0	59.6	60.2

Source: International Air Transport Association, *World Air Transport Statistics* 24 (June 1980):7-9.
Note: Figures include USSR.

qualifications, the reader can glance at the data shown in table 2-12 to get a feeling for the size and type of operations. During 1979, the world airlines carried almost 750 million passengers an average distance of about 1,000 kilometers in domestic markets and about 2,800 kilometers in international markets. Of the total number of passengers carried, about 300 million were carried by airlines of the United States, and about 100 million by the airlines of the USSR.

Traffic share by type of service for the IATA and non-IATA members is shown in table 2-13. The share of traffic carried by IATA members has been declining due to a reduction in membership, primarily airlines from the United States. In 1979, 66.4 percent of total traffic was carried by member airlines of IATA. And since most of the readily available and current data come from IATA, the following information on regional traffic is based on traffic carried by the members of IATA. The North Atlantic is the most important international traffic region in the world, followed by intra-Europe, Europe-Far East, and Europe-Middle East. Table 2-14 shows the relative size of these four and nineteen other international regional traffic bases.

As in the case of U.S. domestic city-pair markets, passenger and freight traffic varies from market to market by orders of magnitude. The high-density routes would include, for example, London-New York, Paris-New York, London-Paris, and Hong Kong-Taipei. As in the case of the United States, there are a number of overseas domestic markets with sizeable passenger traffic. Examples would include Paris-Nice and Tokyo-Osaka. Any statements, beyond these generalizations, would require an indepth analysis of country by country traffic. For example, the top ten markets out of Paris are shown in Table 2-15. There are a number of points worth noting: (1) passenger and

Table 2-13
Traffic Share by Type of Service
(million revenue tonne-kilometers)

IATA Carriers	1975 Volume = 84,047 Percent Share	1979 Volume = 123,040 Percent Share
Scheduled passengers	50.7	46.7
Freight	17.1	15.5
Mail	2.5	1.6
Charter	4.3	2.6
Subtotal	74.6	66.4
Rest of the World		
Scheduled	14.4	25.0
Charter	11.0	8.6
Subtotal	25.4	33.6
Total	100.0	100.0

Source: International Air Transport Association, *World Air Transport Statistics* 24 (June 1980):12.

freight markets do not rank in the same way; (2) the Paris-London market is in the same league as Boston-New York, and New York-Washington, D.C. (top world markets in terms of number of passengers); and (3) five out of the ten markets are domestic. Another way of looking at the passenger traffic in and out of France is to examine the breakdown of passenger traffic handled at the French airports. In 1979, 25.7 percent of the total traffic (about 34 million passengers) was domestic, 41.2 percent within Europe, 14.9 percent Africa, 6.2 percent North America, 3.5 percent South and Central America, and 8.5 percent Orient and Oceania.[2]

For contrast, one can examine the international passenger traffic for Brazil. For its size, relative to the United States and France, Brazil's passenger traffic market is quite small. For example, each of the top ten markets out of Paris generated over 500,000 passengers each year. On the other hand, the top market for Brazil (United States) generated only 406,000 passengers in 1978. Table 2-16 shows Brazil's top twelve international traffic flows. These twelve markets combined generated less than two million passengers, about the size of a single market such as Boston-New York, or Paris-London.

To provide the reader with a broad overview of the diversity of international passenger traffic flows, it is useful to examine the case of trans-Saharan routes. In this region, given the lower economic base (propensity to travel), proliferation of routes and airlines, the traffic bases are relatively small. During 1976, for example, total traffic between Europe and Africa only amounted to 2.6 million passengers. The largest traffic generating routes were located in the West Africa-West Mediterranean region, ac-

Table 2-14
International Regional Operations of IATA Members (1979)

| | Available Tonne-Kilometres (Millions) | | |
| | Scheduled Services | Nonscheduled Services | Scheduled All-Cargo Services |
Route and Areas			
North America-South America	2,495.1	62.9	523.3
North America-Central America	2,311.5	260.8	72.9
North Atlantic	19,674.0	507.7	1,974.4
Mid Atlantic	2,435.9	19.1	47.4
South Atlantic	2,509.9	104.5	250.0
Europe-Northern Africa	2,555.3	300.7	588.8
Europe-Southern Africa	4,085.1	181.3	438.9
Europe-Middle East	5,709.3	503.7	797.3
Europe-Far East (excluding polar route)	6,033.5	94.3	674.5
Europe-Far East (polar route only)	2,373.2	3.9	475.3
Europe-South West Pacific	3,626.5	—	64.2
Middle East-Far East	1,459.6	93.4	287.1
Africa-Far East	292.5	2.9	0.6
North and Mid Pacific	4,426.7	169.3	1,789.9
South Pacific	1,200.7	38.9	46.9
Within North America	1,298.9	54.7	39.7
Within Central America	65.5	2.9	4.6
Within South America	555.4	16.4	32.8
Within Europe	8,340.4	977.6	387.2
Within Africa	406.6	80.0	19.8
Within Middle East	1,500.6	215.2	146.2
Within Far East and South West Pacific	2,937.0	143.0	179.0
Other Routes/Areas	584.1	74.9	5.3
Total	76,877.3	3,908.1	8,846.1

Source: International Air Transport Association, *World Transport Statistics* 24 (June 1980): 22-23.

counting for less than 20 percent of the total traffic (see table 2-17). Other major routes included U.K.-South Africa (9.5 percent), Central Africa-West Mediterranean (7.3 percent), and U.K.-East Africa (7.2 percent). Traffic on these routes, however, is growing at a much faster rate, relative to the more mature routes within Europe and within the United States.

Finally, since Southeast Asia controls some of the world's most popular destinations, it is useful to get an idea of the level of traffic activity in the intra-Orient region. During 1979, the intra-Orient region handled almost 15 million passengers, over 90 percent of which were carried by the eleven members of the Orient Airlines Association. The top ten passenger and freight routes are shown in table 2-18. The regional growth has exceeded the worldwide rate, particularly for freight traffic. Major factors contributing to the recent traffic growth include continued efforts to promote tourism, improved trade, technical, and economic cooperation among the countries in the region, temporary relaxation of restrictions on foreign travel of Chinese residents in Taiwan, and the demand for labor in the Middle East.[3]

Table 2-15
Top Ten Passenger and Freight Markets Out of Paris (1979)

Passenger	Rank	Freight
London	1	New York
Nice	2	London
Marseille	3	Abidjan
Lyon	4	Montreal
New York	5	Chicago
Algiers	6	Tokyo
Toulouse	7	Douala
Geneva	8	Frankfurt
Frankfurt	9	Dakar
Bordeaux	10	Niamey

Source: Institut du Transport Aerien, "Traffic Flows Including Paris in 1979," Bulletin no. 16E (28 April 1980), p. 383.

The Airlines

Figure 2-5 shows the relative size of the airlines of the world. Outside of the USSR, six of the seven largest airlines are from the United States (United, American, TWA, Eastern, Delta, and Pan American); the other one is Britain's flag carrier, British Airways. Each member of this group reported over 20 million passenger miles in 1978. The next group of seven airlines consisted of two from the United States (Western and Braniff), one from Canada (Air Canada), two from Western Europe (Air France and Lufthansa), and two from Japan (Japan Air Lines and All Nippon

Table 2-16
Brazil's International Traffic Flows (1978)
(thousands of passengers: both ways)

Routes	Scheduled	Nonscheduled	Total
Brazil - U.S.	370	36	406
- Argentina	389	12	401
- Portugal	116	4	120
- Federal Germany	78	32	110
- France	106	0	106
- Paraguay	81	4	85
- Italy	79	0	79
- Uruguay	74	0	74
- Spain	73	0	73
- Switzerland	39	18	57
- Chile	54	0	54
- United Kingdom	49	1	50
Total	1,807	114	1,921

Source: Institut du Transport Aerien, "Origin and Destination Brazil: An Overview of Brazil's International Traffic Flows," Bulletin no. 12 (Paris: 24 March 1980), p. 293.

Table 2-17
Europe-Africa Traffic-Generating Centers (1976)
(thousands of passengers)

	Scandinavia/ Benelux	U.K./ Eire	Central Europe	Mediterranean West	Mediterranean East	Total Europe
West Africa	72.5	154.1	90.3	504.8	57.6	879.3
East Africa	70.0	188.3	108.1	47.9	83.9	498.2
Central Africa	63.9	2.2	41.1	191.4	12.5	311.1
Southeast Africa	—	103.3	17.0	137.0	19.4	276.7
South Africa	71.8	248.0	142.0	86.0	106.0	653.8
Total Africa	278.2	695.9	398.5	967.1	279.4	2619.1

Source: Douglas Aircraft Company, *Trans-Saharan Trunk Air Routes* Report no. C1-804-5230 (Long Beach, California: November 1978).

Notes: West Africa = Abidjan, Dakar, Lagos, Douala, Kano, Accra, Ginea-Bissau, Niamey, Bamako, Conakry, Freetown.

East Africa = Nairobi, Khartoum, Addis Ababa, Entebbe, Dar es Salaam, Djibouti, Mogadishu.

Central Africa = Kinshasha, Libreville, Luanda, Brazzaville.

Southeast Africa = Tananarive, Lusaka, Blantyre, Seychelles, Reunion.

East Africa = Johannesburg, Salisbury.

Scandinavia/Benelux = Copenhagen, Amsterdam, Brussels, Oslo, Stockholm.

United Kingdom = London.

Central Europe (including Eastern Europe) = Frankfurt, Hamburg, Dusseldorf, Zurich, Munich, Prague, Moscow.

Western Mediterranean = Paris, Madrid, Lisbon, Nice.

Eastern Mediterranean = Rome, Athens, Milan, Belgrade.

Airways). Other groups, by region of airline domicile, are shown in figure 2-5.

There are two interesting points in figure 2-5. First, many of the airlines in the region of Australia, New Zealand, and Far East have developed into a respectable size considering their relatively late start. Consider, for example, the growth of Korean Airlines and Singapore International Airlines. Korean, beginning operations in late 1962, now ranks with major airlines such as USAir, Varig, and South African Airways. The growth of Singapore Airlines is even more dramatic. Starting in 1972, the carrier now ranks among the world's leading airlines such as SAS and Swissair. The number of airlines in Asia and the Pacific, as well as their growth, explains the gain in their market share (table 2-11). Moreover, the decline in the share of the European carriers results from the fact that the European colonial powers are no longer required to provide air transport services to, from, and within this area to maintain vital communication links. The second point to note is the relative size of the charter carriers. A number of these carriers (Condor, Dan Air, Sterling, and Spantax) also rank among the world's leading scheduled airlines (Sabena, Olympic, Aeromexico, El Al, and Air India). Carrying vacation travelers from the northern to the

Table 2-18
Top Ten Intra-Orient Traffic City-Pairs (1979)

City-Pair	Passengers Number (Both Ways)	City-Pair	Freight Kilograms (Both Ways)
HKG-TPE	1,140,085	HKG-TYO	41,925,711
BKK-HKG	908,378	SEL-TYO	38,920,963
KUL-SIN	945,483	BKK-HKG	28,288,780
TPE-TYO	876,580	TPE-TYO	28,274,353
HKG-TYO	753,647	HKG-TPE	22,727,537
JKT-SIN	748,503	HKG-SIN	18,687,753
SEL-TYO	700,572	SIN-TYO	12,535,888
OSA-TPE	565,720	HKG-SEL	12,492,425
HKG-MNL	538,377	OSA-TPE	11,272,590
BKK-SIN	486,435	JKT-SIN	11,210,893

Source: Orient Airlines Association, "Statistical and Research Report for 1979" (1980).

southern countries in Europe, the European charter airlines have overtaken the scheduled intra-European carriers in terms of passenger traffic handled. This explains the loss of market share for the European scheduled operators and the gain for the charter carriers.

The majority of international airlines are either completely or partly owned by their governments. As a result, their operations reflect a wide spectrum of national interests, some of which extend far beyond the pure economics of the system. And the pursuit of national objectives, ranging from tourism to foreign policy and defense, necessitate the establishment of commercial managerial policies and practices that are in harmony with the national policies. As a result, a number of airlines operate services that are economically not viable and, as such, require state support. The existence of dual objectives, then, makes the operations and their evaluation more complex. And, making profit, although desirable, no longer becomes the ultimate or even an essential goal.

As stated, the extent of government ownership varies from state to state. Many airlines are completely owned by their governments. These include Aeromexico, Air Canada, Air India, Air New Zealand, British Airways, and Qantas. In some cases, the government owns less than 50 percent of the airline. These include Avianca, Japan Air Lines, Mexicana, Pacific Western, and Swissair. Some airlines are privately owned; these include All Nippon, British Caledonian, Varig, and all airlines in the United States. And a few airlines are owned by more than one country; Air Afrique and SAS are examples.

Government ownership has advantages and disadvantages from the viewpoint of airline management. On the positive side, the obvious advantage is a financial one. There are direct and indirect subsidies. The latter include exemption from various taxes, loans that are interest free or guaranteed, generous mail revenues, exemption from customs duty on equipment and parts, and the free use of infrastructure facilities. Moreover,

100,000

AEROFLOT

UNITED AIRLINES

AMERICAN — TWA
EASTERN • PAN AMERICAN
DELTA AIR LINES
BRITISH AIRWAYS

AIR FRANCE

AIR CANADA
LUFTHANSA
WESTERN AIRLINES — BRANIFF
10,000
CONTINENTAL • IBERIA • KLM
NATIONAL • ALITALIA
NORTHWEST
SAS • SWISSAIR

CP AIR

U.S. AIR • CONDOR

RPMs
(millions)

TIA-TRANS INTL.
WORLD AIRWAYS • LAKER • DAN-AIR
HUGHES AIRWEST • OLYMPIC AIRWAYS • SABENA • STERLING • UTA
BRITANNIA
PSA
CAPITOL INTL. FRONTIER • WARDAIR • TAP
• SCANAIR • SPANTAX • BR. CALEDONIAN
FINNAIR
NORTH CENTRAL • AIR INTER • LTU JAT AVIACO
TEXAS INTL. • OZARK • IRISH INTL. • MAERSK • THY
MARTINAIR
PIEDMONT • SOUTHERN AIRWAYS • LOT • BAVARIA
• BA-AIRTOURS • TAROM
• LOFTLEIDIR
PACIFIC WESTERN • SOUTHWEST • CSA HAPAG LLOYD
1,000
• MONARCH • BRAATHENS • TRANSAVIA • BALAIR
AIR CALIFORNIA • INTERFLUG
ALASKA AIRLINES
OVERSEAS NATL. • QUEBECAIR • CONAIR-DENMARK
NORDAIR
FLYING TIGER LINE • AUSTRIAN AIRLINES
• INEX-ADRIA • SOBELAIR • TRANSAIR BR. MIDLANDS
• MALEV • TEA-BELGIUM • ATI
HAWAIIAN AIRLINES • AIR MALTA • TAE-SPAIN
TRANSAIR-CANADA • LINJEFLYG
E. PROVINCIAL • ALOHA TRANSEUROPA-SPAIN • AIR CHARTER INTL. • AIR JUGOSLAVIA • BALKAN-BULGARIA
• AUSTRIAN AT • CYPRUS AIRWAYS • ITAVIA
• AVIOGENEX
SEABOARD WORLD
WIEN AIR ALASKA • KAR-AIR • ICELANDAIR
• EVERGREEN INTL. • EAGLE AIR

AIRLIFT INTL.
• DANAIR/CIMBER
• CAAV
AIR FLORIDA • ALISARDA • LUXAIR • AIR ANGLIA
100

U.S. and Canada   Europe

Source: Boeing Commercial Airplane Company, "Dimensions of Airline Growth" (March 1980), pp. 20-21.

Figure 2-5. Revenue Passenger Miles for Airlines of the World (1978): Grouped by Region of Airline Domicile

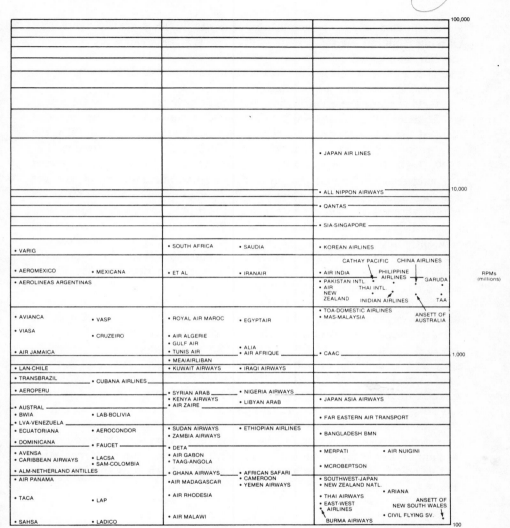

Figure 2-5 *(continued)*

states can also help in the acquisition of desirable fleets, traffic rights, and training facilities. On the negative side, there is state interference with commercial managerial policies and policies relating to employment, investment, routes, and rates. The degree of involvement and the value of net benefits varies from state to state.

Having made the qualification that profit may not always be the essential goal for all international airlines, let us examine briefly the financial state of the world scheduled airline industry. Between 1974 and 1978, the net profit margin had increased from −0.2 percent to 4.1 percent. For 1979, the IATA member carriers achieved a return, after interest, of minus 1.6 percent on investment and minus 1.0 percent on revenue. Total revenues and operating expenses for the year 1979 amounted to $70.5 and $69.8 billion, respectively. On the revenue side the problems related to lower than expected growth in traffic (resulting from the sluggish international economy) and the resistance to fare increases (resulting from political and market pressures). On the cost side, the escalating fuel price continues to be a major problem. And uncoordinated government policies have simply added to the complexity of the problem.

Third-level carriers, as in the case of the United States (commuter and air-taxi operators), have experienced significant growth on a worldwide basis in recent years. And their role and industry characteristics, in general, are also similar to those described for the United States, with respect to stability, concentration, market size and composition, average length of haul, and the type of aircraft in the fleet. However, within each country, there are marked differences with respect to the number, size, and operating environment. For example, in Germany and the Netherlands, the role of these carriers is much more complementary to that of the national flag carriers; the network of the third-level and national carriers is established jointly. A comparative study of the third-level carrier activities and their regulation in five countries is given in an extensive study published by the Institut de Transport Aerien in 1979.[4]

Route Structure

The route networks of international carriers fall within one of three categories: hub and spoke, line, and grid. Intra-European routes are examples of the hub-and-spoke networks where numerous capitals are served from a single capital. The line network is simply a number of different segments connected like a chain. The routes of Air New Zealand and Singapore Airlines are examples of this type of network. Finally, the grid network represents routes interconnected in a self-contained region. Domestic routes of Garuda Indonesian Airways and routes of Indian airlines are examples of grid networks.

Each type of route network has advantages and disadvantages. The hub-and-spoke network can have directional imbalance, low utilization, low load factors, and severe operational difficulties in inclement weather situations at the hub. On the other hand, station density can be reasonably high. The line type of network can produce high utilization but low load factors, low station density, and severe directional imbalance. The grid type of network represents a compromise, no great advantages and no great disadvantages.

In addition to traffic flows and route economics, international route patterns are a function of numerous other considerations such as bilateral agreements, pooling agreements, and the requirement for a national airline to fly a politically desirable route. Most international routes have been negotiated through bilateral agreements based on the principle of Bermuda One, and a few have been negotiated through a multilateral process. In recent years, the regulatory system for the negotiation and operations of international routes has come under severe attack. Problems have arisen as a result of unfair advantage resulting from the transportation of fifth and sixth freedom traffic, diverse national interests and national attitudes to traffic rights, volume and complexity of scheduled operations, the growth and regulation of charter operations, and the proliferation of national airlines.

Pooling represents commercial arrangements to control frequency and capacity to avoid the side effects of excessive competition. In theory, the object is to rationalize schedules, expand the marketing base, and avoid excess capacity and predatory pricing. The proponents claim that pooling arrangements provide better service at lower prices. The opponents claim the reverse, that is, poor service at higher prices. There is, of course, no way to conclusively prove or disprove either claim. It will suffice to say here that there is an element of truth to both claims and the merits of the arguments of each side depend on the routes and airlines under examination.

Finally, the shape of international route patterns is also a function of the decision on the part of the government to force its national airline to operate certain routes that are politically or socially desirable. In the case of an airline that is wholly or partly owned by the government, this requirement is usually not a problem. In the case of a private airline, the government is normally required to pay a subsidy if the route under discussion is not self-sufficient.

Charter Operations

It was shown in table 2-13 that on a worldwide basis charter (or nonscheduled) operations accounted for 11.2 percent of the revenue tonne-kilometres performed in 1979. For the non-U.S. carriers, charter services represented 13.2 percent of total revenue passenger miles (see table 2-11). Moreover, on a regional basis, charter operations are even more significant than on a worldwide basis. Within Europe, for example, based on passenger mile, charter operations account for more than half of the total passenger traffic. On the basis of passengers carried, charter operations account for about 40 percent of the total activity. The other important area of charter activity is the North Atlantic market. Since their beginning during the 1950s, charter operations have become an important and integral component of the total world air transport industry. This growth in charter activity and its maturity reflects the public's increasing awareness of the availability of low-cost air transportation and the general relaxation of government-instituted rules regarding the conditions of charter operations relative to scheduled operations.

Historically, the major charter traffic flows within Europe have been to Spain from the United Kingdom, Germany, Scandinavia, Belgium, and the Netherlands. Recently, some countries have been added to the list as generation centers (see table 2-19) and many more countries (Portugal, Morocco, Tunisia, Malta, Italy, Yugoslavia, Greece, Rumania, and Bulgaria) have become destination centers.

Since the development of the Inclusive Tour Charter (ITC) concept, there has been a continuous debate about the dilution of traffic carried by the scheduled carriers. There are two points worth mentioning: First, many of the destinations served by both types of carriers were originally identified, developed, and marketed by the charter carriers. Second, most of the European national carriers have their own charter subsidiaries which compete actively in the charter market. Recall the relative sizes of Condor, BA Airtours, and Sobelair (figure 2-5). These carriers are wholly-owned subsidiaries of Lufthansa, British Airways, and Sabena. And they are competing not only with the low-fare services offered by the scheduled industry but also with privately-owned charter airlines such as Happag-Lloyd, Sterling Airways, Spantax, and Dan Air. The age-old argument of charter versus schedule carriers must therefore be treated very carefully.

Table 2-19
ITC Flows to Spain Exceeding 100,000 Passengers (1978)

United Kingdom	4,678,400
Germany (FR)	3,792,300
Scandinavia	2,187,800
Netherlands	1,263,000
Belgium	610,100
France	506,800
Switzerland	340,400
Finland	319,500
Ireland	195,800
Austria	112,900

Source: Institut du Transport Aerien, "ITC Traffic in the Europe-Mediterranean Region," Bulletin no. 3 (Paris: 21 January 1980).

Summary

The Airline Deregulation Act of 1978 has made the boundaries and roles of different categories of airlines less clear. Domestic trunk and local-service carriers are rationalizing their networks; intrastate carriers have become interstate and even international carriers; charter carriers are now offering scheduled service; and some freight forwarders own and operate their own aircraft. The bulk of the traffic (62 percent) is still carried by the domestic trunk carriers. Using over 2,500 aircraft and over 340,000 employees, the U.S. airlines offer scheduled air service on some 60,000 city-pairs. The top 1,000 city-pairs account for about 70 percent of the passenger traffic. While the actual number of carriers in a market varies from two to ten, the effective number of competitors generally ranges from two to four.

Although the combination carriers are authorized to transport both passengers and cargo, they have concentrated on passenger transportation. For example, in 1979, the domestic trunks derived almost 88 percent of their revenue from passenger transportation. In August 1980, 65 percent of the total domestic trunks' passenger traffic was carried at discount fares (a discount of 43 percent) and produced 51 percent of the total passenger revenue. The domestic trunks show total assets of 20.4 billion, the cost value of flight equipment (excluding depreciation) represented about 77 percent of the total assets. In 1979 the long-term debt represented almost 21 percent of the total liabilities and equity for the domestic trunk carriers. These carriers netted a 5.4 percent rate of return on investment, a figure considerably below other industries with comparable risk characteristics. During the first six months of 1980 the trunks posted a net loss of $335 million while the locals, including three former intrastate carriers, made a net profit of $28 million. The cost of fuel and the downturn in the economy are the major factors contributing to the financial loss experienced by the trunks.

On a worldwide basis, the U.S. carriers combined accounted for 37.9 percent of the total world passenger traffic. Of the remaining 62.1 percent, the largest share was accounted for by the European carriers. During the last two decades significant gain has been made in the share of traffic carried by the charter carriers, and scheduled carriers in Asia and the Pacific, Africa, and the Middle East. A number of charter airlines and relatively new scheduled carriers (such as Singapore Airlines) now rank with the world's leading airlines. On a regional basis, although the North Atlantic and intra-Europe still maintain the top two positions in terms of traffic activity, routes to and from the Middle East, Africa, South America, and the Pacific are becoming more significant.

During 1979, the financial health of the international industry was extremely poor, resulting from a weak international economy, high cost of fuel, and political and market pressures to keep fares low. And, uncoordinated government policies have simply added to the complexity of the problem. On the other hand, given the diversification of national objectives and policies, making profit, although desirable, is not always the ultimate or even an essential goal for a number of airlines.

Notes

1. K.B. Creddy, "Commuters Provide Vital Link to Worldwide Destinations," *Commuter Air* (15 October 1980), p. 15.

2. Institute of Air Transport, "Medium-Term Forecasts for Traffic at the Paris Airports," Bulletin no. 12 (Paris: 24 March, 1980).

3. Orient Airlines Association, "Statistical and Research Report," 1980.

4. J. Plaignand, et al., *Third Level Activities and Their Regulation* (Paris: Institut du Transport Aerien, 1979).

3 International Aviation

Since 1920 the aviation system has developed from a fledgling industry to a worldwide business contributing to trade, tourism, communications, and international relations. During 1979, the world's more than 200 airlines carried almost 750 million passengers (flying the flags of 143 states), more than 11 million tons of freight, and 8 billion pieces of international mail. The industry's financial performance, particularly recently, has been dismal. For 1979, the world's scheduled airlines (excluding People's Republic of China (PRC) and USSR domestic) posted an operating profit of about $700 million on a revenue of $70 billion. On a net-profit basis the industry experienced a loss. The IATA member carriers achieved a return, after interest, of minus 1.6 percent of investment and minus 1.0 percent of revenue, and the results for 1980 are expected to be worse. This recent poor financial performance is the result of political pressures to reduce fares and rates, negative GNP growth, and soaring operating and nonoperating costs, a substantial portion of which are not within the airlines' control. These include fuel, interest, landing fees, and charges for use of en route navigational facilities. The financial equation is becoming incredibly difficult to solve and, unless it is solved, public interest will undoubtedly be undermined in the long run.

There is a divergence of opinion on the direction of future development for the industry. The minority view, held by the United States, is for elimination of government intervention in the industry, either as a regulator or direct participant. More specifically, U.S. policy is one of uncontrolled competition and elimination of IATA's coordination activities. The majority view is not for more direct government participation but for controlled competition through multilateral cooperation. The proponents of this view believe that, given the different mix of economic, social, and political philosophies around the world, the only realistic way of achieving divergent national objectives is through multilateral cooperation. This chapter provides an overview of the progressive changes to the international regulatory system and discusses some of the recently proposed structural changes designed to meet the challenge of the eighties.

Historical Background

International air transport, as we know it today, began after World War I to meet the needs of official travel after the cessation of hostilities. There were, however, many other factors that provided impetus for the rapid development of the system. These included: (1) the aggressiveness of aircraft manufacturers in finding new markets for aircraft no longer needed for war; (2) the realization by businessmen of the possibilities of faster transport and communications; (3) the desire of ex-military men to continue using their aviation skills; (4) the realization by some government officials of the benefits of aviation with respect to national prestige and national prosperity; and (5) the enormous enthusiasm and fascination with flight of the early pioneers.[1]

Toward the end of World War II, the international community began to realize that the future development of the industry depended on multilaterally negotiated solutions to the economic and regulatory problems. At the Chicago Conference in 1944, an attempt was made to create a multilateral framework to allow the development of commercial air-transportation services by international airlines. At the conference, the British and United States delegations presented the most divergent views on the means of establishing commercial worldwide air routes. The British were in favor of strict regulation, while the United States stressed the need for and the advantages of free competition with the multilateral grant of all five freedoms, without any restrictions of frequencies or capacities. Given the opposing nature of these two views and the inability of the delegations to agree on the fifth-freedom issue, the attempt to negotiate a multilateral agreement on control of competition failed. However, the delegations did agree on a number of important issues. It was agreed, for example, that nations had some right to commercial traffic originating in or destined for their own territories. Since it was impossible to reach a decision on a common multilateral form for establishing principles of shared fifth-freedom traffic, this aspect was left for bilateral negotiation. Finally, it was agreed that there was a need to regulate international fares and rates; the establishment of a mechanism to effect this was left to the airlines themselves.

Because of the failure to develop a multilateral framework at the Chicago Conference, the development of international air-transport services was stalled just after the war. Since the disagreement was primarily between Great Britain and the United States, these two nations attempted to reach a compromise at the Bermuda Conference held in 1946. The attempt was successful when the United Kingdom retreated from its insistence on strict restrictions on capacity and frequency in exchange for letting IATA's traffic-conference machinery establish fares and rates to be recommended to the government for approval. On the issue of fifth-freedom traffic rights, both parties agreed to let the airlines determine the level of capacity offered in relation to the various types of traffic that an airline might carry. Such a compromise provided a fair and equal opportunity for both sides without unduly affecting either party as a result of unreasonably low fares or overscheduling of capacity.

The Bermuda agreement provided the fundamental basis for most of the postwar scheduled route exchange agreements. Through this bilateral process, each nation attempted, to the extent possible, to take advantage of the traffic potential of the points granted in each country. Normally each nation advocated the double-tracking doctrine and attempted, although not always successfully, to provide a fair and equal opportunity for the carriers of the contracting parties. However, in negotiation of each bilateral agreement there were numerous points to be considered, some aeronautical and some totally unrelated to the industry. Consequently the final agreement did not always represent a realistic horse trade and was on occasion more like a horse-for-a-rabbit trade.

In the United States, presidents have always had an active interest in international aviation. As a result, formal policy statements have been issued since 1954 to clarify executive goals and objectives. The first policy statement, although not formal, was issued by President Roosevelt in 1943, calling for limited regulated competition, government subsidy (if necessary), execution of traffic agreements through a bilateral process, and CAB authority to control international fares and rates. President Eisenhower reinforced the need for bilateral agreements in the absence of a multilateral framework for negotiating routes and the need for government authority to resolve fare and rate problems arising from either the inadequate functioning of the IATA machinery or the absence of the IATA forum. President Kennedy proposed continuation of the bilateral regulatory framework on the assumption that a multilateral approach was impractical. However, President Kennedy's policy required the government to obtain adequate access to the market by the U.S. carriers. President Nixon once again advocated the continuation of bilateral agreements but also called for promotion of an environment in which both scheduled and charter carriers had a fair and equal opportunity to compete. The role of the IATA machinery for coordination of fares and rates was reconfirmed.

From President Roosevelt (1943) through President Nixon (1970), U.S. international aviation policies more or less reiterated guidelines with no drastic change with respect to regulation of routes, fares, and rates. However, from just after World War II to the end of 1974, the performance, conduct, and market structure of the international airline industry had changed dramatically. For example, the aircraft had evolved from the piston-engine type to the Boeing 747 with substantial increases in speed and capacity; a number of former colonies had become independent and, for reasons of independence, politics, prestige, and, in a few cases, economics, established their own airlines; the charter industry had made significant inroads in the marketplace; and the price of aviation fuel had increased substantially with the OPEC oil embargo in 1973. As a result, President Ford issued a policy statement calling for implementation (to the extent possible) of U.S. domestic regulatory reform in the international arena.

About the same time that President Ford's steering committee was reviewing the necessary changes to U.S. aviation policy, the British announced their intention to terminate the Bermuda One agreement, effective June 1977. There were many reasons for this decision, but the primary complaint related to the excessive capacity offered by U.S. carriers in the U.S.-U.K. markets (imbalance in commercial activity) and the policies and practices of the CAB in disapproving IATA negotiated fares and rates at the last minute.[2] Bermuda Two, signed on 23 July 1977, represented a compromise that provided some protectionism and some liberalism. Neither the British nor the U.S. carriers as a whole were totally pleased with this agreement but given the desire for continued commerce, both nations viewed the agreement with cautious satisfaction, despite the necessity for mutual compromise. Some new carriers were allowed to enter the market under the new agreement but they were required to submit schedules to their governments for prescreening. By contrast, Bermuda One provided only for an ex post facto review of capacity. Additionally, while the new agreement confirmed the need to obtain government approval of proposed fares and routes, it did not preclude the development of these proposals through the IATA machinery. It should be emphasized that it was the Bermuda Two agreement that allowed Laker to enter the market, and it was Laker's entry that provided the initial impetus for even lower fares on the North Atlantic.

The preceding points highlight briefly the problems and solutions relating to the exchange of commercial rights through 1977. However, magnitude, complexity, and structure of the international airline industry changed so dramatically from 1944 through 1977 that numerous complaints arose about the existing regulatory framework. It was clear from past experience that it was unrealistic to assume that a unique multilateral system could be developed to resolve all the problems. An attempt was made, therefore, on a multilateral basis, to find solutions to the most pressing problems. The result was the sponsorship of a number of international air-transport meetings, the first two of which have already taken place.

ICAO's SATC One

The International Civil Aviation Organization convened its first Special Air Transport Conference (SATC) on 13 April 1977 to examine and formulate recommendations on the following four items: tariff enforcement; policy concerning international nonscheduled air transport; regulation of capacity in international air-transport services; and machinery for the establishment of international air-transport fares and rates. Each of these was of extreme concern to the international air-transport community; 450 conference participants from 110 delegations met for two weeks in Montreal to formulate recommendations on the type of regulation most conducive to the development of an economically stable and efficient international air-transport system, a system that satisfies the varying needs of users throughout the world. However, in view of the periodic difficulties encountered in attempting to find a unique multilateral solution to various problems voiced by the states against the system, the participants decided beforehand to concentrate on the four critical areas.

Tariff Enforcement

In the international air-transport industry the violation of government-approved fares and rates has been a common problem. This is due to the existence of excessive competition (among scheduled carriers and between scheduled and nonscheduled carriers), relatively poor financial performance, the existence of excessive capacity, and the existence of complex fare and rate structures. Under these circumstances many carriers and intermediaries have resorted to violation of approved and coordinated fares and rates in order to gain temporary benefits in share of the market and traffic loads. These malpractices, estimated to run in "losses" of hundreds of millions of dollars, have tended to raise the costs for some users, resulting in the decline in traffic in those categories and, ultimately, to an even greater degree of tariff violations.

Over the years many forms of tariff violations have been practiced. In the background documentation prepared by the secretariat of ICAO, the following were listed as the more common forms of tariff violations:

Passenger Traffic

Selling affinity group tickets to persons not qualified for membership in a group in accordance with IATA Resolution 045 (this was one of the most frequent forms of tariff violation in the past, but it has been largely eradicated by the introduction of advance purchase non-affinity group fares).

Selling charter tickets after flights are fully booked with the knowledge that passengers will be allowed to travel at the charter rate on scheduled flights later.

Upgrading passengers or tickets to a higher class of service without extra charge.

Failure to charge for excess baggage (this is sometimes done on a systematic basis for all full-fare paying passengers).

Selling tickets at full price, but extending passengers a cash refund, usually on arrival at foreign point in a give-away travel bag.

Selling tickets at full one-way fare, with return tickets available at destination at greatly reduced rate, possibly on selected airlines and through designated travel agents.

Improper use of validation stickers (for instance for the purpose of extending the time limits of excursion fares).

Rebate on ticket price by means of a credit arrangement in which no effort is made to collect the outstanding balance.

Rebates to "youth" passengers disguised as compensation for completion of questionnaire in order to circumvent the elimination of youth fares on certain routes.

Gifts, VIP lounges and other preferential treatment for officials, friends, relatives and other favored passengers without full compensatory charges.

Coupon booklets given free of charge entitling the holder to discounts for various purchases and ground services.

IATA agents disposing of their tickets to non-IATA agents at a rebate. (This may be done when an IATA agent is short of the passenger quota required to obtain the higher commission rates applicable to volume sales—in such cases, he may abandon his commission completely on the number of tickets required to achieve his quota.)

Travel agents selling airline seats at "tour-basing fares" directly to individual members of the public without obliging them to pay for the associated ground accommodation. This practice is sometimes followed by tour operators with an over-supply of tour programmes.

Selling ITX and GIT tickets to non-IATA agents who combine them with worthless ground arrangements for sale at a discount to passengers interested solely in the transportation part of the tour.

Selling inclusive tour tickets with the cost of the ground arrangements to be later refunded.

The purchase abroad by agents of tickets in currencies devalued after the date of tariff agreement for resale in home market at a discount from the local prevailing prices. (For example, tickets may be purchased in lire in Italy for Geneva-New York travel when they should have been paid for in Swiss francs, Geneva and Milan being common-rated for New York).

Airlines providing retail agents with tour folders intended for wholesalers. (Retail agents may then print or stamp their name in the space provided and qualify for larger wholesaler commission on which there are at present no industry agreed limits.)

Airlines selling tickets with false price markings (a $200 ticket is sold to an agent for $100 who sells it to the passenger for $150).

Selling counterfeit, stolen or misappropriated airline tickets at a discount.

Unauthorized free transportation and other services extended to agents by airlines.

Merchandise incentive programmes provided for travel agents by airlines.

Passengers and Freight Traffic

Selling air transport (passenger or freight) to agents at regular prices, but giving rebates by devious means—sometimes through deposits made in foreign bank accounts.

Airlines paying secret commissions to major industrial and commercial clients to secure their business.

Abnormally favorable credit terms extended by airlines to certain commercial accounts.

Freight Traffic

Airlines accepting freight shipments without verifying weights.

Accepting freight shipments at weights less than the minimum weight required for the particular commodity classification rates or applicable quantity rebates.

Ignoring the cubic measurements of low-density shipments and charging them by weight.

Stretching commodity classifications to include shipments not corresponding to the description.

Not charging for pick-up, delivery or applicable demurrage or container charges.

Airline rebates to pick-up and delivery operators that promote their service.[3]

Many of the preceding tariff violation problems have been the subject of ICAO assembly resolutions and council study since 1962. At that time the violations had increased significantly, due partly to the financial problems resulting from the introduction of the jet aircraft. Since then the assembly had adopted and revised resolutions asking the contracting states and IATA to strengthen their tariff-enforcement machinery. Although most states require the filing and approval of tariffs for international air transportation, many of these states had encountered problems in enforcing the approved tariffs. According to the survey conducted by ICAO, enforcement problems related to complexity of the tariff structure, frequency of open-rate situations for scheduled carriers, the unregulated environment for the nonscheduled carriers in a number of states, the existence of a number of non-IATA carriers, difficulty in obtaining sufficient and necessary evidence of violation, the lack of sufficiently trained investigators, and, in some cases, the inadequacy of national laws and regulations concerning the activities of carriers and their intermediaries.

Since 1951, IATA has had its Compliance (previously known as the Enforcement) Office enforce the rules and regulations which its members had agreed to and adopted with the approval of their governments. The effectiveness of the IATA system has, however, been limited. To begin with, the IATA compliance system has no jurisdiction over nonmembers or over agreements negotiated outside of its traffic conferences. Furthermore, not only does the association not have a sufficiently large, qualified enforcement staff, but there is not sufficient coordination and cooperation with the national offices and agencies concerned. Finally, not only are the tariffs complex but there have been many open-rate situations. The association urged the governments to take appropriate action to supplement its compliance machinery.

In light of these difficulties many contracting states had recommended that ICAO play a greater role in the enforcement of international tariffs. More specifically, a number of states provided the following suggestions for possible actions by ICAO:

a) intensification of present role of studying aspects of tariff violation, disseminating information to Contracting States, and urging them to take appropriate action;

b) monitoring tariff compliance by collecting data on revenue yields by region and drawing the attention of States to abnormal variations;

c) development of a standard tariff clause for bilateral agreements including the provision of penalties for malpractice;

d) regional coordination of tariff enforcement procedures, including the adoption of recommendations for implementation by regional organizations for their member governments;

e) development of guidelines or international standards and recommended practices on tariff enforcement for use or application by States on a worldwide basis;

f) amendment of the Chicago Convention to provide for penalization of violations of approved tariffs;

g) appointment of ICAO agents to check tickets and airline records;

h) establishment of an international body or procedures to monitor the enforcement of tariffs through officials of national administrations with powers to examine carrier records and determine penalties;

i) involvement in the establishment of international tariffs and in arbitration in cases of difference as to their application.[4]

In addition to the possible action by ICAO, the conference made the following specific recommendations relating to the problem of tariff enforcement:

that States make the violation of such tariffs punishable by deterrent penalties;

that States ensure that active and effective machinery exists within their jurisdiction to investigate tariff violations by airlines, passenger and freight agents, tour organizers and freight forwarders and take necessary corrective measures including penalties on a consistent and uniform basis;

that States whose airlines are members of IATA support the existing IATA compliance system with respect to members of that Association;

that States take the necessary measures to ensure that all carriers operating to and/or from their territories take appropriate measures to ensure application of the tariffs which they have filed with governments and which have not been disapproved;

that States include in their bilateral agreements articles which, to the fullest extent possible, give effect to the foregoing requirements and explore the feasibility of developing a multilateral convention on an overall system machinery;

that States deploy concerted efforts to remove the underlying causes of tariff violations; and

that ICAO should undertake a study to evolve standard practices for enforcement of tariffs by all the Contracting States.[5]

International Nonscheduled Air Transport

Regulation of nonscheduled international air-transport services can be traced to the Chicago Conference of 1944 in which Articles of the Convention dealt in some detail with the rights of nonscheduled flights. However, it is clear from the relatively liberal grant of rights to nonscheduled flights in article 5 that the participants did not consider this type of service to any significant degree relative to the scheduled services. As a result, regulation of nonscheduled service was generally left to the unilateral rules of individual nations. In 1948, the IATA members adopted resolution 045 defining the eligibility to charter aircraft for the purpose of affinity group, own-use, and student study-group charters. Next, in 1952, ICAO prepared and submitted to its contracting states a definition of scheduled international air service as a series of flights with the following characteristics:

a) it passes through the airspace over the territory of more than one state;

b) it is performed by aircraft for the transport of passengers, mail or cargo for remuneration, in such a manner that each flight is open to use by members of the public;

c) it is operated, so as to serve traffic between the same two or more points, either:
   i) in accordance with a published timetable, or
   ii) with flights so regular or frequent that they constitute a recognizable systematic series.

By definition, then, every other flight was nonscheduled. This negative form of definition never received wide acceptance by the contracting states, and many of them were left relatively free to determine the applicability and appropriateness of article 5 of the Chicago convention. It is important to note that the nature of nonscheduled traffic at that time (for example, medical flights) was very different from the current nonscheduled traffic.

Prior to the mid-1950s, there was no real need to develop regulations applicable to international nonscheduled air-transport operations since most international passengers were traveling on business using scheduled services. However, by 1955 significant changes occurred that warranted a review of the need to regulate nonscheduled services. In the United States, the CAB had expressed its desire to liberalize nonscheduled operations in its *Large Irregular Air Carrier Investigation*. In 1956 the *Multilateral Agreement on Commercial Rights on Non-Scheduled Air Services in Europe* was opened for ratification by the members of the European Civil Aviation Conference (ECAC). The object of this agreement was to review article 5 of the Chicago convention concerning the rights of nonscheduled flights and liberalization of such operations in Europe if such liberalization did not harm the scheduled services. In essence, this agreement allowed nonscheduled carriers to offer service with little more than prior notification. In fact, ECAC members agreed during 1958, 1959, and 1961 that ITCs should be treated as nonscheduled services, although they satisfy the criteria defining a scheduled service.

Liberalization of nonscheduled operations allowed this segment of the industry to grow enormously during the next twenty years within Europe and between Europe and North America. Within Europe, for example, the intra-ECAC nonscheduled passenger traffic began to approach the volume of scheduled traffic by the mid-1970s. Similarly, the nonscheduled traffic on the North Atlantic approached 30 percent of the total traffic. The substantial growth of nonscheduled operations in these two markets has had a profound impact on services offered by the scheduled carriers. Consequently, many nations began to question the existing regulatory framework and develop guidelines for allowing both segments of the industry to provide the public with economical and efficient air-transport services.

Historically, whereas the scheduled services have been regulated through bilateral agreements, nonscheduled operations have usually been regulated through unilateral rules, regulations, and laws. From time to time, bilateral or multilateral agreements have been made to regulate certain nonscheduled operations or routes. The nonscheduled operators have been required to obtain prior permission and comply with various restrictions, some of which have limited the degree to which the nonscheduled carriers could compete with the scheduled carriers. For nonscheduled carriers, the first requirement has usually been to obtain prior approval to operate a flight into the territory of another nation. Since the minimum period has varied from a few days to several months, this requirement has influenced long-range planning, which in the case of nonscheduled operations can be even more crucial than for scheduled carriers. In addition to this requirement there are three general types of restrictions on their operations: marketing restrictions through charter definitions and rules, geographical and route restrictions, and capacity control.[6]

The marketing-type restrictions include barring certain types of charters (such as ITC), the three-point rule, the one-stop ITC rule, split-charter rules, and rules relating to back-to-back operations. The geographic and route restrictions are self-explanatory. The capacity-control restrictions can vary from state to state and usually take the form of absolute quotas or some relationship to the existing capacity offered by the scheduled carriers. Finally, price can also be controlled through either a price floor based on estimated costs or a fixed relationship to the existing IATA negotiated tariffs for scheduled operations. All these restrictions exist to protect scheduled carriers, on the one hand, and to provide some opportunity for nonscheduled carriers to compete in the marketplace, on the other hand. After all, the latter segment of the industry does provide a form of service that is in the public interest.

From 1972 on, the difficulties in the regulation of the two types of service became more acute. Personal and pleasure travel was growing at a rate higher than business travel in major international markets. So the CAB in 1972 decided to withhold approval of IATA resolution 045 partly because it had become almost impossible to enforce strictly the rules concerning the composition of groups. The United States, together with Canada and ECAC-member states, decided to replace the affinity-group concept with the nonaffinity-group concept to expand nonscheduled operations on the North Atlantic. This decision, which led to the implementation of advance booking charters (ABC) and travel group charters (TGC), made nonscheduled services more readily available to the general public. Moreover, some of these services were offered with a published timetable and with a frequency that constituted "a recognizable systematic series." In retaliation, the scheduled carriers began to offer service at prices and with features that matched the nonscheduled services. These included part-charters, APEX, and GITs. As a result, the conflicts between the operators of the two services became increasingly difficult to resolve.

While no one denies the need for both types of services, the question is one of balancing competition between the two segments, taking into consideration the needs of different elements of the traffic mix, the desire to promote tourism and foreign trade, and the rights of both segments of the industry to coexist. The difficulty lies, therefore, in being unable to harmonize the aviation policies of different states to achieve the goals and objectives. Moreover, since international air transportation, by definition, involves more than one state, it is important to reconcile the divergent and sometimes conflicting policies and interests of various states to establish multilateral, or even bilateral, agreements that provide for the needs of all participants. Following these objectives the conference made the following recommendations.

The council should undertake studies aimed at—

> establishing a definition or guidelines which characterize international non-scheduled air transport operations and distinguish these from scheduled operations;
>
> establishing guidelines for the world aeronautical community in the regulation of international non-scheduled air transport; and
>
> establishing policy in the field of international non-scheduled air transport giving consideration to important aspects such as capacity, tariffs and prices, variation in operational areas, travel organizers and control of services, and bearing in mind the public interest and tourism development;[7]

The council would examine the feasibility of—

> amending Articles 5, 6 and 96(a) of the Convention so as to reflect the regulatory provisions and principles governing both scheduled and non-scheduled air transport on the basis of the present and future characteristics and structure of the international air transport market; and
>
> revising the Council's Definition of a Scheduled International Air Service.[7]

Pending the conclusion of these studies, the contracting states will be invited—

> to further the development of international air transport as a whole on a sound and economic basis;
>
> to establish and to maintain harmony between scheduled and non-scheduled international air transport operations;
>
> to co-operate in setting up stable, harmonized regimes for scheduled and non-scheduled international air transport operations; and
>
> to provide reasonable opportunities for the traveling public to take advantage of non-scheduled flights without undermining the economic viability of scheduled services.[7]

There is no question about the public need for both scheduled and non-scheduled services. Scheduled services provide the consumer with regular and dependable schedules, flexibility, and worldwide routes. Nonscheduled services exploit the efficiency of plane-load movement to capture the price-elastic traffic and expand passenger and cargo markets. Therefore both types of services are needed. The issues are the balance between the interests of the operators of the two services, the public, and the government, on the one hand, and the harmonization of divergent national policies on the other hand.[8]

Regulation of Scheduled Capacity

The regulation of international air-transport services on a multilateral basis was first discussed at the Chicago Conference in 1944. However, article 6, which states that scheduled international air service cannot be operated without the special permission of a state, implied that the authority to operate such services would require bilateral agreements. It is this form of reasoning that led to the exchange of commercial traffic rights between the United Kingdom and the United States and the resulting Bermuda agreement, which provided for the flexible application of general principles rather than a precise formula. For example, it called for the amount of capacity that took into consideration: (1) traffic between the country of origin and the countries of destination; (2) through airline operations; and (3) the area through which the airline passes after taking account of local and regional services.

This flexible approach to the regulation of capacity has had both advantages and disadvantages, depending on interpretation. For a number of years the approach worked fairly well, given the safety net of an ex post facto review and the existence of pooling arrangements on many routes. But with the growth in the number of airlines (both scheduled and nonscheduled), the changing mix in traffic, the pursuit of divergent national interests and objectives, the divergent national attitudes toward traffic rights, and the unfair advantage taken by some carriers in accessing fifth- and sixth-freedom traffic, the flexible approach implemented in the original Bermuda agreement caused considerable concern in a number of states. The primary concern is that on many routes, capacity does not relate to demand, resulting in an unfair advantage to one partner in a bilateral agreement. The extent of this concern was evident in 1976 when the British announced their decision to terminate the agreement in 1977.

The movement toward a stricter form of capacity control relates, in general, to the question of excess capacity and the question of the financial health of individual airlines and the industry. Sufficient convincing arguments have been advanced to explain the merits of capacity control. For example, given the fixed nature of tariffs, capacity is the only effective tool used to compete in the market. The problem, however, remains one of defining excess capacity. At one extreme it is clear that in scheduled service it is not possible to achieve 100 percent load factor due to the uncertainty in demand and the existence of seasonality, directionality, given size of aircraft, and the need to reposition empty aircraft. At the other extreme, capacity would be in excess if an airline experiences an average load factor too low to provide an adequate return on investment at the existing fare level (a situation that may be desirable from the consumer's point of view). The optimal load factor, and therefore the measure of excess capacity, would lie between these two limits. The question of excess capacity is therefore subjective and complex. The answer varies by airline, route, season, direction, traffic mix, and the degree and nature of competition.

Although the solution for the excess capacity problem is unclear, it is generally agreed that the problem must be dealt with on a bilateral basis. Given the nature of the industry, it is unrealistic to assume that this problem should be attacked by an airline or its government unilaterally. On the other hand, dealing with the issue on a bilateral basis raises other difficulties, some of which are—

a) *differences in interpretation of the term "reciprocity"* involving, for example, conflicting views on right to traffic ranging from the position that each designated national airline is entitled to the traffic originating in its territory to the position that third and fourth freedom traffic should be divided on a 50:50 basis; and disagreement as to the service points to be granted in each partner's territory in such a way as to ensure fair and equal opportunity to each designated carrier.

b) *differences in attitude to capacity control* ranging from the Bermuda concept of no prior control to the concept that control is essential and can only be achieved by predetermination.

c) *conflicting views on the effect of increasing capacity*, whether it stimulates demand by providing better service for the public or merely reduces load factors, encourages tariff violations, and reduces yield; and whether the maintenance of low frequencies and load factors runs counter to the public interest.

d) *disagreements relating to the provision and validity of traffic data*, such data being the basis for estimates of the required capacity on a given route. Problems arise when airlines do not comply with reporting requirements; when capacity is increased by one partner without presentation of data to demonstrate need; and when there is disagreement as to the validity of the data presented particularly in relation to fifth and sixth freedom traffic, or as to the validity of the traffic forecasts required for planning future capacity.

e) *effects of differing aircraft types on capacity question* complicate bilateral negotiations where, for example, the aircraft operated by one partner have a significantly greater capacity or lower breakeven load factor than those of the other. In these situations it may be difficult to agree on frequencies or on the level of capacity required to produce economically satisfactory load factors.

f) *impact of non-scheduled operations*, particularly on competitive routes with excess capacity, make bilateral negotiations on capacity difficult.

g) *difficulties arising from national laws or regulations* where, for example, one partner may consider that the other partner's laws or regulations inhibit airline cooperation or preclude fair and equal opportunity.

h) *effects of considerations outside the air transport field* including particularly political and general economic factors such as international trade balances, development of exports, and the needs of aircraft manufacturing and tourist industries are considered by some States to distort negotiations relating to air transport capacity and the economic viability of international carriers.[9]

Keeping in mind the complexity of the problem and the need for flexible capacity control, the conference recommended:

That the Council undertake studies aimed at:
establishing criteria and using these to formulate alternative methods for regulating capacity on scheduled and non-scheduled international air transport services; and

developing a model clause (or clauses) or guidelines for regulating capacity on the basis of prior determination for consideration, along with other clauses or guidelines by Contracting States.

That, in its studies, the Council take into account:
the need to relate capacity to demand in a flexible manner;

the need to provide effectively for equality and mutual benefit for the carriers of both countries concerned;

the need to encourage the development and expansion of air transport on a sound economic basis and in the public interest;

the needs of airlines and airports for long-term planning of capacity;

in relation to the foregoing points, the distinctive characteristics of scheduled and non-scheduled services and their co-existence within a single market,

the study commissioned (as per previous recommendation) regarding the regulation of international non-scheduled air transport.

That, pending the conclusion of the studies referred to above, Contracting States be invited:
to coordinate their policies and regulations with regard to capacity control;

to include both scheduled and non-scheduled traffic in their considerations;

to ensure that the carriers of both countries concerned have fair and effective opportunity to provide capacity for the carriage of scheduled and non-scheduled traffic,

to encourage their airlines (through arrangements with the airlines of other States if appropriate and subject to government approval) to make the most efficient use of resources consistent with the provision of adequate and regular air transport facilities; and

to monitor closely both load factors and the quality of service to the public.[10]

The majority of the international community feels that the existing system for regulating capacity does not meet the primary objective of permitting the international carriers of all countries to operate under conditions of fair and equal opportunity. Given the unsatisfactory operating economics of the industry and the fact that the regulation of capacity involves many factors that extend beyond the economics of airline operations, the attitude to capacity regulation is changing from one of ex post facto review to one of predetermination.

Machinery for the Establishment of International
Air-Transport Fares and Rates

Tariffs have played such an important role in the development of the international air-transport system that it has become a legitimate interest and
concern not only to the carriers but also to governments and consumers.
The broad and complex nature of this subject restricted conference participants in making their own detailed analysis or recommendations. As a
result, the participants reviewed the report of the *Panel of Experts on the
Machinery for the Establishment of International Fares and Rates* and
recommended that:

> the Contracting States of ICAO should be urged, when reviewing
> tariffs, to consider the views of States whose airlines are not members
> of IATA.

> ICAO be represented by observers at IATA Traffic Conferences.
> These observers would prepare a report on attendance for distribution
> to Member States.

> ICAO should urge States to encourage their national carriers to meet
> on a regional basis to ensure that, in the establishment of international
> fares and rates, the views of all carriers operating on the routes con-
> cerned are taken into account.

> in the interests of both the users and providers of air transport, ICAO
> should endeavor to encourage regular discussions between scheduled
> and non-scheduled carriers, whether members of IATA or not, for
> coordinating tariff policies.

> in the continuation of its work, the ICAO Panel of the Machinery for
> the Establishment of International Fare and Rates initially concentrates
> its efforts on study of the known means by which tariffs, including retail
> seat-prices on non-scheduled services, are established so that measures
> aimed at harmonizing the diverse means by which both scheduled and
> non-scheduled airlines arrive at their tariffs may be proposed.

> the States make every effort to collaborate with ICAO in this study by
> providing in advance data concerning their national non-scheduled
> carriers and any other information that may be considered relevant.

> the Council conduct a joint study . . . on the necessity or not of
> establishing a new intergovernmental machinery for the establishment
> of fares and rates, without excluding the convenience of maintaining
> the existing machinery, if it is justified by the study.

> unilateral action by governments which may have a negative effect on
> carriers' efforts towards reaching agreement should be avoided as far
> as possible.

> influence should be exerted by ICAO towards a simplification of the
> fare structure and types by IATA.

> 1) States not already doing so be invited to require airlines, whether
>   or not participating in multilateral or bilateral tariff agreements,
>   to discuss tariff proposals in advance with their governments;

2) States be invited to require all airlines to submit any resulting tariffs to the governments concerned, requesting their approval; and

3) States take the necessary measures to ensure that Bilateral and Multilateral Air Transport Agreements or the national legislation contain rules with respect to (2) above in order to guarantee an equitable situation between all airlines.

1) all governments should require airlines to submit tariff proposals at least 60 days in advance of their proposed date of effectiveness, it being understood that a shorter period of submission could be permitted by bilateral agreement or in special cases;

2) where airlines have submitted tariff proposals within the period established by the governments concerned, as indicated in (1) above, each government should announce its decision within a reasonable period, if possible within 30 days after the submission of tariff proposals;

when considering fares and rates submitted by airlines or airline associations, governments may require necessary data for justification, and the methodology and/or criteria employed.

the process of tariff filing could be simplified by governments accepting the submission of joint tariff agreements by the national carrier, or in the absence thereof, by a carrier indicated by the government for this purpose. The other carriers involved would indicate in an acceptable manner their concurrence with this form of submission. Approval of tariffs thus submitted would signify that the terms of the bilateral agreements, where applicable, had been met and the carriers involved were bound accordingly.

1) that within the IATA Traffic Conferences or outside the IATA fares-making machinery, airlines should strictly follow the principle that, in adopting tariff agreements, each airline operating on a route or parts thereof should be given equal opportunity to participate in the carriage of the traffic; and

2) that governments in approving tariffs are requested to check that strict adherence of the above principle is followed by airlines.

1) the ICAO Secretariat should endeavor to continue and further develop its work on airline costs and revenues, with particular attention being paid to analyses of regional differences in fares and costs;

2) Contracting States should be urged to assist this project by ensuring that data in respect of their national carrier(s) are made available to ICAO; and

3) that the work described in (1) above should seek to determine the main causes of regional differences in fares and costs and, if possible, measures that might be taken to reduce such differences;

ICAO should, in consultation with States and under the direction of Council, seek practical means, such as Regional Workshops and preparation of relevant ICAO Manuals, to facilitate the task of national administrations, thus enabling governments to fulfill efficiently their role in the process of establishing rates and fares.[11]

From the preceding set of recommendations it is evident that ICAO has expended considerable efforts in the analysis of international fares and

rates. Because the subject is not only vitally important but also full of complexities and controversies, chapter 4 is devoted entirely to a study of
domestic and international air-transport fares.

U.S. International Aviation Policy

Having negotiated the Bermuda Two agreement, the Carter administration
began to view it as excessively protectionist, providing an unfair advantage
for the British carriers. Moreover, encouraged by the CAB's de facto
deregulation of the domestic industry and the initial success of Laker's
Skytrain in the London-New York market, the Carter administration began
to develop U.S. international aviation policy based on free-market competition, with the aim of achieving a wide variety of service and price options
for the consumer.

Policy Goals and Implementation

In developing its procompetitive laissez faire air-transportation policy, the
administration established seven specific goals to be achieved in the negotiation of international agreements:

1. To meet the needs of consumers, new and greater opportunities should
   be created for innovative and competitive pricing by individual airlines.
2. Restrictions on charter operations and rules should be eliminated or at
   least liberalized.
3. Restrictions on capacity, and route and operating rights for scheduled
   carriers should be eliminated to the extent possible.
4. Discrimination and unfair competitive practices faced by U.S. international carriers should be eliminated.
5. Multiple U.S. airlines should be designated in markets that can support
   additional service.
6. The number of gateways should be increased.
7. The opportunity to develop and facilitate competitive air-cargo services
   should be increased.

These objectives and policy goals were established to provide a general
framework for U.S. negotiators to form specific negotiating strategies that
would lead to the development of competitive opportunities. A number of
observers pointed to the weakness of the economic rationale of the free-for-
all competition in international aviation. The list included the following
arguments: not all international airlines are privately owned; air-transpor-

tation policies of their governments include many noneconomic objectives; different nations have different antitrust philosophies. Given the existence of government subsidy, the absence of a common regulatory framework, and the existence of fifth-freedom carriers, the probability of predatory pricing is high. Air transportation is a public service and an integral part of the economy and, as in the case of public utilities, needs some protection from uncontrolled competition. While the free-for-all competitive-market environment may produce the maximum amount of a socially desirable output, what is socially desirable varies from nation to nation. Free competition can only work if all participants operate under the same rules. The international aviation-policy goals may be inconsistent with other national policy objectives. Despite these cautions and the experience of the U.S. maritime industry, the United States continued to pursue its procompetitive policies. (An elaborate discussion of U.S. international aviation-policy goals and implementation strategy may be found in chapter 3 of *U.S. International Aviation Policy* by Nawal K. Taneja.[12])

The International Air Transportation Competition Act of 1979 was signed in 1980 to amend the Federal Aviation Act to provide competition in the international marketplace. Essentially, the act adopts the international objectives of the Airline Deregulation Act of 1978 and encourages the implementation of the U.S. international aviation policy. The primary objectives are—

1. strengthening of the competitive position of U.S. carriers to at least assure equality with foreign air carriers, including the attainment of opportunities for the U.S. carriers to maintain and increase their profitability in foreign air transportation;
2. freedom of air carriers (U.S. and foreign) to offer consumer-oriented fares and rates;
3. the fewest possible restrictions on charter air transportation;
4. maximum degree of multiple and permissive international authority for U.S. carriers so that they will be able to respond quickly to shifts in market demand;
5. elimination of operational and marketing restrictions to the greatest extent possible;
6. integration of domestic and international air transportation;
7. an increase in the number of nonstop U.S. gateway cities;
8. opportunities for foreign carriers to increase their access to U.S. points if exchanged for benefits of similar magnitude for the U.S. carriers or passengers and shippers;
9. elimination of discrimination and unfair competitive practices faced by the U.S. carriers in foreign air transportation, including excessive landing and user fees, unreasonable ground handling requirements, undue

restrictions on operations, prohibitions against change of gauge, and similar restrictive practices; and
10. the promotion, encouragement, and development of civil aeronautics and a viable, privately owned U.S. air-transport industry.

Since early 1978, the United States has negotiated about a dozen liberal bilateral agreements. All of these agreements do not embody all of the principles contained in the policy statement.

Initial resistance to the U.S. policy by Japan, Italy, France, and the United Kingdom led the United States to systematically conclude agreements with neighboring states. It is no secret now that the strategy was to pressure the recalcitrant countries into accepting the U.S. policy rather than experience diversion of traffic to the close, alternative destinations. This argument had particular application to Europe, where much of the North Atlantic market has traditionally been composed of U.S. vacationers whose objective was to "see Europe." Whether such travelers arrived in Paris or Brussels is relatively less important than the price of their airline tickets or tour packages. With excellent ground transportation within Europe and the relatively short distances involved, it is possible to take side trips to most Western European capitals.

The approach adopted by the United States in negotiating pro-competitive air-service agreements has had mixed success. On the negative side, not all states have dropped their resistance to the free-for-all competitive environment. On the positive side, West Germany did change its position on multiple designation, and the United Kingdom made some concessions to the U.S. policy in revision of the Bermuda Two agreement. However, France and Italy remain hold-outs. In the Pacific, a liberal bilateral agreement negotiated with South Korea has not changed Japan's attitude toward the U.S. procompetitive policy.

There is no question that lower fares were introduced on the North Atlantic by scheduled carriers in 1978. In a year characterized by high inflation rates on both sides of the Atlantic, the average fare declined in constant U.S. dollars, resulting partly from the introduction of the Skytrain service by Laker Airways. In 1979, a year during which fuel prices roughly doubled, the average fares charged by U.S. carriers on North Atlantic routes were up only 1.6 percent, a result of new U.S. carriers entering the competitive market. Capitol and Transamerica, for example, respectively introduced New York-Brussels and New York-Amsterdam service at the price of $125 one-way. Data for 1980 are preliminary in nature. While some significant fare increases have been proposed and a smaller number actually implemented, new carrier entry coupled with low promotional fares (most notably those of World Airways) have continued. Furthermore, on former duopoly segments (Miami-London), rate reduction has accompanied increased competition.

The decline in real fares which the United States has listed as a principal objective is undeniable on the North Atlantic routes. Greater diversity is also demonstrated by the number of fares appearing in various markets (the Official Airline Guide lists sixty different fares between New York and London ranging from $384 to $2,380 for the round trip), the absence of the IATA function with respect to U.S. carrier rate setting, and the relative dispatch with which the CAB has acted on new fare proposals as compared to previous lengthy lags between carrier submission and board action.

In its pursuit of low fares, the United States has overlooked the financial stability of the international airline industry since that is not an explicit goal of the procompetitive policy. Fares which do not, in the long run, cover fully allocated costs present a dilemma for an industry with high capital requirements. IATA statistics indicate that its members have experienced an aggregate operating deficit in the North Atlantic operations each year since 1970 and a capital-cost deficit for an even longer period. The first year of the procompetitive agreements' implementation was particularly discouraging: an aggregate loss by IATA members of almost $700 million, the largest in the history of North Atlantic operations; results for 1979 and part of 1980 do not look encouraging either.

Some of the losses on the North Atlantic are being cross-subsidized. In the cases of European carriers with overall operating surpluses, the profitability of other international services have allowed them to maintain transatlantic services. In the cases of other European carriers experiencing systemwide losses, government subsidization will ultimately be responsible for continued airline operation. U.S. carriers cannot avail themselves of government subsidy. Nor does cross-subsidization from domestic services (whose profitability has been eroded by the competitive pressures of deregulation and an economic downturn) appear reasonable in the near term. Consequently, a retrenchment in North Atlantic services (by Pan American and TWA) has resulted in numerous points being deleted and capacity on many remaining services reduced. Finally, exceptionally low fares on the North Atlantic may not be an overall consumer benefit. Cross-subsidization implies that some consumers are paying higher fares than they would otherwise. And elimination or reduction of service suggests a deterioration in product quality.

During 1978, scheduled passenger traffic between the United States and Europe increased 23.4 percent. In accrediting the U.S. procompetitive policies with this impressive figure, the proponents carefully omit data that make it less impressive. They ignore a decline of 18.2 percent in nonscheduled traffic, which pares aggregate growth to only 11.2 percent—significant but not extraordinary growth, as aggregate passenger traffic over the North Atlantic grew at an average rate of 9.7 percent between 1968 and 1978.

Moreover, considering it was a boom year economically on both sides of the Atlantic, the 11.2 percent growth rate might be considered disappointing.

The implementation of additional procompetitive agreements in 1979 did not lead to a substantial increase in total airline traffic: merely 8.5 percent on the North Atlantic (total international traffic to and from the United States increased 14 percent). Growth has further slowed in 1980. In spite of fare wars on certain routes, predictions that the last half of 1980 will show a decline over the corresponding 1979 period in terms of passengers transported are now being made by some experts.

The proponents of U.S. international aviation policy point to large double-digit percentage increases in transatlantic traffic to and from the Benelux countries. It is not clear, however, whether or not the majority of this traffic was, in fact, new traffic as opposed to traffic diverted from other European airports. Figure 3-1 shows that when traffic between the

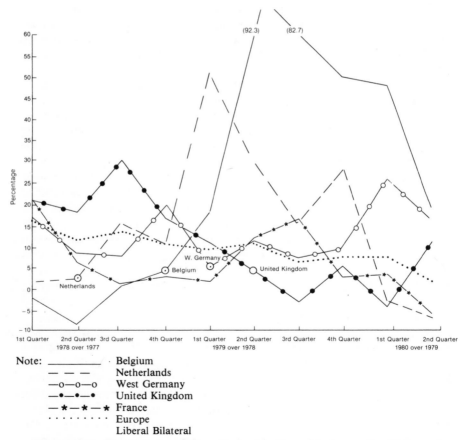

Figure 3-1. Percentage of Growth in Air Travel between the U.S. and Selected European Countries (1977-1980)

Benelux countries and the United States began growing at high rates, the growth rates with respect to nearby European countries (France, Britain, and West Germany) declined; however, after Britain and West Germany implemented liberalized agreements with the United States, their growth rates began to rise, and those of the Belgium and the Netherlands began to fall. France, which has not signed a new bilateral with the United States, has (since the second quarter of 1978) experienced a declining growth rate below the aggregate rate of U.S./Europe traffic expansion. This is particularly interesting since, during the first quarter of 1978 (before the beginning of North Atlantic procompetitive agreements), traffic between the U.S. and France relative to the first quarter of 1977 grew at a higher rate (21.2 percent) than it did between the United States and each of the four other European countries examined. Moreover, in both 1978 and particularly 1979, tourism in France has not declined.

It is important to emphasize that there is a large difference in the absolute size of the markets for the countries shown in figure 3-1. Therefore, a small percentage of the passenger traffic diverted from a large market can result in a high growth rate for a small country.

These patterns in transatlantic passenger traffic suggest that procompetitive agreements have developed little, if any, new traffic. Traffic has merely been diverted from other markets and even then the diversion was temporary. Further substantiating this conclusion is the overall and continuous decline in the growth rate of passenger traffic on the North Atlantic since the implementation of the U.S. procompetitive policy. In the first quarter of 1978, transatlantic traffic was 16.6 percent above that of the comparable 1977 quarter (no procompetitive agreements had been signed at this time), while second quarter 1980 traffic was up by only 2 percent over the comparable 1979 quarter (five procompetitive agreements had been signed by this time). It is argued that the current decline in growth is largely attributable to a downturn in the United States and European economies and that in the absence of procompetitive agreements traffic would be more disappointing than it is now. There is, however, no way to prove or disprove this argument.

The experience in Europe with respect to procompetitive agreements can be related to that in the Far East. There, four states entered into liberal bilaterals with the United States: South Korea (March 1979), Singapore (June 1979), Thailand (June 1979), and the Philippines (October 1980). Following implementation of these agreements, each country experienced a marked increase in passenger traffic to and from the United States well above the aggregate U.S.-Far East growth rate. At the same time, the growth rate relative to a fifth country, Japan (which did not enter into a similar agreement), declined. For the twelve months ending 30 June 1980, passenger traffic between the United States and South Korea increased approximately 76 percent over that of the previous 1978 to 1979 twelve-month period; for Singapore, such traffic increased sixfold; for Thailand, the increase was close to 500 percent. Yet for Japan the increase in traffic during the same twelve months was under 15 percent. In contrast, overall U.S.-Far East traffic increased 20 percent. Since Japan typically generates between 65 and 75 percent of U.S.-Far East traffic, very small diversions of traffic from Japan to other Asian states can produce startling growth rates in the latter.

It must also be noted that what increases there have been in the transatlantic traffic have not been evenly spread on both sides of the Atlantic. The U.S. procompetitive policies were implemented at a time when the value of the dollar was declining with respect to the major European currencies of West Germany, Great Britain, and France. This, coupled with the fact that ground transportation costs are now a much higher percentage of total trip cost and air fare is a correspondingly lower percentage, has encouraged European discretionary travel to the United States and discouraged American discretionary travel to Europe. Therefore, non-U.S.-citizen traffic has been increasing at a considerably faster pace over the North Atlantic than has U.S.-citizen traffic. In 1978, for example, non-U.S.-citizen traffic between the United States and Europe increased 25.3 percent; U.S.-citizen traffic, a modest 7.2 percent. In 1979, non-U.S.-citizen traffic rose 10.8 percent, while its complement fell 0.9 percent. And in the first half of 1980 (the first period during which European passengers have outnumbered Americans among transatlantic passengers), the noncitizen component was up 13.2 percent versus a 3.9 percent drop in the U.S.-citizen traffic.

The disparity in these figures indicates that low fares do not automatically mean increased traffic. That non-U.S.-citizen traffic on the North Atlantic routes increased at a rapid rate between 1978 and the first half of 1980 while the growth in U.S.-citizen traffic slowed and ultimately became negative shows that net increases in passengers transported was significantly influenced by factors other than fares, such as ground transportation costs and currency exchange values. In comparing the relative costs of goods and services between the United States and Europe, a difference of 65 percent has developed in the past three years. And the relative inflation index (product of CPI and the exchange rate index) has made travel to the United States by Europeans a real bargain.

In negotiating procompetitive agreements, the United States has sought multiple designation. In the case of the five European nations that have signed procompetitive agreements, multiple designation has been granted—restrictively, in the case of the United Kingdom, but essentially without restriction for Belgium, the Netherlands, and West Germany. With the exception of the United Kingdom, where Laker and British Caledonian compete with British Airways, CAB reciprocal concession of multiple foreign-flag-carrier entry is not particularly meaningful because for any given European nation there is generally only one carrier authorized to provide service.

The effects of multiple designation on the highest volume routes involving procompetitive agreement partners of the United States appear to be minimal. For example, Capitol and Transamerica replaced rather than supplemented Pan American's Benelux services. And a large number of carriers designated to begin new services never did. It appears that the multiple designation objective of the United States may be appealing theoretically but practically impossible because of insufficient density and existing overcapacity.

European carriers historically have been able to capture a disproportionately high market share of their national passengers traveling to the North Atlantic. This, coupled with the fact that multiple designation generally only applies to U.S. carriers, means that U.S. carriers could merely be dividing a constrained market share among themselves. In a few cases, the share of U.S. carriers has increased in markets that have procompetitive agreements. Belgium is a case in point (see table 3-1). The share of U.S. flag carriers for two countries that did not sign procompetitive agreements (France and Italy) is also shown in table 3-1. In the case of France the U.S. share was 60 percent in August 1978, 57 percent in August 1979, and 56 percent in August 1980. For the same periods, the U.S. share for Italy was 57 percent, 57 percent, and 54 percent, respectively. In the case of the service to the Far East, the results have been mixed; the share increased between the United States and South Korea but decreased between the United States and Singapore (see table 3-2).

The U.S. purported objective of enhancing its flag-carrier-market share is responsible for much of the criticism from the international aviation community. However, on the basis of available traffic data, such criticism is unwarranted on a systemwide basis. In 1977, U.S. flag-carriers-market share on the North Atlantic was approximately 45 percent. In 1978 it declined to 44 percent and remained at that level for calendar year 1979. But during the first eight months of 1980, this share had eroded further.

The CAB has relied essentially on two factors to improve U.S. flag-carrier-market share: multiple designation, and the relatively lower operating costs of the U.S. carriers, which can be translated into lower fares. Multiple designation is theoretically more appealing than practically possible, and, although lower fares can be charged by U.S. carriers because of lower operating costs, not only are potential subsidies available to state-run airlines for maintenance of competitive posture, but the likelihood of unfair policies and practices is much greater with some foreign carriers and their governments.

A principal example of the failure of U.S. policy to improve market share for U.S. carriers involves the bilateral agreement with the Netherlands. At the time the agreement was negotiated (March 1978), there were no scheduled U.S. carrier operations between the two countries. The new bilateral essentially designated an unlimited number of U.S. carriers to initiate service between various continental U.S. points and the

Table 3-1
U.S. Flag Carrier Market Share between the United States and Selected European Countries
(percent)

| | Countries that Have Signed Procompetitive Agreements | | | Countries that Have Not Signed Procompetitive Agreements | | All Europe |
	Belgium	Netherlands	West Germany	Italy	France	
1978						
January	13	2	49	56	44	40
February	8	2	46	55	44	39
March	9	5	48	55	50	42
April	15	2	44	61	53	45
May	21	6	41	62	53	45
June	30	16	45	61	51	45
July	39	21	46	62	58	46
August	34	17	43	57	60	44
September	19	15	44	56	54	44
October	17	10	40	59	49	44
November	2	3	54	64	46	46
December	9	15	43	58	44	43
1979						
January	16	20	40	59	43	42
February	16	12	39	65	39	39
March	8	17	39	91	45	43
April	5	23	45	64	55	43
May	31	26	41	61	51	43
June	46	22	48	62	52	47
July	56	26	49	61	57	47
August	54	27	48	57	57	44
September	44	28	46	57	54	44
October	17	26	42	60	52	44
November	17	18	49	60	47	42
December	37	20	45	58	44	46
1980						
January	40	17	45	59	43	41
February	39	12	45	58	41	39
March	37	6	48	57	43	40
April	43	6	52	58	51	42
May	41	10	49	61	51	43
June	47	14	52	58	51	44
July	56	14	53	54	55	45
August	55	11	54	54	56	44

Source: U.S. Department of Transportation, Transportation Systems Center.

Table 3-2
U.S. Flag Carrier Market Share between the U.S. and Selected Far East Countries
(percent)

	Countries that Have Signed Procompetitive Agreements		Countries that Have Not Signed Procompetitive Agreements		Total Far East
	S. Korea	Singapore	Japan	Philippines	
1978					
January	4	N.A.	48	48	46
February	14	N.A.	46	47	44
March	11	98	47	43	45
April	10	98	50	47	47
May	0	96	37	45	35
June	2	95	34	42	33
July	0	95	33	43	33
August	2	97	35	41	34
September	10	98	41	45	41
October	9	97	48	49	45
November	23	100	52	44	49
December	10	95	50	46	46
1979					
January	11	94	47	47	46
February	7	94	44	46	44
March	15	100	46	52	47
April	8	2	46	42	44
May	10	18	46	41	43
June	8	32	48	54	45
July	11	30	48	53	45
August	18	20	46	49	44
September	16	14	45	46	45
October	10	17	45	49	46
November	16	34	45	43	45
December	16	24	48	48	43
1980					
January	15	24	45	42	42
February	16	26	43	39	40
March	13	30	42	34	40
April	27	34	44	34	41
May	25	38	45	34	43
June	20	34	45	37	42
July	21	19	47	41	42
August	22	19	46	40	42

Source: U.S. Department of Transportation, Transportation Systems Center
Note: N.A. means the information was not available.

Netherlands. Among those to take advantage of the new bilateral was National Airlines, which began Miami-Amsterdam service and, later, daily New York-Amsterdam service. Its service was later supplemented by Transamerica, which began New York-Amsterdam flights at $125 one way. In Boston, Pan American began service to Amsterdam at $50 one way (later raised to $285 round trip before Braniff replaced it in that market). The traffic stimulated by these services caused U.S.-carrier-market share to peak at 28 percent in September 1979. But thereafter it declined markedly as demand diminished and the incompatibility of very low fares with a medium density market during a period of large fuel price increases became apparent. As of August 1980, U.S. market share had declined to 11 percent. In the fall of 1980, KLM is offering two daily 747 round trips between New York and Amsterdam; Transamerica, the only remaining U.S. competitor on that route, will offer thrice-weekly service with a DC-8.

Improvement of the competitive posture of U.S. airlines will probably depend on more than multiple designation and low fares. Specifically, such airlines are subject to distribution disadvantages in Europe. It is ironic that by discouraging U.S. carriers from their participation in IATA's North Atlantic conferences, the U.S. government is removing an important mechanism for rectifying such a marketing imbalance, since it was an IATA sales-agency program that assured access for all carriers to travel agencies worldwide.

The negotiation of fifth- and sixth-freedom traffic in procompetitive agreements between the United States and European states has generally taken a lower priority than other objectives for the U.S. negotiators. This is because establishing such rights involves a third country, which may or may not be amenable to the U.S. policy; and the extension of such rights could likely enhance the position of European carriers more than it would that of the U.S. airlines.

With regard to the second point, U.S. carriers already have considerable unused fifth-freedom rights in Europe, and many of their intra-European-tag ends to transatlantic services have never been profitable because of the much higher level of service offered by European carriers. Further, any significant additions to beyond rights from European cities for U.S. carriers could probably only be negotiated at considerable concession. For example, for a U.S. carrier to receive the London-Cairo route, a U.K. carrier might insist on the New York-Mexico City route, an exchange that would hardly be of equal value. Therefore, because of differences in geography, market size and composition, and competition, it is difficult to negotiate beyond rights with equal commercial value. Sixth-freedom rights represent an even greater problem.

In exchange for concessions with respect to the objectives of the U.S. policy, the CAB has designated additional U.S. gateways for its procompetitive agreement partners. Reciprocity is not possible on the Europeans' part, however, since because of geographical size there are generally not more than two plausible points for nonstop transatlantic service in any given European country (more often, there is only one).

The increase in U.S. gateways for transatlantic service has been justified as an increase in level of service and consumer convenience. But it is not without a trade-off. Proliferation of gateways means a reduction in economies of scale as they preclude the use of high-capacity aircraft. Fuel savings are lost and ground support expenses increase appreciably.

To state that the procompetitive policy has been a failure with respect to North Atlantic operations would be an exaggeration. However, when evaluated in terms of all of the stated policy goals, it has not been an unqualified success. On the other hand, the pursuit of these policy goals clearly has been accompanied by considerable criticism from foreign states and consequent feelings of distrust within the international aviation community.

The International Air Transport Association

Show-Cause Order. Most of the international passenger and airfreight rates have been coordinated and negotiated through the IATA multilateral forum. However, in 1978, the CAB issued an order directing IATA and other interested parties to show cause why it should not make final its tentative finding and conclusion that the tariffs negotiated through the IATA traffic-conference machinery were no longer in the public interest and therefore should no longer be approved. This unilateral action caused concern in the international community and raised serious questions about the CAB's wisdom in its declared position.

Over the years, four general complaints have been lodged against the IATA rate-making machinery: (1) fares and rates have been too high and would have been lower in the absence of IATA; (2) the unanimity rule has led to the establishment of high fares and rates and inefficiencies in the conference machinery; (3) IATA's compliance machinery has not worked; and (4) the traffic-conference activities and procedures have been conducted in secrecy. The validity of these criticisms is questionable. For example, critics, complaining about IATA negotiated fares and rates being too high, have usually compared international fares and rates with U.S. domestic operations. Fares and rates vary by route because of variations in operating costs and service levels. The unanimity rule, adopted first at the insistence of the CAB, has provided a process of give and take, protecting each carrier and preserving the interrelationship of international fares and rates. There are valid reasons for holding meetings behind closed doors. The process is complex and the need to compromise may not be possible in a completely open environment. In any case, the final negotiated tariffs have always required approval of each and every government. The complaint about compliance is perhaps the only valid criticism.

As a result of some of these criticisms and the drastically changed operating and marketing environment, IATA members recognized the need for modernization and liberalization of the rate-making process. The modernization process started in 1975 at the general meeting in Oslo and resulted in the following features for the tariff-coordinating activity: freedom to participate or not; third-party presentations; attendance of observers; greater recognition of the role of third- and fourth-freedom carriers; additional fare- and rate-development flexibility; greater use of subarea agreements; the role of compliance reoriented to a preventative rather than punitive approach; and the development of less rigid agreements.[13]

Despite the monumental efforts by IATA members to restructure the activities and procedures of their organization, the CAB continued its attack on the proceedings relating to the show-cause order. The basic tenet of the CAB stand was a view of competition and not regulation as the best method for allocation of scarce resources. Moreover, the CAB pointed to the Sherman Antitrust Act of 1890 which states that every contract or combination in restraint of trade among the states or with foreign nations is illegal. In the past the CAB provided antitrust immunity to the U.S. international airlines. However, the appropriateness of the Sherman act is not clear. It assumes, for example, that if there were no private agreements, a competitive market would exist. But in international air transportation, a purely competitive market cannot exist, even in the absence of a private agreement. And since the IATA-coordinated tariffs are ultimately presented to the affected governments for their review and approval before they become effective, it is debatable that they are cartel agreements and not in the public interest.

Almost all of the international airlines and their governments questioned the wisdom of the CAB's proposed action to dismantle the IATA traffic-conference machinery. They pointed out that the IATA multilateral forum was technically and politically necessary to the smooth functioning of the international air-transport system. It is necessary, for example, to ease the direct and interline scheduled operations and currency-exchange problems. The system also facilitates the coordination of reservations and baggage-handling practices, development of fare construction and prorate rules, and routing practices and procedures. Despite their validity, arguments such as these did not convince the CAB members. Some nations pointed out that the absence of an IATA-type multilateral forum would actually reduce competition, not expand it, particularly on routes involving third-world countries. The CAB was unconvinced. Finally, pressure from other U.S. government departments (such as state and transportation) compelled the CAB to give conditional approval to the tariff-coordination process.

On 15 April 1980, the CAB issued a statement of tentative findings, giving antitrust immunity for the continuation of intercarrier tariff discussions for a period of two years. However, the U.S. carriers are discouraged from participation in traffic conferences concerning the North Atlantic. The CAB feels that the two-year approval will provide sufficient time to test results of the new traffic-conference organization and procedures. In the interim a new unit has been set up at the board to study developments in the next two years, as well as examine other alternatives to IATA that are less anticompetitive. The threatened denial of antitrust immunity for the U.S. carriers was based on two reasons. According to the board, the exclusion of U.S. carriers would provide a useful yardstick for assessment of the need for and the impact of the reorganized IATA structure and procedures. Second, for some time now (given the existence of open-rate situations), the operations in the North Atlantic market have not depended on the conference machinery. One should be careful of this last argument. It is the existence of the IATA coordinated rules and procedures that have prevented the North Atlantic situation from becoming totally chaotic. Not only is there no realistic alternative to IATA, there is no evidence that its activities reduce competition.

Competitive Marketing of Air Transportation. One of the major roles of IATA is the administration of its worldwide passenger- and cargo-agency programs for its member airlines. These programs establish standard procedures and financial responsibility criteria for the accreditation of passenger and cargo agents. At the present time there are about 30,000 passenger and 3,000 cargo agents who have qualified under these criteria and entered into a standard agreement with IATA allowing them the possibilities of writing tickets and waybills on any member carrier. The function and role of the agent becomes clear when one realizes that almost 80 percent of all international passenger travel services are sold by agents.

In 1979, the CAB instituted an investigation into the competitive marketing of air transportation to examine why an exclusive conference system of jointly appointed agents is the best method of marketing air transportation. The CAB's claims that in the deregulated environment the exclusivity aspects of the IATA agency programs tend to eliminate options or innovations. The accreditation standards are enforced in such a way that agents are forced to generate new sales rather than "intercept" existing business. This is achieved through the premises or location standards. Furthermore, claims the CAB, the personnel and financial standards act as a barrier to entry into the agency field. As a result of these and other miscellaneous standards, the CAB felt that the IATA/ATA agency programs could be anticompetitive and as such not in the public interest. Behind the board's investigation was the desire to encourage greater retail price competition. This desire is evident from the comments that the board has solicited on its proposals, namely:

1) a complete exemption allowing carriers and/or other retailers to
    engage in total pricing freedom;
2) a limited exemption for carriers and/or ticket agents conditioned on
    charging rates keyed to the zone established by the Act and the
    Board's policy statement creating a non-suspend zone;
3) a policy statement concluding that tariffs may provide for price
    ranges, which would gradually widen over time;
4) a policy statement permitting tariffs with two-tiered pricing, one price
    for sales by the carrier directly to the public and a second price, fixed
    or open, for sales to the public by non-airline retailers;
5) a policy statement permitting tariffs to stipulate a single price for all
    sales made by air carriers, with retailers adding their own charges; and
6) a policy statement permitting carriers to issue tickets to retailers at a
    price which would not include the airline's own marketing costs.[14]

The IATA agency programs have provided significant benefits to its
member airlines and consumers. An individual airline cannot possibly
maintain its own ticket office in every city, let alone multiple offices in a
given city. It simply is not cost effective. Take the examples of British Airways, which maintains only twenty-eight sales offices in the United States
but because of the existence of the IATA sales-agency program can sell its
services through any one of almost 17,000 agents. Not only can an individual airline take advantage of this comprehensive distribution network,
but the IATA-agency program prevents an airline from any misuse of its
market power. For the consumer, the agents provide access to worldwide
services offered by the airlines (including interline), an explanation of the
various available service-price options, and standard transportation
documents recognized and accepted worldwide. The passenger is also
assured that the airline will honor the ticket issued by an agent.

There is competition among travel agents. Any agent who meets the
IATA-agency objective standards can enter the market. Ironically, in the
absence of the IATA-agency program, the competition might be reduced
rather than increased. For example, the large and influential agents would
be able to established exclusive agreements with individual airlines, or
monopolize certain territories, or settle for lower commission but higher
volume. Any of these conditions could force out the small agent.

The issue of retail price competition deserves a serious and careful
analysis since the marketing of air-transportation services is different from
marketing other products. A retailer could promise the consumer a certain
type of service and charge an appropriate price. There is no guarantee,
however, that the airline will provide the service promised, since the airline
cannot know what has been promised and the price that has been charged at
the retail level. Retail pricing, or net fare, is therefore not likely to be in the
public interest. An agent is not just a retailer in the traditional sense. He is
accountable to both the airline and the consumer since the customer buys a

complex service to be consumed at some future date at a point which could be on the other side of the globe. The IATA-agency program ensures the existence of this accountability.

ICAO's SATC Two

Since the conclusion of ICAO's first Special Air Transport Conference in 1977, radical changes have been introduced by the United States in the international air-transport system, ranging from the free capacity determination in the liberal bilateral negotiations to the abortive attempt to dismantle the IATA rate-making machinery. Partly because of these changes, the international air-transportation community met at ICAO's Second Air Transport Conference (12 to 28 February 1980) to shed light on the divergent aviation policies on capacity and nonscheduled operations and determine ways of improving the machinery for the establishment of international fares and rates.

Regulation of international air-transport services was the first item on the agenda and it was subdivided into three categories: distinction between categories of international air-transport service, scheduled and nonscheduled; regulation of capacity in international air-transport services; and regional multilateral air-transport agreements. International air-transport fares and rates were divided into five categories: scheduled passenger fares; nonscheduled passenger tariffs; scheduled and nonscheduled airfreight rates; coexistence and harmonization of methods by which fares and rates are established; and tariff enforcement. Each of these areas was addressed in detail resulting in five recommendations on the first agenda item. The second agenda item that contained twenty-six recommendations is discussed in chapter 4.

The relationship between scheduled and nonscheduled operations has been an issue for some time, one that has become more serious with the implementation of programmed or scheduled charters. Some members of the international aviation community feel that the original ICAO definition established in 1952 is outdated and should be revised. A panel of experts has examined this possibility along with outlining different ways to distinguish scheduled from nonscheduled and programmed charters. Neither approach yielded ideal solutions. If the 1952 definition is changed, the definition needs to be tightened but still kept flexible. In the case of distinguishing features, the experts made an attempt to classify criteria into two groups; economic, and legal and regulatory. Again, it was impossible to cover every case completely satisfactorily. In the end, the panel of experts recommended and the conference supported the retention of the 1952 definition with a certain amount of modification of the existing notes on the application of the definition. The desire for maintaining flexibility was the basis of this recommendation since it would allow the accommodation of different economic and political circumstances and the continuously evolving conditions.

The next issue related to the criteria and methods of regulating capacity, both scheduled and nonscheduled, with emphasis placed on the regulation of scheduled capacity. Many participants in the international aviation community feel that in recent years the regime for regulation of capacity had not promoted the contemplated objectives, namely: a close relationship between supply and demand; a fair and equal opportunity for all carriers; a coexistence of scheduled and nonscheduled service in the same market; an efficient use of the resources, including airport and airway facilities, and fuel; and the maximization of public interest encompassing three elements, airlines, governments, and consumers. The panel of experts was therefore asked to establish criteria, formulate alternative methods for regulating capacity, and develop a model clause or guidelines for regulating capacity on the basis of prior determination.

The panel identified three alternatives to the methods for regulating capacity: predetermination, Bermuda One, and free determination. In the first case, governments establish or approve capacity with varying degrees of flexibility, depending on market requirements. In the second case, governments establish principles only; carriers are free to establish capacity according to the market requirements but subject to governments' ex post facto review. In the third case, carriers are completely free to establish capacity in the marketplace.

The United States, together with ten other nations (Belgium, Finland, Germany, Iceland, Israel, Jamaica, the Netherlands, Singapore, Sweden, and Switzerland), promoted the free-determination method on the premise that it allows the carriers to match capacity to traffic and prices, resulting in higher load factors and consequently lower fares. Additionally, it provides incentives for innovation, which benefits the consumer. The opposite point of view was expressed by Australia, which claimed that the only rational way to achieve low fares is through increased productivity which is achieved through the predetermination of capacity. By contrast, the majority of the community feels that since the marketplace is not perfect, a certain amount of regulation is required to protect public interest and achieve international cooperation. Moreover, given the heterogeneity of markets and the divergence of national policies, the free market-oriented philosophy for capacity regulation is infeasible. The developing nations favor this viewpoint. It is difficult for the carriers of developing nations to acquire the latest technology aircraft, yet without such aircraft the national flag carrier would be at an operating-cost disadvantage. They feared that free determination would lead to uneconomic fares and capacity "dumping," an environment which would eliminate the tiny flag carrier.

Having examined the criteria, the alternative methods, and the relationship between the criteria and the methods for regulating capacity, the panel of experts embarked on the development of typical capacity clauses for each alternative method. At the time the SATC Two had convened, only the guidelines for the predetermination method for regulating capacity had been examined. The conference recommended that the list of six criteria and a total of sixteen guidelines shown in figure 3-2 be submitted to the contracting states for their consideration. The conference emphasized the need for harmonization of capacity with resources and the environment.

The panel of experts had made an initial attempt to outline the guidelines for the free determination and the Bermuda One type of capacity. These guidelines are shown in figures 3-3 and 3-4, respectively. The conference recommended that the panel analyze the relationship between these two methods and the objectives and criteria approved by the conference.

The third subcategory within the first agenda item called for an exchange of views on regional multilateral air-transport agreements. A number of multilateral arrangements by regional groups of states (such as ACAC, AFCAC, ECAC, LACAC, and the Yaounde Treaty groups of states) already exist to harmonize national civil aviation laws, regulations or practices within one regional group of states. Additionally, there are multinational airlines (such as Air Afrique, Gulf Air, and SAS) and multinational technical cooperative arrangements (such as the ATLAS and the KSSU). A number of conference participants expressed a desire to examine the ways and means of strengthening such arrangements. In the past, when some of these arrangements failed, the problems were usually related to practical applications.

On the issue of fares and rates, the United States pushed its double-disapproval and country-of-origin concepts, while Australia promoted its concept of point-to-point service pricing based on the needs of the third-and fourth-freedom traffic. This method of pricing, combined with predetermined capacity, would produce the lowest fares, according to Australia's paper and the recent experience. The majority of participants rejected both positions and favored the continuation of a multilateral system. The LACAC agreed that the optimal system would be multilateral coordination. However, in its absence, the second choice should be the coordination at regional levels among the countries involved and the bilateral process should be reserved as a last resort. The conference recommended that IATA's worldwide traffic conference machinery, wherever applicable, be adopted as a first choice, and that carriers should not be discouraged from participation in the machinery.

A. *The need to relate capacity closely to demand in a flexible manner:*

- Determination of capacity is made by specifying types of aircraft, frequency of services, and in some cases number of seats and/or cargo capacity by volume or weight that may be made available.

- Determination of demand (traffic requirements) is usually made empirically, based on statistics for existing traffic and on reasonable estimates for future traffic, taking into account the economic environment, including tariffs and other relevant factors.

- Relating capacity closely to demand requires the provision of capacity at a level to achieve a reasonable load factor—that is, a load factor that will provide on-demand passengers with a reasonable chance of obtaining accommodation, and assure reasonable economic return to the airlines.

- Flexibility in the provision of capacity may be achieved by such means as closely monitoring load factors to detect changes in demand, arranging for periodical and ad hoc consultations, and facilitating the provision of extra flights, or extra sections, or of temporary capacity by one airline on behalf of the other participating airline to meet short-term fluctuation of demand.

- Flexibility may also be gained by providing objective criteria within which limited capacity increases shall be approved—for example, increases up to an agreed limit provided that relevant load factors during the same period of the previous year reached an agreed level.

B. *The need that the capacity to be provided should primarily be governed by the demand for traffic between the territories of the two contracting parties.*

- Traffic other than the traffic between the territories of the two contracting parties is usually regarded as complementary only, but, in some cases it may be of considerable importance for the consumers and the airlines concerned.

- With regard to the provision of supplementary capacity for such traffic the following should be taken into account, depending on the circumstances:

—the overall balance to be achieved by any bilateral agreement,

—basic differences which may exist between "beyond" and "intermediate" traffic needs,

—the requirements of through airline operations and the traffic requirements of the area through which the service passes, taking account of the needs of local and regional services.

- In many cases the provision of supplementary capacity for such traffic may not be justified since the capacity provided for the traffic between the territories of the two contracting parties may suffice to cover other traffic needs as well.

C. *The need to provide effectively for equality and mutual benefit for the carriers of both countries concerned.*

- Equality and mutual benefit will usually be related to the overall balance of the bilateral agreement and their effective achievement may be arrived at by measures relating to flexibility in the provision of capacity, such as those in "A" above.

- These criteria are of great and increasing importance and may be best reflected in the preamble to an agreement. However, capacity may need to be scheduled so as to achieve efficient use of airport and airway facilities to economize the use of resources through optimization of load factors, and to minimize environmental nuisance. (These requirements may some times require reconciliation with those related to "A" above.)

D. *The need to encourage the development and expansion of air transport on a sound economic basis and in the public interest.*

- This criterion, which is general and fundamental, is normally reflected in the preamble to an agreement rather than in individual clauses.

- The "public interest" is composed of three principal interest factors: the airline industry, users of air transport, and other national interests.

- Capacity should be offered at a level which provides the on-demand passenger with a reasonable change of obtaining accommodation, assures a reasonable economic return to the carriers, avoids the "dumping" of capacity, and is scheduled to meet the convenience of the public to the greatest extent possible.

E. *The need to match traffic with airport and airway capacity, to make efficient use of human and material resources (particularly fuel), and to protect the environment from air and noise pollution.*

- These criteria are of great and increasing importance and may be best reflected in the preamble to an agreement. However, capacity may need to be scheduled so as to achieve efficient use of airport and airway facilities, to economize the use of resources through optimization of load factors, and to minimize environmental nuisance. (These requirements may sometimes require reconciliation with those related to "A" above.)

F. *The need to harmonize the provision of non-scheduled and scheduled capacity in relation to total demand.*

- When certain services, particularly so-called "programmed" or "schedulized" charters, are classified as scheduled by both contracting parties, special measures may be necessary to designate the carriers and routes involved so that the capacity they offer may be regulated together with other scheduled capacity.

- In order to have the necessary information for harmonizing capacity, States may agree to exchange any data that may be useful on the level of capacity offered by non-scheduled services.   □

Source: International Civil Aviation Organization, *Bulletin* (May 1980):21.

Figure 3-2. Guidelines for the Predetermination Method of Capacity Regulation

(1) Each Party shall allow a fair and equal opportunity for the designated airlines of both Parties to compete in the international air transportation covered by this Agreement.

(2) Each Party shall take all appropriate action within its jurisdiction to eliminate all forms of discrimination or unfair competitive practices adversely affecting the competitive position of the airlines of the other Party.

(3) Neither Party shall unilaterally limit the volume of traffic, frequency, or regularity of service, or the aircraft type or types operated by the designated airlines of the other Party, except as may be required for customs, technical, operational, or environmental reasons under uniform conditions consistent with Article 15 of the Convention.

(4) Neither Party shall impose on the other Party's designated airlines a first refusal requirement, uplift ratio, no-objection fee, or any other requirement with respect to the capacity, frequency, or traffic which would be inconsistent with the purposes of this Agreement.

(5) Neither Party shall require the filing of schedules, programs for charter flights, or operational plans by airlines of the other Party for approval, except as may be required on a non-discriminatory basis to enforce uniform conditions as foreseen by paragraph (3) of this Article or as may be specifically authorized in an Annex to this Agreement. If a Party requires filings for information purposes, it shall minimize the administrative burdens of filing requirements and procedures on air transportation intermediaries and on designated airlines of the other Party.

Source: International Civil Aviation Organization,'' Panel of Experts on Regulation of Air Transport Services,'' Report of the Third Meeting (15-26 October 1979).

Figure 3-3. Model Capacity Clause: Free-Determination Method

Summary

Drastic changes have taken place in the regulatory system since the Chicago Convention of 1944 and the Bermuda One agreement signed in 1946. Since then, not only have more participants entered the marketplace, but air transportation has become a major element in the economic, political, and social development of all countries. These developments combined with advances in aviation technology have produced an air-transportation system that is massive in size and complexity. In recent years, airlines and their

(1) The air transport facilities available to the travelling public should bear a close relationship to the requirements of the public for such transport.

(2) The designated airline or airlines of each Contracting Party shall have a fair and equal opportunity to (compete) (operate) on any agreed route between the territories of the two Contracting Parties.

(3) Each Contracting Party shall take into consideration the interests of the airlines of the other Contracting Party so as not to affect unduly their opportunity to offer the services covered by this Agreement.

(4) Services provided by a designated airline under this Agreement shall retain as their primary objective the provision of capacity adequate to the traffic demands between the country of which such airline is a national and the country of ultimate destination of the traffic. The right to embark or disembark on such services international traffic destined for and coming from third countries at a point or points on the routes specified in this Agreement shall be exercised in accordance with the general principles of orderly development of international air transport to which both Contracting Parties subscribe and shall be subject to the general principle that capacity should be related to:

(a) the traffic requirements between the country of origin and the countries of ultimate destination of the traffic;

(b) the requirements of through airline operations; and

(c) the traffic requirements of the area through which the airline passes, after taking account of local and regional services.

(5) Consultations between the Contracting Parties shall be arranged whenever a Party requests that the capacity provided under the Agreement be reviewed to ensure the application of the principles in the Agreement governing the conduct of the services.

Source: International Civil Aviation Organization, "Panel of Experts on Regulation of Air Transport Services," Report of the Third Meeting (15-26 October 1979).

Figure 3-4. Model Capacity Clause: Bermuda One Type Method

governments have found the regulatory system developed after World War II to be incapable of accommodating the continuously changing air transportation system. As a result, the United States has adopted new aviation policies and attempted to change certain aspects of the existing regulatory system.

This unilateral action on the part of the United States has been received unfavorably by the international aviation community, which, as evidenced from ICAO's two SATCs, has recommended that the difficulties faced by the system must be discussed and resolved through common approaches, taking into consideration the interests of all participants.

Notes

1. International Air Transport Association, "World Air Transport: 60th Anniversary 1919-1979" (December 1979).

2. N.K. Taneja, *U.S. International Aviation Policy* (Lexington, Mass.: Lexington Books, D.C. Heath Co., 1980).

3. International Civil Aviation Organization, *Tariff Enforcement*, Circular 135-AT/41 (September 1977), pp. 21-23.

4. Ibid., pp. 16-17.

5. International Civil Aviation Organization, *Special Air Transport Conference Report*, Doc. 9199 (1977), pp. 6-7.

6. M. Karamoko, "International Nonscheduled Passenger Air Transport: Origins, Characteristics, Development, Issues," M.S. thesis, M.I.T., (June 1979), pp. 38-40.

7. International Civil Aviation Bulletin, *Special Air Transport Conference Report*, Doc. 9199 (1977), pp. 11-12.

8. _____ . *Policy concerning International Non-Scheduled Air Transport*, Circular 136-AT/42 (September 1977).

9. _____ . *Regulation of Capacity in International Air Transport Services*, Circular 137-AT/42 (September 1977), pp. 22-23.

10. _____ . *Special Air Transport Conference Report*, Doc. 9199 (1977), pp. 16-17.

11. _____ . "Panel of Experts on the Machinery for the Establishment of International Fares and Rates," Report of the First Meeting (6-17 December 1976).

12. N.K. Taneja, *U.S. International Aviation Policy* (Lexington, Mass.: Lexington Books, D.C. Heath and Company, 1980).

13. International Air Transport Association, *Review*, vol. 14, no. 3 (July-August 1979):16.

14. U.S. Civil Aeronautics Board, "Investigation into the Competitive Marketing of Air Transportation," Order no. 79-9-64 (Docket 36595) (13 September 1979), pp. 16-17.

4 Domestic and International Air Fares

Since 1977 there has been intensive activity in the field of domestic and international air fares, resulting partly from the changing regulatory environment and partly from the economic environment. De facto deregulation of the U.S. domestic industry by the CAB, ICAO's first SATC, procompetitive guidelines for the negotiation of U.S. bilateral agreements, the CAB's attack on the IATA traffic-conference machinery, passage of the Airline Deregulation Act of 1978 and the International Air Transportation Competition Act of 1979, and ICAO's second SATC have all had significant influence on tariffs. Fares have been influenced by increasing fuel prices, high inflation and interest rates, and changing currency exchange rates. This chapter reviews major developments relating to the structure and level of domestic and international scheduled passenger fares.

Domestic Fares

Until the conclusion of the domestic passenger fare investigation (DPFI) in 1974, the CAB did not have comprehensive standards for evaluating the reasonableness of tariffs proposed by the industry. The objective of the nine-phased DPFI was to develop these standards. The result was the establishment of an inflexible normal fare structure for coach service based on the industry's average costs by length of trip, at standard load factors that averaged 55 percent but varied by distance. The formula was inflexible in that it produced identical fares for all equal-distant markets even though a higher or lower fare might be warranted, based on cost or marketing considerations. Individual carriers were allowed to file across-the-board changes (upward or downward) in the entire structure but could not adjust fares in particular markets. The only way to compete on price in an individual market was either to offer a restricted promotional fare or establish a new class of service. However, the CAB felt that some measure of price competition was necessary to obtain improved carrier efficiency and an improvement in the allocation of resources.

The domestic passenger fares began to deviate from the DPFI standards in the spring of 1977 when the CAB approved "Peanut Fares," filed by Texas International, and "Supersaver Fares," filed by American Airlines. The latter fare represented, for example, a 40 percent discount of the normal coach fare and was more than likely outside the range allowed under the DPFI criteria. Similar discount fare proposals continued to be filed when on 3 September 1978, the CAB adopted its fare flexibility rule PS-80, designed to introduce market-by-market price competition by eliminating DPFI rules requiring fares to be established uniformly on a mileage basis (phase 9). The DPFI also required the first-class fares to be established at a fixed percentage above the coach fares (phase 9) and the discount fares not only had to be justified on the basis of the profit impact test but contained an expiration date not to exceed 18 months (phase 5). These and other DPFI criteria were replaced in the Airline Deregulation Act of 1978, by the Standard Industry Fare Level (SIFL) to be adjusted at least twice a year to reflect changes in actual industry costs.

In the PS-80, the CAB established a suspend-free zone ranging from 10 percent above to 70 percent below the existing DPFI (phase 9) coach fare.[1] Within this range, carriers were allowed to file fares without economic justification and they were expected to be approved unless another party could demonstrate that their approval would cause irreparable damage to competition. In markets where four or more carriers had nonstop authority, the upper limit was 10 percent above the SIFL; in all other markets the upper limit was 5 percent; and local-service carriers were allowed to set their fares up to 30 percent above the SIFL ceiling. The lower limit was generally 50 percent below the SIFL and could be as much as 70 percent below for up to 40 percent of a carrier's weekly available seat-miles. For carriers operating aircraft with less than sixty seats, there was no upper or lower limit on fares.

The PS-80 ceilings were based on the DPFI phase 9 formula as adjusted by the CAB's fare level standards and for cost increases. The Airline Deregulation Act of 1978 ratified PS-80's zone-of-reasonableness concept but called for a slightly different method of establishing the ceiling fare. The CAB was required to determine a SIFL for each pair of points and each class of service, using the fare level in effect on 1 July 1977 and updated by the percentage change in operating costs per available seat-mile. The basic fare for SIFL (effective 15 July 1977) was given by the following formula:

$$\$16.16 + 8.84 \text{ cents per mile (0-500 miles)}$$
$$+ 6.74 \text{ cents per mile (501-1500 miles)}$$
$$+ 6.48 \text{ cents per mile (over 1500 miles).}$$

Some carriers supported the CAB policy, some suggested modifications to the flexibility zone, and some opposed the policy on legal grounds. Eastern favored maintaining status quo on the grounds that the new policy would create anomalies in that passengers in high-volume markets would benefit while in other markets they would receive lower service at higher fares. The CAB was not persuaded by Eastern's equity argument and instead reemphasized the benefits of its policy, namely, that the public would benefit if fares are based on actual costs in particular markets rather than on broad industry average costs.

A number of carriers objected to the concept of computing ceiling fares based on the DPFI formula which was established on the basis of industry average costs in both high- and low-cost markets. The phase 9 formula produced fares in the long-haul markets that were above the corresponding costs and fares in short-haul markets that were below the costs. Under the new policy, cross-subsidization of markets would no longer be possible since carriers would reduce their fares in the long-haul markets but would be prevented by the ceiling from increasing their short-haul fares. Carriers submitted various proposals to overcome this difficulty. The CAB decided to ignore these arguments on the assumption that not only are there applicants willing to provide service in all markets at fares below the DPFI level but that local-service carriers could still establish fares up to 30 percent above the coach fares and all carriers could raise their load factors above the 55 percent standard incorporated in the DPFI formula. As to the adjustment of the fare ceiling, the board proposed to make the changes on the basis of costs alone. Finally, some of the carriers also raised an issue with respect to the floor of the zone, set at 50 percent below the ceiling level and 70 percent below for the off-peak period. However, based on the experience of the intrastate carrier, Southwest, the board decided to ignore the comments filed by the major carriers.

After passage of the Airline Deregulation Act, the SIFL continued to be updated to reflect the increases in airline costs, particularly the increases in fuel costs. At the same time, the CAB continued its liberal policy of issuing multiple permissive awards where all fit applicants were granted authority regardless of whether an applicant actually intended to operate service in the market.[2] As a result, an airline was in a position to offer service in almost any domestic market. In 1977, the U.S. trunk and local-service carriers had authority to serve about 25,000 city-pairs. By the spring of 1980, they held authority to serve over 100,000 city-pairs.[3] Open entry began to cause the carriers to shift toward longer-haul service. However, the CAB was of the opinion that this widespread shift may also have been the result of the SIFL formula, which made long-haul service more attractive than short haul.[4] As a result, the CAB proposed several possible changes to make its fare policies more flexible during the remaining transition period (through 31 December 1982). The following alternatives were proposed by the CAB for domestic fare flexibility:

1. Full downward flexibility in all markets.
2. Ten percent upward flexibility in two- and three-carrier markets.

3. Full upward flexibility for markets up to 200 miles and 30 percent (or more) upward for 200 to 400 mile markets.
4. Full upward flexibility for a portion of each carrier's capacity each week (or some other period) in each market (or system).
5. Thirty percent upward flexibility in all markets (or 50 percent for 0 to 200 or 0 to 400 mile markets).
6. Full upward flexibility in all markets.

The CAB requested comments on its proposed alternatives after having pointed out the pros and cons of regulation through the SIFL formula. On the positive side, the use of SIFL protected the consumer from potential abuses of monopoly power. On the negative side, SIFL was biased in favor of long-haul markets; in some markets it facilitated tacit price coordination, and it served as a practical disincentive to innovative pricing. The commenters were asked to focus on remaining barriers to entry. At the time the Notice of Proposed Rulemaking was issued, this SIFL formula was in effect:

$$\$23.86 \ + \ 13.05 \text{ cents per mile (0-500 miles)}$$
$$+ \ 9.95 \text{ cents per mile (501-1500 miles)}$$
$$+ \ 9.57 \text{ cents per mile (over 1500 miles).}$$

On 12 June 1980, the CAB issued its interim policy statement (PS-94) in which it broadened the fare zone: full downward flexibility in all markets; full upward flexibility in 0 to 200 mile markets; up to 50 percent above SIFL in 200 to 400 mile markets; and up to 30 percent above SIFL for flights over 400 miles. The SIFL formula as of 1 July 1980 was

$$\$25.92 \ + \ 14.18 \text{ cents per mile (0-500 miles)}$$
$$+ \ 10.81 \text{ cents per mile (501-1500 miles)}$$
$$+ \ 10.39 \text{ cents per mile (over 1500 miles).}$$

Most of the commenters supported the full downward fare flexibility (option 1). Carriers in general argued for unlimited pricing freedom as the way to achieve greater service and price options resulting from innovation by management. The majority of the commenters supporting increased upward flexibility opposed the option of full upward flexibility for a portion of each carrier's available seat-miles as administratively unworkable. Parties opposing substantially broadened upward fare flexibility argued their case on the basis of inconsistency with the congressional intent to pursue deregulation on a fixed timetable. Having taken into consideration all comments, the CAB decided to establish the full 50/30 percent scheme of upward flexibility.

The proponents of airline deregulation claim that it has produced low fares and high growth in passenger traffic. It must be pointed out that the declining trend in real yield is not a new phenomena; the real yield has been declining since 1950 (see table 4-1). Moreover, in 1980, the real yield is expected to increase by 12 percent; actual yield by 27 percent. Turning to the question of traffic growth, while it is true that a reduction in yield will in general lead to higher growth in traffic, there is no specific relationship between the two in any given year. In 1959, for example, an increase in real

Table 4-1
Actual and Real Airline Yield for Domestic Trunks

| Year | Actual Yield | | Consumer Price Index | | Real Yield | |
	Cents	Percent		Percent Change	Cents	Percent
1949	5.75	0.4	71.4	(1.0)	8.05	1.3
1950	5.54	(3.6)	72.1	1.0	7.68	(4.6)
1951	5.59	0.9	77.8	7.9	7.19	(6.4)
1952	5.54	(0.9)	79.5	2.2	6.97	(3.1)
1953	5.43	(2.0)	80.1	0.8	6.78	(2.7)
1954	5.37	(1.1)	80.5	0.5	6.67	(1.6)
1955	5.32	(0.9)	80.2	(0.4)	6.63	(0.6)
1956	5.28	(0.7)	81.4	1.5	6.49	(2.1)
1957	5.25	(0.6)	84.3	3.6	6.23	(4.0)
1958	5.58	6.3	86.6	2.7	6.44	3.4
1959	5.80	3.9	87.3	0.8	6.64	3.1
1960	6.01	3.6	88.7	1.6	6.78	2.1
1961	6.19	3.0	89.6	1.0	6.91	2.9
1962	6.35	2.6	90.6	1.1	7.01	1.5
1963	6.07	(4.4)	91.7	1.2	6.62	(5.6)
1964	6.01	(1.0)	92.9	1.3	6.47	(2.3)
1965	5.94	(1.2)	94.5	1.7	6.29	(2.8)
1966	5.69	(4.2)	97.2	2.9	5.85	(7.0)
1967	5.50	(3.3)	100.0	2.9	5.50	(6.0)
1968	5.45	(0.9)	104.2	4.2	5.23	(4.9)
1969 (48 states)	5.70	4.6	109.8	5.4	5.19	(0.8)
1969 (50 states)	5.59	—	109.8	—	5.09	—
1970	5.77	3.2	116.3	5.9	4.96	(2.5)
1971	6.09	5.6	121.3	4.3	5.02	1.2
1972	6.16	1.2	125.3	3.3	4.92	(2.0)
1973	6.38	3.6	133.1	6.2	4.79	(2.6)
1974	7.24	13.5	147.7	11.0	4.90	2.3
1975	7.35	1.5	161.2	.9.1	4.56	(6.9)
1976	7.79	6.0	170.5	5.8	4.57	0.2
1977	8.24	5.8	181.5	6.5	4.54	(0.7)
1978	8.08	(1.9)	195.4	7.7	4.14	(8.8)
1979	8.50	5.2	217.4	11.3	3.91	(5.6)
1980E	10.80	27.0	246.6	13.4	4.38	12.0

Source: Merrill Lynch, Pierce, Fenner and Smith, Inc., "Aviation Log," *Institutional Report* vol. 3, no. 12 (3 September 1980):4. Reprinted with permission.

yield of 3.1 percent was accompanied by an increase in traffic of 15.1 percent. This counter-intuitive trend continued through the next three years and also existed in 1971 and 1976 (see table 4-1).

It is noteworthy that the so-called bargain fares are available, in general, only in the longer-haul, high-density markets. For example, the low fare of $99 in the New York-Los Angeles market was only $2 more than the fare in the Boston-Washington market. On the other hand, the New York-Los Angeles length of haul is about seven times that of Boston-Washington. The situation, therefore, is one where the benefits have been redistributed: consumers in some markets are enjoying significantly lower fares, while in other markets fares are significantly higher. In any case, the large volume of traffic generated by the bargain fares has not translated into long-term profits. The losses in the highly competitive markets are already being, or will ultimately be, subsidized by the excessive profits in other markets. This topic is explored in detail in chapter 5.

International Fares

The IATA Traffic-Conference Machinery Controversy

Until recently, the majority of the scheduled international tariffs (both passenger and cargo) have been coordinated through the IATA traffic-conference machinery. Beginning with the Bermuda One agreement of 1946, most bilateral agreements have made direct reference to the IATA rate-making machinery and a few have made indirect reference to it. Even in the case of governments whose airlines are not members of IATA and whose bilaterals do not contain specific mention of IATA, the non-IATA airlines are still indirectly bound, to some extent, by the existing IATA tariffs due to the dominance in international markets by IATA members. In recent years, this highly publicized system has been criticized and now a controversy exists on two questions: Is the system unnecessarily complex and perhaps unnecessary altogether?, and Has the system caused scheduled international fares and rates to be higher than those under some other system? With respect to the first question, the system is complex but for valid reasons. As to the need for such a system, the answer is unequivocally yes; there is no realistic alternative. The answer to the second question is probably no, given that there is no realistic alternative available to replace the existing multilateral process—at least no alternative that would provide a long-term solution. Any analysis beyond superficial criticism will show that the imperfections and deficiencies often raised with respect to the IATA machinery are invalid. The real problem is lack of understanding about the process on the part of the critics.

Before proceeding with the general criticisms, let us briefly review the IATA rate-making process. International tariffs are coordinated through traffic conferences. The original pattern of nine different regional conferences was replaced by one consisting of three areas that collectively cover all regions of the world. These three are supplemented by joint conferences to deal with matters that affect more than one conference area and a composite conference that deals with matters on a worldwide basis. Under normal circumstances each conference meets once every two years and is supported by a host of permanent committees, specialized subcommittees, and working groups. Conference resolutions are reached by votes and used to be valid and binding on the carriers only if accepted unanimously. In 1976, the concept of limited agreement was implemented to surmount the problem of achieving unanimity. This agreement applies only to carriers operating under third- and fourth-freedom rights in a given conference zone.

The first step in the establishment of tariffs is to agree on a comprehensive pattern of specified fares based on the use of the basic currencies (U.S. dollar and pound sterling). The next step is to compute, using the agreed construction rules, all other normal fares to meet the particular needs of individual carriers. This step is a reasonable one given the almost half-million fares in use. The basic normal fares are established after taking into account a number of factors. These include distance, specified needs of the carriers primarily interested in the routes in question, specific needs of governments with respect to promotion of tourism, price elasticity of demand, anticipated demand patterns in related city-pairs, availability and nature of competition (non-IATA carriers, nonscheduled carriers, scheduled carriers, and surface carriers), and, of course, costs. Added to this general list of factors are the route-linking strategies of individual carriers, a factor that affects not only traffic but also costs.

Numerous IATA committees provide supporting material to serve as a basis for deliberations on fares. These include, for example, the Cost Committee and the Commercial Research Committee which collect and analyze data supplied by individual members to establish industrial guidelines to determine the overall impact of various fare and rate patterns.

Through the conferences IATA members develop very detailed tariffs for approval by their governments. The tariffs coordinated are extremely comprehensive and include fare and rate levels, types, and conditions of service. With the changing and increasingly diverse market conditions, the coordination process began to get increasingly so complex that it became quite difficult to reach traditional agreements. As a result, a special task force was established to review the traffic-conference machinery. This task force concluded that, while the association was a necessity, changes were warranted if the association was to remain effective. The task force recommended that:

1. the activities of IATA should be regrouped into two categories as
    follows:
    a. trade association activities with mandatory membership;
    b. tariff coordination activities with respect to passenger, cargo, or
        both matters with optional membership;
2. a. the existing three individual traffic conferences and the four joint
        traffic conferences be retained;
    b. the existing subarea provisions be redefined;
    c. the existing voting rights be maintained;
3. the provisions with respect to limited agreements be made permanent;
4. the traffic conferences recognize the prime interest of third- and fourth-
    freedom carriers in establishing the fare levels for the traffic carried at
    the lowest fares, and the interest of other carriers in carrying traffic at
    such fares;
5. members should be able to introduce innovative fares and rates between
    their own countries and other countries;
6. a. conditions of service pertaining to meals, bar service, sales on
        board, and in-flight entertainment should no longer be the subject
        of agreements;
    b. conditions of service should be reviewed with respect to giveaways;
    c. all resolutions should be reviewed to eliminate any unnecessary
        regulation;
7. a. third parties be allowed to present their position to the traffic con-
        ferences;
    b. the ICAO secretariat be invited to attend traffic conferences with
        observer status;
8. the compliance program of IATA be modified so as to place greater
    emphasis on the preventive rather than the punitive aspects;
9. the Executive Committee redefine the terms of reference of the Traffic
    Committee and the Industry Policy Committee.

All of these recommendations were implemented in 1979 to restructure
the association and its tariff-coordinating activities. For example,
observers from ICAO and AEA have attended the conference meetings. In
addition, third parties (such as the UFTAA, the International Chamber of
Commerce, and the International Organization of Consumers' Unions)
have been given an opportunity to provide their input. New fare-
construction rules now provide that mileage flown be measured over
ticketed points instead of over the actual aircraft routing. Maximum
deviation allowed (previously 20 percent) has been reduced in many areas
and the deviation surcharges have been modified. The modifications,
therefore, provide the needed flexibility to make the tariff-coordinating
process more responsive to the changing market and regulatory conditions.

In the past, there may have been an element of validity in some of the criticisms raised by the opponents of IATA. These included, for example, the excessive delays resulting from the use of the unanimity rule, and the influence of fifth-freedom carriers on tariffs relating to third- and fourth-freedom operations. Many of these criticisms no longer apply with the restructured conference machinery (that is, two-tier structure and an opportunity available for significant fare innovations). On the other hand, the following general criticisms, perhaps unwarranted, continue to be made about the association and its tariff-coordination process.

The first deficiency cited by critics relates to the lack of input by the user, either consumers or, more likely, governments representing consumers. But, governments have always had, directly and indirectly, the opportunity to provide their input. Not only have they been in a position to accept or reject the ultimately negotiated tariffs, but each and every government can provide policy guidelines to their carriers prior to the meetings. The fact that, in some cases, a carrier regulates the government rather than the other way around is hardly a fault of the IATA machinery. Direct participation by government is neither a realistic nor a desirable solution. The process is sufficiently complicated as it is without involving added bureaucracy. And, in a number of cases, there is a lack of expertise and manpower in the appropriate government agency to deal adequately with the full complement of tariff issues. Some government officials feel that they are not given sufficient time to review the coordinated tariffs. Again, that is often an inherent problem of bureaucracy.

The second general criticism relates to the inability of some carriers to acquire equal opportunity to access certain markets, given the restrictions on such access and the elimination of interlining and stopovers through the introduction and modification of IATA resolutions. Although there is some validity to this criticism, the real problem is not with any inadequacy or deficiency with the tariff-coordination system but rather with the definition and the ultimately negotiated traffic rights.

Third, a criticism is often lodged against the IATA tariff-negotiation system that nonscheduled carriers, not being members of IATA, are unable to participate in the traffic-conference machinery. This is an unfair criticism. To begin with, it is not clear why such participation is necessary. Although these carriers provide a needed service, they are usually subject to different government regulatory policies than scheduled carriers. In any case, IATA has been willing in the past to have their participation; not only did the nonscheduled carriers refuse to participate, but the CAB objected to the proposal.

The fourth criticism is often directed at the complexity of tariff structure. Once again, while the criticism is valid, one must understand the reasons behind the complexity. Fares are a function of cost, marketing, and political factors. Each one of these three factors varies by market, airline, and time period, and the influence of each factor is not necessarily independent of the other two factors. Finally, a large percentage of the operating costs of an international airline are not under the direct control of its management. These include, for example, fuel costs and user charges. Given these constraints, it is difficult to see how much the tariff structure could be simplified. Recently, the CAB has pointed to the need to unbundle international fares. This concept would create two types of fares: the basic point-to-point fare with no extra privileges (such as interlining, stopovers, and different routings), and the bundled fares with all the trimmings. While the concept has some theoretical appeal, it should be noted that it would simply redistribute benefits in that some travelers would pay less while others would pay more.

There is no question that multilateral negotiations produce balanced tariffs that are available for travel over all scheduled carriers. Moreover, the IATA coordinating process has resulted in lower fares not higher ones. Consider the following hypothesis. Since all airlines do not have uniform costs, one would expect that a low-cost carrier would propose a low fare. This carrier would undoubtedly have a strong bargaining position since failure to reach an agreement on its terms would mean no agreement at all and the possibility of unilateral fare filings, which could in turn introduce the lower fare proposed initially. Has this mode of operation existed? If it has not, then why has the industry produced such a meager return on its investment? And, during the last ten years, why has the average transatlantic economy fare increased by only half as much as the OECD-weighted composite price index for the United States, Canada, and Western Europe?

There is no question that IATA's multilateral process, despite its weaknesses, represents the optimal method of negotiating international tariffs. The system provides definite benefits to consumers, carriers, and governments. For the consumer, the system provides access to a worldwide system with an interline network that allows travel between any point in the world on a single ticket paid for in the national currency. For the carrier, the system provides an opportunity for participation in tariff coordination, interline, and prorated arrangements, and the establishment of standardized procedures—all necessary elements in the long-term planning process. Finally, the system allows different governments to reconcile their conflicting national objectives and interests in an apolitical forum.

Interlining. The *interline system* represents the heart of the integrated global scheduled air-transportation system, whose maintenance and integrity requires a great deal of airline cooperation. The interline system requires the availability of standardized documentation (including contractual conditions of transportation), commonly agreed industry practices (regarding reservations and traffic handling), and the availability of an intercarrier clearing and settlement system. All these requirements are met by the interline system established through the IATA multilateral forum for coordinating international tariffs on a worldwide basis.

The coordination of international tariffs is a prerequisite to the development and maintenance of an effective interline system. For example, an airline would want to establish interline agreements only if the existence of such agreements makes a reasonable contribution to its online services. In the case of through fares, this condition can only be met by the development of a satisfactory proration of revenue. The multilateral tariff-coordination process allows interline tariffs to be developed to provide the consumer with a more flexible air-transportation system.

The unilateral decision of the U.S. government to attempt to dismantle the IATA tariff-coordinating process would set back, and possibly eliminate entirely, the interline process. Even with the CAB's interim decision to let IATA function for two more years, the lack of participation by U.S. carriers in the tariff-coordination process will reduce the effectiveness of interlining. The only reason that the situation on the North Atlantic routes has not become totally chaotic is because carriers continue to use basic procedures discussed, debated, and adopted at the past traffic conferences. But this situation cannot continue forever without a coordinated system. Also, the proliferation of international tariffs outside of the IATA regime, resulting from country-of-origin, double-disapproval, and point-to-point principles, are inhibiting the continuation of the interline system.

The value of interlining is even more pronounced in the case of air cargo because charges can include elements other than transportation by air (pick-up and delivery, customs clearing, and so forth) and can be collected either from the shipper or from the consignee. Moreover, the exact routing is not always specified in the case of air-cargo movements. Interlining is therefore more a function of the exchange of transportation documents and establishment of common procedures and practices than of the number of carriers involved. In the case of industry practices, IATA's efforts have been devoted to reservations; agency automation; cargo automation; passenger, cargo, and general traffic handling; baggage handling; and special cargo services. In addition to these industry practices, interlining requires a number of multilateral facilities established by IATA. These include, for example, the Clearing House, the Prorate Agency, the Bank Settlement Plan, the Cargo Accounts Settlement System, and the Multilateral ULD Control Agreement.

The following hypothetical example, taken from IATA's March-April 1980 *Review*, illustrates the complexities of a traditional interline process. A travel agent in Mexico City issues a ticket from Mexico City to Bombay via Los Angeles, Tokyo, and Bangkok with return travel via Singapore, Manila, Honolulu, and Los Angeles (figure 4-1a). The ticket is charged on a Universal Air Travel Plan (UATP) credit card issued by United Air Lines.

(a)

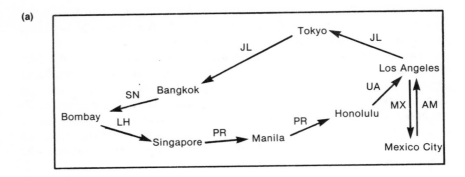

(b)

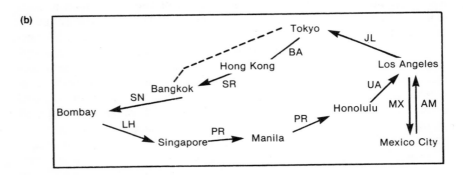

(c)

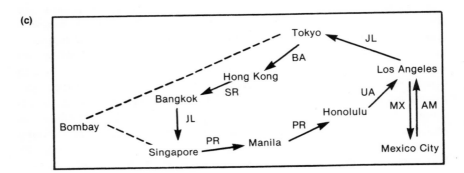

Source: International Air Transport Association, *Review* vol. 15, no. 2 (March-April 1980):13-15.

Note: AM: Aeromexico   JL: Japan Air Lines   BA: British Airways
SN: Sabena   SR: Swissair   PR: Philippine Air Lines   UA: United
MX: Mexicana   LH: Lufthansa

Figure 4-1. The Interlining Multilateral Facilitative Activity

The multilateral process requires the travel agent to communicate the passenger's itinerary to Aeromexico (the first carrier) which uses the multiaccess reservation system to arrange the rest of the itinerary shown in figure 4-1a. The travel agent will be advised by Aeromexico of the fare ($2,034) based on multilateral construction and routing practices and common-currency basis. The agent will in turn issue a standard multilateral interline ticket on Aeromexico stock, with nine flight coupons and three auditor's coupons which, along with the credit-card script, are sent to a local Mexican bank appointed under the bank Settlement Plan. The agent would have deducted his standard commission. The local bank will send the script and the auditor's coupons to Aeromexico.

Aeromexico, in turn, will bill United, since this airline will have collected the money through its UATP card. The actual billing is undertaken through the IATA Clearing House, which arranges for net settlements having processed the various billings submitted by different member and nonmember carriers. At this stage, Aeromexico has been credited the total fare. In the first stage, Japan Air Lines (JL), which has a claim for the Los Angeles-Tokyo portion of the trip, will bill Aeromexico through the clearing house for the multilaterally established portion of the charges in U.S. dollars.

Now suppose that before leaving Tokyo, the passenger is required to go to Hong Kong before arriving in Bangkok. The passenger would contact the next carrier on the itinerary (Japan Air Lines) to make the necessary change and issue a ticket using its own identification plate and at no additional charge to the passenger. The revised itinerary is shown in figure 4-1b. Now JL will collect from Aeromexico the remaining portion of the total fare. On the new ticket issued by JL, the first coupon shows transportation on British Airways (BA) from Tokyo to Hong Kong. This carrier will now claim a portion of the fare from JL in pounds sterling. The next portion of the trip is on Swissair (from Hong Kong to Bangkok) and, as in the case of BA, it also makes a claim against JL.

In Bangkok, the passenger, deciding that the trip to Bombay is no longer required, contacts Sabena, the next carrier on the itinerary. Sabena makes a new reservation on JL from Bangkok to Singapore, computes the refund totaling $306 (7,038 Mexican pesos), and issues a new ticket. This refund is made using a miscellaneous charges order with a credit to the UATP account with United. The revised itinerary is shown in figure 4-1c. Now Sabena makes a claim against JL for the remaining portion of the total fare.

The next portion of the trip is in fact on JL, which will now make a claim against Sabena for the Bangkok-Singapore sector. Next, Philippine Air Lines will submit a claim against Sabena for the Singapore-Manila and the Manila-Honolulu sectors. Similarly, United and Mexicana will claim from Sabena the portions of the fare for the Honolulu-Los Angeles and

Los Angeles-Mexico City sectors, respectively. However, Mexicana's claim will be handled through the Airlines Clearing House, the U.S. counterpart of the IATA Clearing House. Finally, United bills Aeromexico for the amount of refund and Aeromexico, in turn, bills Sabena. All financial transactions will ultimately be performed through the IATA Clearing House. (During 1979, the two-way turnover through the clearing house amounted to over $20 billion.)

There is no question that passengers and carriers could perform the interlining function without the multilateral machinery of IATA. However, it is likely to be less convenient and more expensive to passengers. For example, a passenger would need to negotiate with multiple carriers and agents using multiple currencies, rules, and regulations concerning the conditions of travel. At the same time, for cases other than point-to-point travel, costs could be higher if the inbound and outbound travel is made on different carriers or if the routing is changed.

Critics of the IATA multilateral tariff coordinating machinery often compare the U.S. domestic to the international interlining system. Unfortunately, neither are the two systems identical nor can the domestic system be automatically extended to include international operations. In the first place, all financial transactions in domestic operations occur in the same currency. Also fare structure and level are established with a more consistent and less complex formula (for example, as a function of distance). Finally, the U.S. domestic system is more developed than many segments of the international system with respect to level of frequency and number of nonstop and direct flights. For these reasons, it would be unrealistic to assume that the U.S. domestic interlining system could simply be transferred to the international arena.

Fare Anomalies. Consumers, with little or no knowledge of airline economics, have often questioned the numerous anomalies in international passenger fares and cargo rates. Typical questions are: Why are transatlantic fares lower than intra-European fares? Why are fares higher during peak periods? Why are scheduled fares higher than nonscheduled fares? Why are cargo rates higher and lower in different directions? There are no simple answers to these questions. Among other factors, fares and rates are a function of cost considerations, traffic mix on a route, season, density, direction (in the case of cargo), degree of competition (including other modes of transportation), and government policy such as the development of tourism.

Consider the case of transatlantic fares versus intra-European fares. The greater length of haul and traffic density on the North Atlantic routes allows the introduction of larger and more efficient aircraft. Unit cost of transatlantic operations is therefore lower than for the intra-European operations. Operating costs of European operations are also higher compared to the U.S. domestic operations because of the differences in the price of fuel and user charges, such as landing fees. Marketing considerations also have an influence on costs. Passenger traffic on intra-European routes is more business-oriented than on transatlantic routes. The exceptionally high level of business traffic forces airlines to increase frequency by using smaller aircraft, which in turn increases operating costs. Finally, intra-European passengers traveling for nonbusiness purposes tend to use the services of nonscheduled carriers. These are only some of the reasons why costs and, in turn, fares tend to differ between transatlantic and intra-European markets.

The comparison of intra-European fares with transatlantic fares is often extended to include U.S. domestic operations. Unfortunately, such comparisons are meaningless. At the outset it should be pointed out that some critics, in order to make their point, end up comparing normal economy fares in one region with discount fares in another. Such comparisons are loaded and misleading. Nevertheless, it is a fact that intra-European fares are higher than U.S. domestic fares. But there are often valid reasons for this differential. Besides the differences in operating costs cited earlier, the U.S. carriers operate in a homogeneous market with no international boundaries to cross, no political philosophies to reconcile, and no economic interests to protect. The U.S. carriers also operate in markets that are broad based, that is, the scheduled carriers transport business travelers as well as those traveling for vacation or personal reasons. In other words, the last two categories are not inaccessible to the scheduled carriers. In Europe, the nonscheduled carriers account for more than half of the total revenue passenger miles. Therefore, more of the traffic carried by scheduled carriers tends to be business oriented. Finally, the star-shaped route structure of the intra-European carriers tends to introduce greater inefficiencies relative to the collection of stars or galaxy-type route structures of U.S. domestic carriers. The European carriers are therefore operating under different rules and in a different environment. As a result, their tariffs are different from those available in the U.S. domestic or transatlantic markets.

The issue of higher fares during peak periods is slightly more complex. The scheduled airlines provide service on a year-round basis in all markets—dense as well as thin markets. However, traffic fluctuates tremendously from market to market and from season to season. While it would be possible for a scheduled airline to reduce the fares in some markets during peak-period travel, it would then be impossible for that airline to offer any service during off-peak periods. In order to provide service on all routes throughout the year, carriers cross-subsidize their operations across markets and across seasons. The question sometimes asked is, ''If the load factor is low during off-peak periods and the airline is unable to meet its operating costs, why not raise fares?" Unfortunately, such a strategy, depending on the value of price elasticity and the traffic mix, could reduce load factors even further, resulting in the necessity for even higher fares.

The question of the difference between nonscheduled and scheduled services is raised so often that it deserves some explanation. To begin with, the operating costs of nonscheduled operations are lower. Generally, these carriers use older and more densely seat-configured aircraft. Their indirect costs are also much lower. But it is the difference in load factor that allows the nonscheduled carriers to offer lower fares. Whereas the scheduled carriers operate at approximately 60 percent load factor, the nonscheduled carriers operate at load factors closer to 95 percent. If one assumes, perhaps in an oversimplification, that fare is equal to cost divided by load factor, then it is clear that lower cost accompanied by high load factor provides an opportunity to offer low fares. One must remember, however, that the two services are not identical. Nonscheduled carriers offer service only at certain times of the year, in certain markets, to large groups, and with almost no flexibility to change reservations, routings, airlines, and destinations. The lower fare is therefore accompanied by lower quality of service.

In the case of air cargo, rates tend to vary by direction and commodity. Here again, cost considerations, marketing considerations, and political pressures can be used to explain the anomalies. In the case of costs, densities of certain commodities can make the aircraft cube out before it weighs out. As a result, the cost per ton-mile can vary significantly from commodity to commodity. The variation in rates by direction can be explained by the one-way nature of air cargo. Whereas passengers, in general, make round trips, air cargo moves in one direction only; from the place where the goods are manufactured to the place where they are consumed. Finally, governments can influence rates in order to encourage export of certain commodities or discourage the import of other commodities.

The preceding examples illustrate the reasons for the anomalies that exist in international fares and rates. As shown, there are usually good reasons for the regional variation in tariffs. In addition to the cost, marketing, and political reasons cited, there are also unique characteristics of the airline industry. According to an IATA study, the differences between the airline and other industries can be explained by three facts: (1) productivity of an airline depends almost completely on its fleet; (2) output (seat departure) cannot be inventoried; and (3) a large percentage of the operating costs are outside of an airline's control. It is these differences that can help explain the economic performance and conduct of the industry.

Special Drawing Rights. The agreement on a multilaterally acceptable pricing unit has been the topic of an on-going study for a number of years but with greater urgency since 1973 when currency conversion rates were frozen.

Prior to this the fares were coordinated in two basic currencies: the U.S. dollar and the U.K. pound. Conversion rates were then agreed for each country for application to the basic currencies to establish local selling fares. Under this system, the currency fluctuations beginning in February 1973, if reflected in the full fluctuations against the basic currencies in the IATA conversion rates, would have resulted in substantial changes in local selling fares. The changes would not have been commensurate with other cost changes and market conditions within the countries in question. To overcome this difficulty and maintain fares at the required selling level, the conversion rates were frozen and adjustment factors were established to relate local selling fares with the basic currency fares. The adjustment factor, in the form of either a surcharge or a discount, is computed in the following manner:

$$\text{Adjustment Factor} = \frac{\text{Local Selling Fare}}{\text{Frozen Exchange Rate} \times \text{Basic Fare}}$$

For tariff construction purposes carriers use artificial fare construction units (FCU) which in reality are the pre-February 1973 U.S. dollar fares.

Since a large portion of a carrier's revenue is derived from sales within its own country, there is a need for a common basic currency so that fare structures can be established that are fully integrated on a worldwide system. The basic common currency unit was required to meet the following criteria:[5]

1. highest possible degree of stability in the value of the unit;
2. compatibility in the face of any conceivable kind of exchange rate movement, with or without a parity system (that is, floating situations, widening of trading margins, joint floats, crawling pegs, and changes in any other financial indicators);
3. practicability in its actual use for industry purposes (that is, in establishing traffic-conference fares and rates, in publication, selling and in the application of traffic procedures and practices; also for interline accounting and filing with regulatory agencies);
4. ease of convertibility into selling fares and rates combined with the greatest possible degree of stability in the levels of selling fares and rates;
5. capability of avoiding differentials in selling fares and rates but nevertheless enabling any system of directional fares and rates to operate; and
6. neutrality and credibility as regards its content and application in the eyes of governments, the public and IATA members.

The SDR proposal was first discussed in 1973 and it was approved by the IATA members, in principle, in 1975. The primary objective of the plan was to bring some stability in international fares which were experiencing large fluctuations caused by rapid and wide swings in the values of various currencies (see figure 4-2). The SDRs are monetary units established through a complex formula using, effective January 1981, a weighted average value of the currencies of the five countries having the largest exports of goods and services during the period 1975 to 1979. At this time, the group is composed of the United States, West Germany, France, Japan, and the United Kingdom. This system will replace the current situation where a sixteen-currency basket has been used for the valuation of the SDR while a five-currency basket has been used to determine the interest rate on the SDR.

Effective 1 January 1981, the SDR, defined by the International Monetary Fund (IMF), will be determined using the weights shown in table 4-2. According to IMF, these weights reflect broadly the relative importance of these currencies in international trade and finance. In any case, the currency composition of the basket can be adjusted at five-year intervals beginning 1 January 1986.

The position of U.S. carriers on the SDR plan is unclear. Initially, Pan American, when it was still a member of the IATA, thought that the plan would not have any significant impact since certain governments would not accept an automatic system that would change international fares. Moreover, believing that the U.S. dollar would consistently gain strength, it was Pan American's opinon that the plan would put downward pressure on the U.S. dollar selling fare, resulting in an adverse impact on its revenue. Now that Pan American and most other U.S. carriers are no longer members of the IATA tariff-coordinating-conference machinery, it is questionable whether their objection to the implementation of the SDR plan can have any impact. However, if the plan should be implemented, the U.S. carriers may find it to their advantage to accept the new unit because of their substantial interline traffic.

The Role of Governments

International tariffs negotiated through the IATA traffic conferences have always had direct or indirect input from governments. Participation by the governments has come about in one or more of three ways: review of the tariffs after they have been negotiated at the traffic conferences; preconference briefings to inform airlines of the governments' particular needs and requirements; and direct government orders to national carrier(s) to provide special fares. However, in recent years, the role of government has increased, in several cases, from one of approval-granting agency to direct participation and, in a few other cases, to unilateral action. The increase in

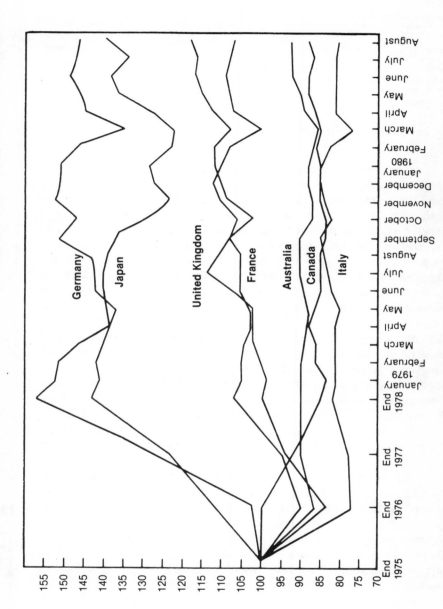

Source: International Air Transport Association, "The State of the Air Transport Industry: Annual Report" (Montreal: 27-30 October 1980), p. 19.

Note: End of Period Exchange Rates in Local Currencies Relative to the US Dollar, Index End of 1975 = 100

Figure 4-2. Recent Comparative Exchange-Rate Developments for Seven Major Countries

Table 4-2
Components of SDR

Currency	Weight (percent)
U.S. dollar	42
Deutsche mark	19
French franc	13
Japanese yen	13
UK Pound	13

Source: International Air Transport Association.

the role of governments stems from a number of perceived deficiencies with the IATA multilateral forum: inability of the national carrier to comprehend the overall national policies and priorities; inability of the government to have direct participation in the conference machinery; inability of the machinery to take sufficient account of consumer interest; inability of conferences to reach decisions in reasonable time periods to provide sufficient opportunity for governments to review the ultimate tariffs; submission of negotiated tariffs (to governments for approval) with insufficient cost and other justification; lack of participation and direct input from nonscheduled and nonmember carriers; monopolistic attitudes of some carriers and their governments; and the ineffective enforcement of the tariffs.

The preceding issues were discussed in great detail at the first SATC of ICAO. The general conclusion was that not only were many of the deficiencies perceived unfairly but that government-established tariffs did not represent a realistic alternative to the existing IATA traffic-conference machinery. As a result the ICAO Council developed the concept of a Standard Bilateral Tariff Clause for the guidance of states. This clause specifically required the carriers to discuss their tariff proposals in advance with their governments and submit the ultimately negotiated tariffs for government approval.

The U.S. government was not totally satisfied with the standard clause and put forward two different concepts that have recently been introduced in some of the bilateral agreements: country-of-origin rules and the double-disapproval rate clause. According to the United States, the addition of these two concepts to the standard one proposed by the ICAO Council would provide not only sufficient flexibility to take account of diversity of markets and operations but also would be consistent with the existing multilateral tariff negotiating machinery. It should be evident that the implementation of the U.S. concepts can lead to unilateral action by some governments. These concepts are predicated on the desirability and existence of free competition, which is very rarely acceptable to developing nations who normally envision free competition to benefit larger carriers at the expense of their small carriers. Because the concepts put forward by the United States have been accepted only by a few nations, they cannot be considered as standard clauses to be admitted into all bilateral agreements. Moreover, their incorporation would undoubtedly lead to the incorporation of many other concepts that are beneficial to other nations. As a result, the U.S. proposal was withdrawn.

Negotiation of special bilaterally agreed fares may be suitable for the two countries involved, but they may restrict or eliminate interlining or stopover privileges. An example of this situation in the Far East and the Pacific Region led to the development of resolutions by multilateral governmental bodies against discriminatory practices. During 1979, actions were taken by two particular bodies, the Association of South East Asian Nations (ASEAN) and the Fifth United Nations Conference on Trade and Development (UNCTAD-V). In both cases, the object was to eliminate in civil aviation the discriminatory practice of systems of duopoly where specially negotiated bilateral fares become an exclusive arrangement between two developed nations. It was assumed that developing countries could not possibly compete with the enormous capacity potential of the developed nations' carriers. (It is interesting that the UNCTAD resolutions are not binding.)

ICAO has had, from time to time, the power to review and recommend changes in international tariffs established by airline associations. In the late fifties, ICAO had received the authority, although it was not used, to study international tariffs and the methods used to establish them, their justification, and the consequences and effects of the delegation of functions to IATA in this field. In 1963, ICAO's Air Transport Committee voted against the need for ICAO to undertake specific studies on other economic work on the subject of international tariffs. Two years later the decision was reversed and the council was authorized to undertake studies to explore and analyze measures to further the development of international travel.

In recent years, however, more positive action has been forthcoming from ICAO beginning with the annual surveys of international air transport fares and rates, followed by studies on regional differences in fares and costs for international scheduled passenger transport. The purpose of the surveys is to provide an overview of international tariffs and to perform comparisons of the levels of fares and rates in different geographical areas. The purpose of regional studies is to provide basic information useful in establishing an objective basis for examining the fare-setting machinery and ultimate agreements. More recently, ICAO has convened its two SATCs to examine air-transport regulatory problems including the tariff machinery. In summary, while ICAO's role in international tariffs has generally been passive, it has become much more active in the last five years.

Standard Foreign Fare Level. The *Standard foreign fare level* (SFFL) is the international equivalent of the domestic SIFL that was established in the Airline Deregulation Act of 1978. The SFFL applies to passenger fares on all routes to and from the United States and contains an automatic approval zone of 5 percent above to 50 percent below the standard level established by the CAB. Any carrier, U.S. or foreign, is allowed to adjust fares within this range without CAB approval unless, on retaliatory or discriminatory grounds, the CAB considers a particular fare not to be in the public interest. The carriers were in favor of this provision since it was a means of reducing the regulatory lag in the introduction of international fare increases, needed to keep up with the increases in the price of fuel.

According to the International Air Transportation Competition Act of 1979, the SFFL was required to be set at the level of fares filed with and approved by the CAB to go into effect on or after 1 October 1979 (with appropriate historical adjustments). Moreover, the standard fare levels were to have been established between each pair of points, for each class of fare, and each class of service existing on 1 October 1979. The act made provisions for the CAB to make adjustments to the base levels where the fare level in effect on 1 October 1979 was determined to be unjust or unreasonable. However, the CAB was allowed only to make such adjustments between a number of points which, in aggregate, combined to a total of 25 percent of all passengers transported internationally by U.S. airlines. This restriction was presumably intended by the U.S. Congress to limit CAB discretion to adjust fare standards on an unlimited basis.

The introduction of fare flexibility in international markets did raise some problems. For example, the CAB considered some markets to be noncompetitive due to the existence of government restrictions on pricing and entry. In any case, unlike the domestic fares that were determined on the basis of DPFI, international fares were coordinated through the IATA traffic-conference machinery, and these were not cost related in the CAB's opinion. In September of 1979, the CAB released a staff study of international fares that concluded that some normal economy fares were high. As a result, an investigation was initiated to examine fare levels in the following twelve markets: New York-Rio de Janeiro, New York-Caracas, Miami-Buenos Aires, Miami-Caracas, Miami-Lima, Los Angeles-Lima, Los Angeles-Tokyo, Seattle-Tokyo, New York-Tokyo, New York-Paris, New York-Athens, and New York-Milan. It is interesting that the CAB decided to attack markets where U.S. bilateral liberalizing initiatives had not been successful. It is also noteworthy that the fares in question had been properly filed prior to 1 October 1979 and none was suspended or considered unreasonable so as to warrant consultation.

In establishing standard levels, the CAB was required to use all relevant or appropriate information which presumably included foreign carriers' costs. With the possible exception of Argentina, all bilateral agreements with respect to the countries in question were of the Bermuda One type, requiring the establishment of rates to take into consideration all relevant factors, including the cost of operation, reasonable profit, and the rates charged by other carriers. According to this provision, the CAB cannot determine the reasonableness of a rate based solely on the costs of U.S. carriers. It must also consider the costs of foreign carriers since the agreements contemplate the establishment of a fair and equal competitive opportunity for the carriers of both contracting parties. Since foreign carriers' costs are in general higher than are those of U.S. carriers, the CAB was in fact attempting to force foreign carriers to set rates below their costs. In fact, the CAB was using inconsistent arguments. On the one hand, it was argued that foreign states cannot disapprove low fares filed by U.S. carriers if such fares are justified by the cost of operations of U.S. carriers. On the other hand, it finds quite appropriate disapproval of higher fares (if indeed the fares in question were higher) based on the higher operating costs of foreign-flag carriers.

The CAB Bureaus (combined) concluded that the fare levels in the twelve markets under consideration were unjustly or unreasonably high resulting in excess profits. However, not only did the methodology proposed by the CAB Bureaus fail to take into account costs or revenues of non-U.S. carriers, they considered only revenues and costs for the specific point-to-point city-pair segments. The difference in costs between the two groups of carriers was in fact substantiated by Pan American in its exhibits which showed that its costs were lower, on the average, than any of its non-U.S. competitors. The need to take foreign-carrier costs into account was not only implied in the Bermuda One type of bilateral agreements in force with the countries relating to the markets in question, but it is also implied in the International Competition Act of 1979.

The CAB Bureaus had outlined three approaches for determining the existence of excess profits in the markets in question. First, total revenues from all passengers on the segment were compared with total costs for all segment costs. Second, the weighted average published fare (in effect on 1 October 1979) was compared with the weighted average unit costs under version six cost methodology developed in the DPFI for point-to-point traffic. The third approach focused on fare classes and separated economy and first-class fares from coach and first-class unit costs.[6] For the markets under consideration, the staff had recommended the first approach where segment revenues had been utilized, based on an allocation of through fares' revenues. Thus while this approach did include the effects of interline prorate dilution, it did not account for the impact of beyond or feeder traffic in terms of contribution to the reduction of average costs for the primary segments.

The fares in effect on 1 October 1979 in the twelve markets were negotiated and coordinated through the IATA's traffic-conference machinery, which is a far more realistic means of evaluating the carrier economic implications of fares than the methodology used by the CAB Bureaus. The IATA method analyzes fares on an area rather than a segment basis; it attempts to relate revenues with costs for an entire tariff period rather than a single point in time; it uses the information provided by the IATA Cost Committee, reflecting the costs of all members; and it attempts to recommend fares that will cover full economic costs. And, in reality, despite its endeavors to recommend fare levels that recover all economic costs, the conference normally ends up recommending lower fares. For example, on a fully allocated cost basis, the fares should have been increased by 12.2 percent for the North-South America area whereas the final resolution increased fares by only 5 to 10 percent. On the North and Central Pacific routes, costs were expected to increase by 31 percent, and yet the resulting IATA agreement adopted the fares in effect then in the market.[7] It is highly unlikely, therefore, that the industry is earning the 17 percent return (generally considered to be an adequate return on investment) and even more unlikely that it is making an excess profit.

During the investigation, the CAB staff was unable to provide any significant evidence to support the claim that any 1 October 1979 fare in the twelve markets at issue was either unjustly or unreasonably high. Even the CAB's own administrative-law judge criticized the staff work for having errors in calculations, not providing persuasive evidence for the existence of excessive profits, and for providing evasive answers during questioning. In addition, the judge was particularly concerned about the lack of consideration given to the beyond and feeder-route segments. In his opinion, the traffic carried on such segments allows a carrier to achieve high load factors on the main segment, thereby producing lower costs for the point-to-point traffic on the main segment. Unfortunately, the CAB Bureaus had failed to consider the network aspect of the problem.

A member of the CAB's staff defended the CAB's position that fares coordinated through the IATA's traffic-conference machinery are high as they are based on the operations of the most inefficient carriers. The irony in this situation is that it is the U.S. carriers that are pressing for higher fares and the foreign governments are not giving their approval. Consider the denial by Italy to the fare increases proposed by Pan American and Trans World Airlines and the denial by the Japanese government to approve fare increases proposed by Pan American. Similarly, the decision by Air France not to increase its Vacances fare over the 1979 level forced Trans World to lower its fare.[8]

The administrative-law judge issued his initial decision on 2 July 1980, concluding that the CAB Bureaus had not met their burden of proof in establishing that the fares at issue were unreasonable and recommended that the case be dismissed. The CAB issued its decision on 12 August 1980, indicating that while it agreed to end the investigation, in its opinion excess profits did exist in several of the markets and attributed these excesses to tickets purchased in foreign countries with foreign currency. The CAB felt that the excess profits resulting from the directional imbalance in international fares could be handled in other ways after the deadline of 13 August 1980.

In ending the preceding investigation, international fares in effect on 1 October 1979 became the SFFL base for the zone. However, the act makes provisions for the adoption of cost pass through, particularly for fuel-cost increases, by adjusting the SFFL base periodically by percentage changes in actual operating costs per available seat-mile. In establishing the SFFL (for the four-month period) beginning 1 October 1980, the CAB is allowing international fares to be increased by the following adjustment factors over the 1 October 1979 level: Atlantic, 1.1706; Latin America, 1.2372; and Pacific, 1.1667. Alternatively, the two-month adjustment factors are: Atlantic, 1.1625; Latin America, 1.2251; and Pacific, 1.1576.

SATC Two Revisited. The recommendations of ICAO's SATC Two were reviewed in chapter 3 in detail for the first agenda item (regulation of international air-transport services) and briefly for the second agenda item (international air-transport fares and rates). Detailed discussion of the conference's recommendation on international fares was postponed until other aspects of the fare development process, presented in this chapter, had been covered. The reader may therefore find it useful to go back to the conference's recommendations listed in chapter 3.

As stated earlier, the conference agenda item number two was divided into five areas: mechanisms for the establishment of scheduled passenger fares; mechanisms for the establishment of nonscheduled passenger tariffs; mechanisms for the establishment of freight rates (scheduled and nonscheduled); coexistence and harmonization of methods by which fares and rates are established; and tariff enforcement. The conference made a total of twenty-six recommendations in these five categories. Most of these recommendations were based on the analysis and studies produced by the Fare and Rates Panel, which, by September 1979, had met four times to discuss these issues.

First the conference focused on the mechanisms for the establishment of scheduled passenger fares. In general the participants favored the multilateral coordination of international tariffs, both at the carrier and government levels. The participants recommended, to the extent possible, that tariffs should be cost related and initially developed by the carriers with subsequent approval by the governments. The need to ensure the economic viability of the scheduled carriers was reiterated. In other words, the need to safeguard the economic viability of a carrier is as important as that of safeguarding the public interest. In any case, multilaterally-coordinated tariffs at the worldwide level are in the public interest since they ensure the maintenance of a rational system that provides significant benefits to consumers, carriers, and governments.

Consider the benefits to the consumer. Multilaterally-coordinated tariffs serve the diverse interest of consumers and improve efficiency of the system by, for example, reducing tariff anomalies, increasing the choices of available services, and providing the benefits of through pricing. For the carriers, multilaterally-coordinated tariffs minimize organizational and administrative costs, establish a common basis of practices and procedures, provide the means of ensuring equal opportunity to serve a market, and enable the execution of long-term planning. For governments, the multilateral coordination process is more cost-effective, allows reconciliation of conflicting policies and objectives, and minimizes confrontation. It is for these reasons that the conference recommended that ICAO contracting states be urged to consider the views of the states whose airlines do not participate in the IATA-tariff-coordinating activities.

The majority of the participants did not view favorably the proposals put forward by the United States—concepts containing country-of-origin and double-disapproval rate clauses. The United States proposed that these concepts be incorporated into the standard tariff clauses. However, the majority rejected the idea of elevating these concepts to the status of standard. The group claimed that, as such rate clauses were based on the principle of free competition, they would favor large carriers at the expense of the small carriers, particularly those belonging to developing countries. The conference did not object to the examination of new types of tariff clauses but to the incorporation of any such concept in the standard clause unless it was widely accepted by the international community. The conference also recommended that unilateral actions taken by governments should be avoided since such actions may have a negative effect on carriers' efforts toward reaching agreement. Moreover, when international tariffs are established at a regional level, participants should give consideration to the multilateral system.

Next the conference turned its attention to mechanisms for the establishment of nonscheduled passenger tariffs and focused on three types of charter traffic: affinity group, nonaffinity group, and inclusive tour. In each area, the conference examined the roles of carriers, governments, and intermediaries in the establishment of tariffs. While some participants did not consider it judicious to regulate nonscheduled operations, most thought that the regulation of the two types of service should be harmonized since the distinction between them has become increasingly vague. The conference recommended, for example, that in order to protect the interest of consumers and contribute toward stabilizing the economics of both types of carriers, states should maintain an appropriate balance between the passenger tariffs for both types of service, and impose a minimum restraint on nonscheduled tariffs. If it should become necessary for a state to regulate nonscheduled fares unilaterally, then the particular tariff controls should be decided with participation from all concerned parties; controls should be kept flexible and should be announced as far in advance of implementation as possible. As for the intermediaries, given their important role, they should be subject to licensing and regulatory procedures, for a state's own originating traffic.

The conference did not take up the issue of part-charters since the Panel on Fares and Rates itself had not reached any conclusion. The basic problem relates to the lack of an explicit definition of part-charter; any attempt at clearer definition is limited by the nebulous nature of the concept. In a general way, the concept involves the sale of a block of seats on a scheduled flight but only under charter conditions. There is, therefore, a special relationship between scheduled and nonscheduled fares. Moreover, if charter traffic can be accommodated on scheduled flights, then in theory (on the basis of reciprocal rights) nonscheduled carriers should be allowed to carry individual-ticketed passengers. But in most regions of the world, such a situation would warrant an inherent change in policy. Because of such issues, the Panel on Fares and Rates recommended that the part-charter issue be examined first by the Panel on Regulation of Air Transport Services in order to provide the necessary guidelines for developing recommendations for the establishment of part-charter tariffs. The conference concurred with the recommendation.

Mechanisms for the establishment of freight rates was the third category of international tariffs examined by the conference participants. While the IATA machinery for coordinating freight rates is similar to that for passenger fares, the process is more complicated, given the complexity and heterogeneity of airfreight. The role of freight forwarders and agents received substantial attention during the conference. Since this group plays a significant role in the development, movement, and pricing of airfreight, its input in the development of airfreight rates was considered essential. Some participants considered a regulated multilateral environment to be a necessity although they had serious objections to many aspects of the existing IATA system. Simplification, by elimination of the discriminatory elements of many specific commodity rates, is considered high on the list of priorities. It would also reduce tariff violations and improve the enforcement process. As to governments, some participants recommended that the forwarders and agents be licensed, at least for their own originating traffic.

The conference recommended that carriers should provide governments with timely, accurate, and adequate information to expedite the government decision-making process.

On the agenda item concerning coexistence and harmonization of methods of establishing tariffs, the participants noted an increase in the number of different methods used to establish tariffs due to the increase in activities by regional organizations and government intervention. The Panel on Fares and Rates had recommended that these methods should all be coordinated for interregional harmonization and that the secretariat's work on differences in regional fares and costs would be of immense value in this area.

The conference also examined two recommendations made in a working paper introduced by Australia, Ethiopia, Italy, Trinidad and Tobago, and the United Kingdom. These states were concerned with the impact of fuel availability and price on the future viability, stability, and growth of the industry. These states pointed first to the need for recognizing the relationship between costs, tariffs, carrier viability, and technological change, and second, to the need for consultation among states relating to fuel availability, price stability, and conservation. Both recommendations were adopted by the conference. However, some participants pointed out that while fuel prices were of substantial concern to the aviation community, one should not overlook the importance of increases in other cost factors, such as the currency exchange rates.

Finally, on the subject of tariff enforcement, the conference noted that the situation relating to the enforcement of tariff had not changed since 1977, except for the restructuring of IATA in which the emphasis had shifted from punitive to preventive enforcement-compliance programs. However, the extent to which these enforcement procedures can be applied on a worldwide basis depends on the degree to which multilateral agreements are in effect. It is therefore necessary for governments to support even more strongly the establishment of multilateral agreements. In cases where multilateral agreements do not exist, there is a pressing need for national enforcement programs, requiring the filing and approval of tariffs, authorizing the investigation of violations, and the imposition of penalties.

Summary

In recent years, domestic and international passenger air fares have come under scrutiny from all directions. Within the United States, the CAB has departed from the standards established in its DPFI by introducing fare flexibility designed to introduce market-by-market price competition. The old DPFI criteria have been replaced in the Airline Deregulation Act by the new SIFL formula which is to be adjusted periodically to reflect changes in industry costs. As of 12 June 1980, the fare zone has been broadened to include full downward flexibility in all markets, up to 50 percent above SIFL in 200 to 400-mile markets, and up to 30 percent above SIFL for flights over 400 miles.

Internationally, the CAB has concluded its Show-Cause Order with a decision that prevents, at least temporarily, the U.S. scheduled carriers from participating in the North Atlantic tariff-coordination activities. The International Air Transportation Competition Act was passed in February 1980, which, among other things, established a SFFL formula that in some ways is similar to the domestic SIFL. As a result, the CAB now has limited control over international passenger fares. The use of SFFL (a cost-adjusted zone) required as a benchmark the fares in existence in October of 1979. The CAB selected twelve markets and claimed that the existing fares were unduly high. However, based on the findings of its own administrative-law judge, the case was dismissed.

The problems facing the international aviation community continue to mount, resulting in the organization by ICAO during February 1980 of the Second Air Transport Conference. This conference, like its predecessor, firmly supported multilaterally coordinated fares. Additionally, the conference recommended that the worldwide IATA multilateral traffic-conference machinery should, wherever applicable, be adopted as a first choice in the establishment of international tariffs. This method provides benefits to the consumer, the carrier, and the government and as such any tariffs established at a regional level should give full consideration to the worldwide multilateral system.

Notes

1. U.S. Civil Aeronautics Board, *Part 339—Statements of General Policy*, Regulation PS-80 (Dockets 31290 and 30891) (25 August 1978).

2. _____ . *Oakland Service Case*, Order 78-9-96 (1978).

3. _____ . testimony of Chairman Cohen before the Aviation Subcommittee on Commerce, Science, and Transportation on Fare Flexibility Regulation, May 20, 1980.

4. _____ . Part 399—Statement of General Policy, PSDR-66 (Docket 37982) Notice of Proposed Rulemaking (3 April 1980), p. 3.

5. International Air Transport Association, "Mechanisms for Establishment of Scheduled Passenger Fares: The Currency Situation," Working Paper WP-21 presented at the ICAO's Second Air Transport Conference, 14 February 1980, Montreal.

6. U.S. Civil Aeronautics Board, *Standard Foreign Fare Level Investigation* (Dockets 37730 and 37744) (12 August 1980).

7. International Air Transport Association, "Statement of Position of the International Air Transport Association," *Standard Foreign Fare Level Investigation* (Docket 37730) (30 May 1980).

8. James Ott, "Foreign Fare Issue Splits CAB," *Aviation Week and Space Technology* (28 July 1980):20-21.

5 Economic Behavior

The observed changes in the economic behavior of the industry are only partially the result of deregulation of the domestic industry. Uncertainty and increasing fuel prices, the state of the U.S. economy, and its standing relative to the economies of other countries have also had a major impact on the current situation.

Regulation

Since passage of the Airline Deregulation Act of 1978, the CAB has significantly relaxed regulatory requirements with respect to entry, exit, and pricing. By January of 1985, when the CAB will cease to exist, the airline industry will be completely deregulated except to the extent that other U.S. government agencies may retain some regulatory control. Until then, Congress has given broad powers to the CAB for management of the transition. It must be remembered that certain aspects, such as subsidy, will continue to be regulated by the government.

For a few years, a number of economists have claimed that characteristics of the airline industry do not and should not be compared to those of a public utility. The airline business is, in fact, just like any other business. Therefore it was not necessary for a government agency to encourage competition (through regulation), foster sound economic conditions, and assure continuation of service. In their opinion, the establishment of a free marketplace was the optimal method of achieving the desired result—a way to produce the service most efficiently through an efficient allocation of resources and sell these services at reasonable prices. In a nutshell, a totally competitive marketplace will produce the optimal quality, quantity, price, and variety of the services to be offered.

Whereas the preceding points are rather theoretical in nature, the proponents of deregulation cited the following specific points to support their case.

Based on the experience of the intrastate carriers, the short-haul interstate markets were being served inefficiently due to the high cost structure of the regulated carriers. Freedom of entry would have encouraged innovative entrepreneurs to enter these markets and freedom

111

of pricing would have allowed different services (for example, high density, high load factor) to be tailored to individual market requirements.

The licensed route authority prevented some carriers from optimizing their total network resulting in the operation of inefficient services as evident in the existence of low load factors. Free-market entry and exit would have allowed individual carriers to rationalize their routes leading to more efficient operations and eventually lower priced service.

The fares in the longer-haul (and dense) markets were kept at an artificially high level in order to cross-subsidize the inefficient operations in the short-haul markets. Any competition that existed in the longer-haul markets was based on service and not price. Free entry and pricing freedom would have lowered fares by raising load factors and reducing excess profit.

Opponents to deregulation argued that not only is the airline industry at least a quasi utility but that the CAB had allowed competition in major markets (although with a limited number of carriers) to the extent that it was economical, efficient, and feasible. In return for limited competition and protected route authority, individual airlines were obligated to serve large and small communities under controlled tariffs, avoid unfair and anticompetitive practices, and report accounting, financial, and traffic data to the CAB. Under this system, a majority of markets received competitive service. While the total number of trunk carriers had decreased, a number of other categories of carriers (such as local service, all cargo, and commuter) had been authorized by the CAB. As to the reasonableness of prices, passengers in the United States under the old system were not only provided with fares substantially below those existing in other parts of the world but had access to numerous discount fares. The only real problem with the regulatory system was its cumbersome nature, such as excessive regulatory lag and the antiquated operating restrictions on route authority.

The proponents' arguments prevailed and the Airline Deregulation Act of 1978 was passed. Phased transition will end all entry control by the end of 1981 and price regulation by the end of 1982. All forms of airline regulation by the CAB is targeted to end early in 1985. The CAB is using all its powers to speed up the transition process for several reasons: because of consumer benefits experienced in the short term, because of the belief that speed would minimize the distortions of change, and because there would be time to take remedial action in case of error.[1]

During the transition period, market entry is just about automatic. A route certificate can be obtained through a simple application and with very little delay. Exit, on the other hand, is a different story. An airline cannot leave a market if the service received by a community falls below the *essential air service* level, a term which has no statutory definition. The CAB has established standards and guidelines for essential air service. These guidelines provide for the availability of subsidy should the free marketplace be unable to induce a replacement carrier. During 1978 more than 200 notices were filed with the CAB by airlines wishing to stop scheduled service at various points. In about 15 percent of the cases, the CAB did force the carriers to continue providing service, but was obliged to pay them subsidy for doing so. In some cases a replacement carrier entered the market. For example, USAir replaced United between Charleston, West Virginia and Pittsburgh. In other cases service was replaced by a commuter carrier with often better frequency but lower total number of seats and non-jet equipment.

In the area of price regulation, the CAB until recently has been more than accommodating in the approval of price reductions. As of May 1980, the CAB has broadened significantly the flexibility zone for airlines to lower as well as raise fares to cope with inflationary pressures. Reduction in the regulatory delay in approving fare adjustments required for cost increases (particularly fuel) represents a positive step taken by the CAB when one considers the impact of a one penny per gallon increase in the price of fuel accompanied by a two-month regulatory delay in the adjustment of fares.

In the area of consumerism, regulation has been expanded rather than relaxed. For example, the CAB, with speed comparable to that used in relaxing route and price regulations, has moved to develop and rigorously enforce consumer protection. The Bureau of Consumer Protection, the Federal Trade Commission of the airline industry, was established to solve consumer protection problems such as marketing rules with respect to charter-tour packages sold by tour operators, overbooking, advertising, baggage liability, and smoking on aircraft.

It cannot be stated with certainty that the airline industry will ever be completely free from federal regulation. There is no guarantee that the CAB will actually cease to exist. A quick glance at the continually increasing role of the Bureau of Consumer Protection and the need to monitor and control market exit indicates perpetuation of regulatory activity of some sort. Even if the CAB sunset did occur, the industry must deal with other government committees and departments. As one airline executive recently pointed out, ". . . at last count, there were 114 federal programs involving the transportation of people and on Capitol Hill there are seven House committees, with twelve subcommittees, and seven Senate committees with eight subcommittees, plus one congressional commission, all dealing—or attempting to deal—with transportation issues."[2] Moreover, let us not forget the Departments of Transportation, State, and now Energy and Labor. With or without the CAB, the federal regulatory system is not likely to disappear in the foreseeable future.

Operating Costs

In recent years high inflation rates worldwide have had a serious impact on airline operating costs. Table 5-1 shows the inflation rate (measured in increase in consumer prices) of world regions and selected countries. These high inflation rates, added to the increase in the price of oil, have increased airline operating costs at unprecedented rates. In 1978, cost per available ton-mile for IATA scheduled services increased 21.0 percent over the previous year; in 1979, it increased 17.0 percent; and in 1980, it is expected to increase 16.8 percent. Table 5-2 shows a breakdown of unit operating costs for 1979 for the IATA scheduled international services. It should be noted that fuel and oil, which accounted for 22.6 percent of total costs in 1979, increased 60.8 percent from 1978. En route charges, although a very small percent of total costs, are also increasing at an above average rate. In 1979, the increase in this category was 27.0 percent, 10 percent above the average increase in unit operating costs.

For U.S. domestic operations, cost increases have been similar but not as severe as those in international operations. Tables 5-3 and 5-4 show the trend during the last thirteen years for various categories of airline costs. The composite index increased from 100 in 1967 to 280.2 in 1979 and stood at 315.1 for the year ending in the second quarter of 1980. The largest increase was in the fuel component where the index was at a level of 555.8 for the year 1979 and 747.1 for the year ending in the second quarter of 1980.

The extraordinarily high costs of fuel have changed the economics of airline scheduling and network planning. In the new environment, variable costs for a flight are now higher than fixed costs, leading management to think twice about tag-end operations. The decision to develop an undeveloped market must now be evaluated with care, given the high level of incremental costs. Higher operating costs in general and fuel costs in particular are forcing the decision to ground older aircraft. Aircraft such as the older B-707 and the B-727-100 are generally not economically viable, given the price of fuel. For example, the use of B-727-100 is limited to high yield markets. The block hour cost per seat, based on the 1979 aircraft direct operating costs for the trunk carriers, varies from about $11 for the widebody aircraft (B-747, DC-10, and L-1011) to about $14 for the B-707-100 and the B-727-100.[3] (These data are not adjusted for stage length).

It should be noted that the increase in operating costs is related more to traffic than to capacity (see figure 5-1). Between 1971 and 1979 capacity-related costs for U.S. scheduled carriers (flying operations, direct

Table 5-1

Inflation Patterns of World Regions and Selected Countries: Consumer Price Increases

| | Percent Average Annual Increase | | Percentage Change from Previous Year | | | | |
| | | | Actual | | | Forecast | |
	1965-1970	1971-1976	1977	1978	1979	1980	1981
Developed market economies							
Total OECD nations	3.5	9.1	8.7	7.7	9.9	12.5	10.0
United States	4.3	7.0	6.5	7.7	11.3	13.5	9.5
Canada	3.9	8.3	8.0	9.0	9.1	10.0	10.5
Japan	5.5	12.0	8.1	3.8	3.6	9.0	7.5
Australia	3.1	11.8	12.3	7.9	9.1	10.7	10.0
France	4.4	9.6	9.4	9.1	10.8	13.0	10.0
Germany	2.4	6.0	3.7	2.7	4.1	4.8	3.5
Italy	3.0	13.8	17.0	12.1	14.8	21.0	16.0
United Kingdom	4.6	14.5	15.9	8.3	13.4	18.0	15.0
Developing market economies[a] total	13.0	25.0	27.1	23.6	29.4	29.6	n.a.
Latin America[b]	17.0	41.5	51.1	41.7	48.7	47.6	n.a.
Argentina	19.3	d	d	d	d	80.0	60.0
Brazil	27.5	25.0	43.7	38.7	52.6	66.0	60.0
Mexico	3.5	14.2	29.0	17.5	18.2	22.0	19.0
Africa	5.0	14.0	16.9	14.7	20.1	19.7	n.a.
Ivory Coast	5.4	10.3	27.4	13.0	16.6	13.0	12.0
Kenya	1.8	12.8	14.9	16.9	8.0	n.a.	n.a.
Nigeria	5.7	14.8	21.5	24.3	7.0	n.a.	n.a.
Asia[c]	8.0	10.6	7.9	5.9	10.3	11.4	n.a.
India	6.8	9.1	8.4	2.5	6.3	10.0	7.0
Indonesia	d	23.0	11.0	8.6	24.4	11.0	10.5
Philippines	6.0	14.0	7.9	7.6	18.8	15.0	10.0
Middle East	4.0	15.6	18.7	21.0	26.8	35.0	n.a.
Major oil exporting nations	10.0	12.7	15.4	9.7	11.0	11.8	n.a.

Sources: Historical data for industrialized countries from OECD and for developing countries from IMF. Forecasts from IATA Macro-Economic Forecast Exchange Scheme and IMF for groups of developing countries. Taken from International Air Transport Association, "The State of the Air Transport Industry: Annual Report," Montreal, 27-30 October 1980, p. 18.

[a]Non-oil developing countries.

[b]Includes Caribbean.

[c]South and East Asia includes Afghanistan and Pakistan.

[d]Excessively high rates of inflation.

maintenance, maintenance burden, and aircraft servicing) increased by 180 percent; traffic-related costs (passenger servicing, traffic servicing, reservations and sales, advertising, and promotion) increased by 178 percent; and all other costs increased by 88 percent. However, after inflation, in particular categories (such as labor and fuel), is factored out, the increase in capacity-related costs during this eight-year period was only 4 percent, com-

Table 5-2
Unit Operating Costs: IATA Scheduled International Services

1979	US Cents per ATK	Percent Change	Percent Composition
Flight deck crew	2.6	+ 8.3	7.1
Fuel and oil	8.2	+ 60.8	22.6
Flight equipment insurance, depreciation, and rentals	2.6	+ 4.0	7.1
Maintenance and overhaul	3.8	+ 8.6	10.5
Landing fees	1.8	+ 12.0	4.9
En route charges	0.5	+ 27.0	1.4
Station and ground operations	4.0	+ 8.1	11.0
Cabin attendants and passenger service	4.0	+ 8.1	11.0
Ticketing, sales, and promotion	6.7	+ 9.8	18.4
General administration	2.2	+ 4.8	6.0
Total	36.4	+ 17.0	100.0

Source: International Air Transport Association, "The State of the Air Transport Industry: Annual Report," Montreal, 27-30 October 1980, p. 21.

pared to 50 percent for the traffic-related cost category. In other words, during this eight-year period, a 42 percent increase in capacity was achieved with a 4 percent increase in real costs while an 80 percent increase in traffic was achieved with a 50 percent increase in costs. Therefore, attention should now be focused on improving productivity through improvements in traffic-related costs.

As stated before, the new economics of the industry brought about by the increase in airline costs in general and fuel costs in particular is impacting airline scheduling and network planning. Four areas where major changes in service have taken place are the concentrated effort to develop hub-and-spoke networks, an increase in average length of haul (by adding longer-haul routes and deleting short-haul routes), route diversification, and taking advantage of the elimination of operating restrictions.

The move toward a hub-and-spoke network is not a new one; Delta (at Atlanta), Northwest (at Minneapolis), and United (at Chicago) have always operated such a network. However, the level of activity has increased in this area after passage of the Airline Deregulation Act of 1978. Table 5-5 shows the hubs for domestic trunk carriers that are being developed as well as expanded activity at existing hubs. The reasons for expanded activity in this area are, first, that such networks lead to significant traffic development, traffic control, and high load factors on connecting flights, and, second, that the process can lead to lower operating costs. The real benefit, however, is related to an improvement in the flow of traffic and the advantage of feeder traffic. Consider the case of USAir. Figure 5-2 shows the hub at Pittsburgh. Prior to deregulation, USAir was carrying passengers into Pittsburgh from smaller and intermediate-sized points and turning these passengers over to competitors for transportation to their ultimate destination. By expanding service into long-haul markets such as Tampa, West Palm Beach, Orlando, Houston, and Phoenix, USAir is able to hold on to its own traffic at Pittsburgh and increase its length of haul and average passenger trip length, resulting in a measurable improvement in productivity. No longer does USAir carry a passenger from Erie to Pittsburgh (109 miles) and hand him over to another carrier for the connection to Phoenix (1800 miles); instead, the passenger stays on the USAir system the entire way.

The second modification in route network is that of the addition of longer-haul routes and deletion of shorter-haul routes. In 1979, the domestic trunk carriers deleted routes averaging 366 miles and added new services on routes averaging 797 miles. Likewise, the local-service carriers added routes averaging 428 miles in length and deleted those averaging 181 miles. This process continued in 1980.[4] For example, during the first quarter of 1980, the local-service carriers increased their average length of haul by 12.3 percent over the same period in 1979. The motivation for this move is derived from the fact that, whereas unit operating costs are higher for short-haul operations, the fare increases (until May 1980) had all been fairly straight across the board. Figures 5-3 and 5-4 show, for trunk and local-service carriers, the net change in frequency by range class between August 1978 and August 1980. Table 5-6 shows some specific examples of the trend to move into longer-haul markets. In some cases, service added or deleted related to the population of the cities. Table 5-7 shows an example of the cities restructured on this basis for USAir. In the case of USAir, cities dropped out of the system are now being served by the Allegheny Commuters so that the connecting traffic is still retained by USAir.

The desire to increase average length of haul by adding longer-haul routes is based on the expectation of increased profits. It is claimed, for example, that in short-haul operations unit costs tend to be high and fares cannot be raised indefinitely due to the existence of competition from other modes. However, the implication of this line of reasoning should be evaluated with caution. It has been shown that increased fares in short-haul markets do not always result in reduced traffic. Furthermore, in longer-haul markets high fares are usually accompanied by a variety of discount fares not to mention increased competition. Therefore, lower unit costs accompanied by greater competition and discount fares may not necessarily increase profits.

The third development toward route rationalization is that of diver-

Table 5-3
Annual Airline Cost Index

	Labor		Capital		Fuel		Passenger Food		Advertising and Promotion	
	Index (1967 = 100)	Percent Increase Over Prev. Yr.	Index (1967 = 100)	Percent Increase Over Prev. Yr.	Index (1967 = 100)	Percent Increase Over Prev. Yr.	Index (1967 = 100)	Percent Increase Over Prev. Yr.	Index (1967 = 100)	Percent Increase Over Prev. Yr.
1967	100.0		100.0		100.0		100.0		100.0	
1968	108.0	8.0	105.5	5.5	98.0	(2.0)	104.0	4.0	99.8	(0.2)
1969	119.0	10.2	112.5	6.6	107.9	10.1	105.9	1.8	103.9	4.1
1970	134.7	13.2	119.8	6.5	105.8	(1.9)	114.1	7.7	96.3	(7.3)
1971	147.0	9.1	113.8	(5.0)	110.6	4.5	113.2	(0.8)	95.8	(0.5)
1972	163.6	11.3	113.7	(0.1)	113.5	2.6	119.2	5.3	96.7	0.9
1973	176.2	7.7	128.4	12.9	123.1	8.5	125.7	5.5	94.0	(2.8)
1974	190.4	8.1	142.8	11.2	232.7	89.0	131.2	4.4	91.4	(2.8)
1975	208.6	9.6	133.4	(6.6)	279.8	20.2	140.6	7.2	97.1	6.2
1976	230.8	10.6	132.1	(1.0)	303.8	8.6	141.1	0.4	94.3	(2.9)
1977	257.6	11.6	135.9	2.9	349.0	14.9	148.0	4.9	102.0	8.2
1978	283.8	10.2	152.5	12.2	376.9	8.0	149.0	0.7	97.9	(4.0)
1979	305.6	7.7	155.8	2.2	555.8	47.5	159.9	7.3	102.3	4.5

Source: Air Transport Association of America.

sification of routes to reduce seasonality, improve market traffic mix base, or improve fleet utilization. Republic (formed by the merger of North Central and Southern) was interested in adding a few more good winter destinations to its system when it made the decision to acquire Hughes Air West. For USAir the route system concentrated in the northeastern quadrant was highly susceptible to disruptions inherent in the winter weather. The strategy, presumably, was to move to the sunbelt-vacation markets. In the case of Eastern, it is alleged, the decision to enter the transcontinental market was based on the desire to improve fleet utilization. With the delivery of additional A300s, the carrier had some spare L-1011s. These aircraft, substantially depreciated, could be used to offer lower fare service in transcontinental markets. Such a strategy would not only improve L-1011 fleet utilization but be a competitive response to TWA and United for entering its Florida markets. In the case of American, the decision to enter the Hawaiian market would not only increase its feeder traffic and improve its competitive posture with United, it would also provide a cost-effective use for its depreciated DC-10s when they are replaced by the B-767 fleet.

The fourth area of route rationalization evolves from a desire to eliminate operating restrictions in order to improve traffic flow and aircraft productivity. This movement is clearly evident from an analysis of the USAir system. The lifting of one-stop restrictions on flights enabled the carrier to begin a number of new services, including Pittsburgh-Minneapolis/St. Paul, Pittsburgh-Houston, Washington-Detroit, Nashville-Houston, and Philadelphia-Cincinnati.

Landing Fees		A/C Maintenance		Passenger Traffic Commission		All Other		Composite	
Index (1967=100)	Percent Increase Over Prev. Yr.	Index (1967=100)	Percent Increase Over Prev. Yr.	Index (1967=100)	Percent Increase Over Prev. Yr.	Index (1967=100)	Percent Increase Over Prev. Yr.	Index (1967=100)	Percent Increase Over Prev. Yr.
100.0		100.0		100.0		100.0		100.0	
118.6	18.6	90.3	(9.7)	100.4	0.4	104.5	4.5	104.4	4.4
121.6	2.5	82.0	(9.2)	106.8	6.4	109.7	5.0	111.8	7.1
139.8	15.0	75.5	(7.9)	124.6	16.7	115.6	5.4	120.0	7.3
165.4	18.3	66.7	(11.7)	137.1	10.0	121.5	5.1	126.5	5.4
172.7	4.4	77.3	15.9	151.0	10.1	126.6	4.2	135.5	7.1
188.3	9.0	82.9	7.2	165.9	9.9	134.0	5.8	145.1	7.1
216.9	15.2	96.4	16.3	200.7	21.0	147.4	10.0	170.6	17.6
232.0	7.0	99.9	3.6	231.2	15.2	161.0	9.2	188.7	10.6
258.9	11.6	106.9	7.0	268.8	16.3	169.3	5.2	204.0	8.1
273.2	5.5	114.9	7.5	287.0	6.8	179.6	6.1	224.8	10.2
273.6	0.1	114.5	(0.3)	300.7	4.8	192.2	7.0	242.5	7.9
309.5	13.1	115.7	1.0	346.4	15.2	209.3	8.9	280.2	15.5

Carefully planned route rationalization adjustments have helped some carriers become more profitable. USAir is undoubtedly the best example. The carrier reported a net income of $22.4 million in 1978, $33.4 million in 1979, and $26.6 million during the first six months of 1980. The marked improvement in TWA's third-quarter profit is also partly the result of route rationalization. Uncontrolled expansion, on the other hand, has led some carriers to post substantial losses. In the case of Braniff, operating losses have been incurred since the third quarter of 1979. Total operating losses for four quarters (from the third quarter of 1979 through the second quarter of 1980) have amounted to $125 million. If nonoperating charges are included, the pretax losses for these four quarters amounted to $168 million. Although a retrenchment process has already begun, only a small percentage of the costs incurred to initiate new service can be recouped. As a result, the carrier has had to sell some of its fleet in order to strengthen its poor financial performance.

A number of small intrastate carriers have expanded their service into new and major routes. This list includes Air Florida, PSA, and Southwest Airlines. Air Florida, a small intrastate carrier, now flies major international routes such as Miami-Amsterdam and Miami-Brussels. PSA, a large intrastate carrier in California, now serves Nevada, Utah, and Arizona in the United States, and Mazatlan and Puerto Vallarta in Mexico. Similarly, Southwest Airlines, a small intrastate carrier in Texas (serving Dallas, Houston, and San Antonio) now serves fifteen cities in Texas, Oklahoma, Louisiana, and New Mexico. However, while important, the expansion of these carriers has had little statistical effect on the total industry.

Table 5-4
Airline Cost Index for U.S. Trunk and Local-Service Carriers (Year Ending Second Quarter 1980)

	Index (1967 = 100)	Percent Change over Year Ending Second Quarter 1979
Labor (employment cost per employee)	318.3	9.5
Capital (interest on long-term debt)	175.1	12.9
Fuel (cost per gallon)	747.1	82.4
Passenger food (cost per revenue passenger mile)	172.8	14.4
Advertising and promotion (cost per revenue ton-mile)	112.2	16.5
Landing fees (cost per aircraft ton landed)	322.1	11.7
Aircraft maintenance materials (cost per available ton-mile)	119.9	2.9
Traffic commissions: passenger (cost per revenue passenger mile)	400.7	29.5
All other (implicit deflator: GNP)	218.8	9.1
Composite	315.1	25.2

Source: Air Transport Association of America.

Fare Competition

Despite the claims of deregulation proponents, fare competition is not a new concept. It has been in existence before and since the establishment of the CAB. What is new is the degree of fare competition in certain dense long-haul markets. As a result, a certain segment of the population is enjoying considerable bargains in the short term, while losses in these markets are subsidized by consumers in other markets. Consider the introduction of the $99 fare on transcontinental routes. Some analysts have noted that it would require a load factor of of 150 percent for a wide-body aircraft to break even at such a fare. Furthermore, the one-way fare between Boston and Washington was only $2 more than the $99 transcontinental fare. Such examples provide much more than circumstantial evidence that either losses incurred on the high density long haul routes are being subsidized by excess profits earned in other markets, or they are contributing to the overall system losses.

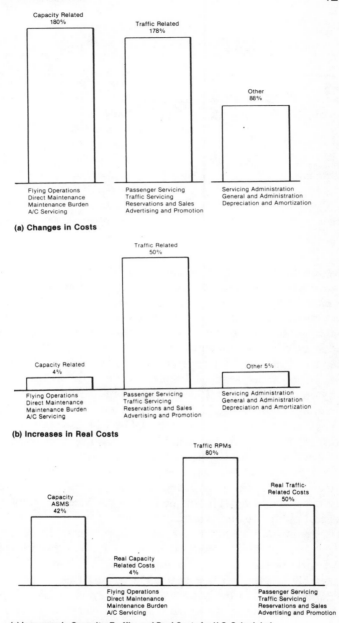

(a) Changes in Costs

(b) Increases in Real Costs

(c) Increases in Capacity, Traffic, and Real Costs for U.S. Scheduled
     Airlines

Source: Air Transport Association of America

Figure 5-1. Changes in Real Costs of U.S. Scheduled Airlines (1971-1979)

Table 5-5
Hubs Existing or Being Developed by U.S. Trunks

Carrier	Principal Hubs
American	Chicago, Dallas, St. Louis
Braniff	Dallas, Kansas City
Continental	Denver
Delta	Atlanta, Dallas
Eastern	Atlanta, Charlotte, St. Louis
Northwest	Minneapolis
Pan American	Houston, New York
Trans World	Chicago, Pittsburgh, St. Louis
United	Chicago, Denver, Memphis, Kansas City
Western	(No significant hub-and-spoke pattern)

Proponents of deregulation had hoped that consumers would be offered more diversified price and service options in the deregulated environment. But choices have always been available to the traveling public, ranging from low prices offered by charter carriers to the high-priced, first-class service offered by scheduled carriers. Now the lower priced (but also lower quality) service is offered by scheduled carriers as well. In June of 1977, TWA reduced its regular coach fare from $156 to $99 between Chicago and Los Angeles. The carrier reduced frequency from five to two and increased capacity on the B-707 to 187 seats. The idea was to maintain presence in a market at minimum costs. The same year, Delta offered a $55 fare between New York and Miami on a stretched DC-8 with 244 seats. In June 1980, World offered a $99 fare between New York and Los Angeles on its high-density configured DC-10. In each case, the deregulators pointed to the benefits of their much touted gospel. The consumer, however, was rarely informed about the lower quality service associated with lower fares. In many cases, the capacity available for the low-fare service was restricted. Again, the general public was unaware of this fact.

It is debatable how much new traffic was generated by the low fares. The CAB first allowed the introduction of deep discounts in April of 1977, and the Airline Deregulation Act was passed in October of 1978. It is not unreasonable to consider the year 1976 as one free of any influence of deregulation, actual or de facto, and 1979 as a year impacted by deregulation. In 1976, domestic scheduled traffic (measured in revenue passenger miles) increased by 10.3 percent, while real yield increased by 0.4 percent. During 1979, traffic increased by 11.1 percent even though real yield had decreased by 5.2 percent.[5] Admittedly, there were two other factors worth consideration in 1979: United was on strike and the DC-10 had been grounded

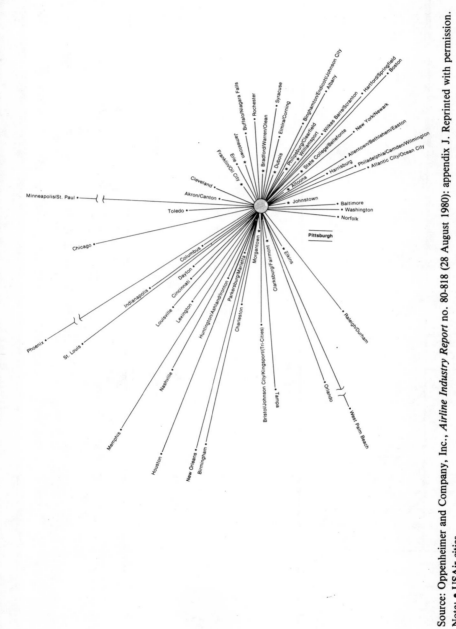

Figure 5-2. USAir Pittsburgh Hub

Source: Oppenheimer and Company, Inc., *Airline Industry Report* no. 80-818 (28 August 1980): appendix J. Reprinted with permission.

Note: • USAir cities
★ Allegheny commuter cities

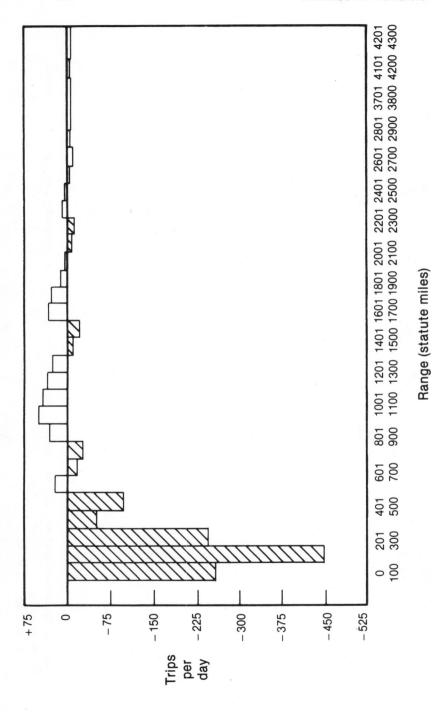

Source: Douglas Aircraft Company.

Figure 5-3. Trunk Carriers: Net Change in Frequency by Range Class (August 1978 versus August 1980)

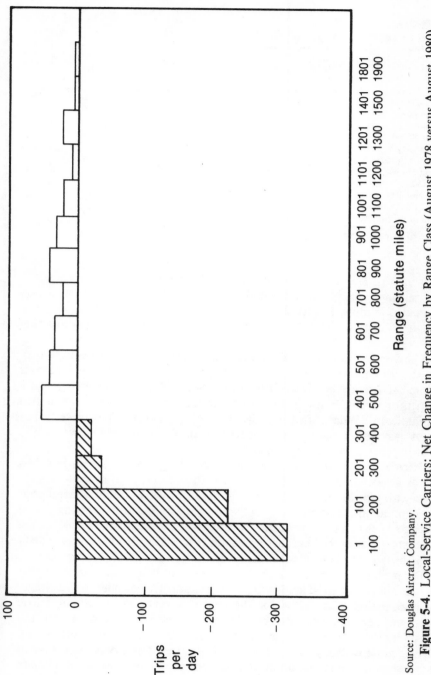

Source: Douglas Aircraft Company.

Figure 5-4. Local-Service Carriers: Net Change in Frequency by Range Class (August 1978 versus August 1980)

Table 5-6
Trend to Increase Length of Haul

Market	Number of Nonstop Carriers Serving	
	Before Deregulation	After Deregulation
Dallas-Seattle	2	4
Minneapolis-Phoenix	1	3
Atlanta-Seattle	0[a]	2
Chicago-Seattle	2	3
Kansas City-Seattle	1	2
St. Louis-Seattle	1	2
Detroit-Phoenix	0[a]	1
Detroit-Las Vegas	1	2
Cleveland-Las Vegas	1	2
Miami-Los Angeles	2	3
Miami-San Francisco	1	2

[a]No certificated route authority.

for a month. However, affected passengers were indeed able to travel on other airlines and aircraft. It would appear that the new fare competition has had minimum effects on total traffic on a total system basis, even though individual airlines or routes may have experienced some fluctuations.

The decision to offer a new low fare is a complex one and should be supported with detailed analysis in a number of areas. Unfortunately, there is seldom sufficient time available for evaluation of fare-change decisions if a competitor offers a lower fare first. Should the new fare be matched automatically? What if the new fare is lower, or higher? The answer is not always easy and, in any case, is dependent on the situation. However, the following factors almost always enter into such analysis.

Price elasticity of demand is usually the first area explored. Is it less than or greater than unity? If it is greater than unity, total revenue will increase with a price reduction. But what about profits? If management considers minimal dilution and only marginal costs of carrying extra passengers, chances are good that profits will also increase. Consider the load factor: if average load factor has not reached intolerable levels, a decision is usually made to go ahead with the introduction of a lower fare.

The problem is actually far more complex. One needs to examine not just average- but peak-period load factor. It is necessary to consider both average- and peak-period load factor for the next few years when normal traffic growth has been factored into the calculation. Based on past experience, the probability is high that a carrier experiencing high load factor would end up ordering more capacity. When the cost of this new capacity is factored into the calculation, the reduction in fares may no longer be reasonable. Despite

Table 5-7
USAir Route System since Deregulation

Points Added		Points Dropped	
Cities	Population	Cities	Population
Houston	2,659,900	Utica	323,800
Tampa	1,439,900	Youngstown	543,500
West Palm Beach	495,900	Morgantown	71,500
Orlando	611,200	Clarksburg	78,700
Birmingham	820,800	New Haven	763,900
Phoenix	1,340,200	Williamsport	114,100
Raleigh/Durham	503,700	Bradford	53,300
New Orleans	1,152,200	Newport News	367,400
Tucson	473,900	White Plains	47,400
Total	9,497,700	Trenton	320,700
		Total	2,684,300

Source: Oppenheimer and Company, Inc., "Airline Industry Report" no. 80-818 (28 August 1980): Appendix A. Reprinted with permission.

its simplicity, few carriers have probed the long-term implications on profitability before introducing a new promotional fare. As one veteran analyst explains, ". . . rather than fill empty seats, promotional fares seem to have generated them."[6] To fill the added capacity, some carriers go on to consider the introduction of even more promotional fares.

In light of the poor financial performance by the airline industry, it is necessary to control any further proliferation in fares. If the airline industry is to become economically viable, it is also necessary for individual carriers to establish pricing policies in which fares are not only market oriented but also cost based. Management can no longer maintain the premise that equitable division of total operating cost among the different classes of passengers on board is impossible. On the contrary, management must divide the total market into segments of differing needs and abilities to pay. And there must be some assurance, in so far as it can be determined, that each segment pays in full for the services it gets and gets only the services for which it pays. The actual price charged for various types of services must then be evaluated with respect to its impact on long-term profitability.

Consider one segment of the market: the business traveler. The key requirement of this segment is flexibility with respect to seat availability on short notice and the ability to cancel reservations or change flights, routings, or destinations. Unfortunately, given the stochastic nature of demand, the inability to inventory aircraft seats, and the "batch production" nature of scheduling, productivity (measured in load factor and aircraft utilization) is usually quite low. In order to improve the level of productivity, management can offer a variety of fares to attract other types of traffic. While promotional fares can generate some additional traffic (and, in turn, revenue), the new traffic generated by these fares also results in additional activities to be performed and costs to be incurred. An important aspect of pricing policy should be a requirement that the passenger pay any and all costs incurred specifically for activities related to his transportation. For example, if management acquires an additional fleet of aircraft to transport certain traffic during peak periods, then that segment of the traffic must pay a fare that not only recovers the direct and indirect costs of this additional fleet but also makes an appropriate contribution to overhead costs.

Most airlines offer a variety of discount fares to attract or direct a certain type of traffic to particular flights in order to improve productivity. If traffic generated by these fares does not require the acquisition of additional capacity, one need only consider the noncapacity costs, that is, flight-related and passenger-related costs. If, however, new capacity is required either now or in a subsequent year to transport either the discount fare-generated traffic or other traffic which may have been displaced, then capacity costs must be factored into the fare-level decision. Increasingly, carriers are beginning to realize that specific promotional fares should be tailored to short-run market situations and should not be used as a foundation for long-term capacity acquisition. On the other hand, if the newly generated traffic requires no additional factors of production (aircraft, reservation system, staff, airport ticket counters) but improves the productivity of existing resources, then this improvement must also be reflected in computation of the fare level. It is this improvement in productivity and the lack of resource-related costs that should allow management to offer promotional or discount fares.

In the past, the industry has offered many discount fares that neither recovered appropriate per passenger costs nor fulfilled their desired role of improved productivity. This may have been caused by the abnormally low level of these fares or, more likely, by the level of service provided which did not match the fare. In fact, many discount-fare passengers received almost identical service to the full-fare passenger. As a result, airlines received less revenue and provided real incentive for the full-fare passenger to take advantage of the lower fare. Such pricing policies produce poor economic results in the long run and should be replaced by those in which each type of service offered is market oriented and cost based. For example, advance purchase excursion service can be restricted by method of distribution and should carry restrictions that are strictly enforced.

It is emphasized that the preceding criteria for sound pricing policy do not require each and every fare to make an equal contribution to long-term profitability. Such a requirement would be unrealistic. The only require-ment is that each segment of traffic pay a fare that recovers the cost of all activities related to transportation of that segment. After the basic costs have been recovered, each fare can make a different contribution to the total system-wide profitability. In that sense, a certain amount of cross-subsidization is inevitable.

The implementation of sound economic pricing policies has been made more difficult in the deregulated environment. The reason, according to one experienced airline executive, lies in the difference between the microeconomics of the individual competitive decision and the macro-economics of what the air-transport system as a whole needs for ongoing viability.[7] It is this difference that can lead a mature and responsible management to make a series of individual decisions which, while each ap-pears advantageous to the carrier making it, is disastrous for the industry as a whole when all such decisions are aggregated.

As an example, take a new carrier that has made a decision to cut drastically the fare in a given market, "M." Let us assume that the existing carrier "A" had been making a 20 percent return, which was used to offset a lower return in some other market. The nature of the air-transport in-dustry requires a certain amount of cross-subsidizing in order to produce on-going economic viability. A reduction in the profitability from opera-tions in market M for carrier A will not only influence the viability of ser-vice offered in some less-favorable market but it will also influence the overall system results. Since market M is not an integral part of carrier "X's" route system, it has no comparable significance for X. As long as the lower fare produces revenue sufficient to recover costs, it is in the interest of carrier X to offer such a service. As a result, the new carrier is able to reduce the profitability of a route that has been vital to the existing carrier in con-tributing to its system-wide average needs. Now if another carrier repeats the process in another market considered vital to carrier X, one can see how a reasonably sound individual decision can have serious drawbacks when all such individual decisions are aggregated.

Few carriers have implemented economically viable pricing policies even when the industry was regulated. With deregulation, the situation has become worse at least during the transitional years. Figure 5-5 shows the in-crease in the proportion of traffic carried at discount fares. Figure 5-6 shows the trend in the reduced-fare yield as a percentage of the full-fare coach yield. The combined effect of these two trends has been an increase in the reduced fare revenue as a percent of total coach revenue (see figure 5-7). Finally, table 5-8 shows the revenue and traffic data for domestic trunks for August 1980, disaggregated by type of service.

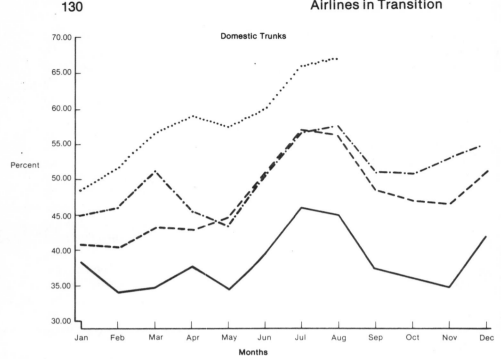

Source: Air Transport Association of America.
Note: _____ 1977
      — — —   1978
      -.-.-   1979
        1980

Figure 5-5. Reduced Fare RPMs Percentage of Total Coach, Forty-Eight States

Load Factor

The average load factor in U.S. domestic operations for the trunk and local-service carriers increased from a low of 45.9 percent in the first quarter of 1971 to a high of 69.0 during the second quarter of 1979, and then declined to 60.0 percent a year later during the second quarter of 1980. The steady increase in the average-system load factor has improved efficiency of airline operations resulting in a reduction in per passenger costs or at least kept the fares from increasing even higher. But the lower fares resulting from higher load factors have been accompanied by lower quality of service; the higher the load factor, the lower the quality of service (in terms of convenience).

In a recent study, the Air Transport Association of America (ATA) produced a detailed analysis of individual daily data on load factor for the month of August 1975. Although a peak-season month then, such load fac-

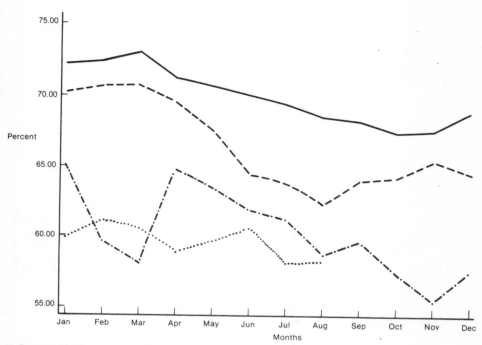

Source: Air Transport Association of America.
Note: _____   1977
          — — —   1978
          - . - . -   1979
            1980

Figure 5-6. Reduced Fare Yield Percentage of Full Coach, Forty-Eight States

tors are now comparable to the year-round averages. Using these actual data, the ATA study showed the extent to which passengers are turned away beyond an average load factor of about 60 percent, despite the availability of seats at departure time.[8]

Consider the data in figure 5-8a which show the distribution of load factors on the Chicago-Denver route. In this case the monthly average load factor was 66 percent. The curve follows approximately the normal distribution at the lower end whereas the right-hand side is cut short by the limited number of seats on the aircraft. If a normal curve is superimposed over the actual distribution plotted in figure 5-8a, one can get an idea of the unaccommodated demand, that is, a passenger who desired to travel on a given flight but could not be accommodated due to the flight being sold out. See figure 5-8b. It should be noted that in addition to the lack of capacity to

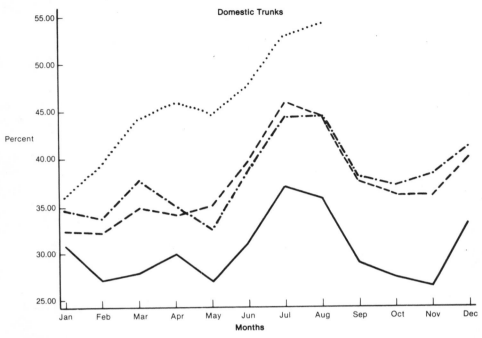

Figure 5-7. Reduced Fare Revenue Percentage of Total Coach, Forty-Eight States

the right of the 100 percent capacity line, the level of unaccommodated demand increases with an increase in the no-show factor.

The preceding analysis used an entire month's data. The problem becomes worse when one considers the distribution by the day of the week. Table 5-9 shows, for example, the distribution of average load factors by day of the week in the same Chicago-Denver market during August 1975. The daily average load factor varies from 59 percent on Wednesday to 72 percent on Sunday. Compare this with the monthly average load factor of 66 percent. One can go further in the analysis and show that 72 percent level was an average of all flights on Sundays; in fact, more than 25 percent of the flights on Sundays departed with a 90 percent or high load factor (see figure 5-9). The unaccommodated demand therefore increases on heavily traveled days, and it increases even more on the popular flights on the heavily traveled days.

In recent months, the carriers have attempted to cope with the high-

Table 5-8
Revenue and Traffic Data Domestic Trunks Forty-Eight States, August 1980

Service/Fare	RPM's			Revenues			Yield		Enplanements		
		Percent			Percent			Percent		Percent	
	(000)	Total	Change	($000)	Total	Change	¢/RPM	Change	Pax	Total	Change
Coach											
Full	4,656,399	33.0	(29.5)	683,561	45.9	(4.4)	14.68	35.7	6,450,995	39.9	(33.6)
Reduced	9,441,786	67.0	4.9	807,017	54.1	41.2	8.55	34.6	9,733,820	60.1	4.2
Total	14,098,185	100.0	(9.7)	1,490,578	100.0	15.9	10.57	28.3	16,184,815	100.0	(15.1)
First											
Full	660,971	71.0	(29.1)	123,653	81.2	1.0	18.71	42.4	772,758	77.4	(34.9)
Reduced	270,023	29.0	(24.2)	28,597	18.8	13.3	10.59	49.4	225,854	22.6	(24.4)
Total	930,994	100.0	(27.7)	152,250	100.0	3.1	16.35	42.7	998,612	100.0	(32.8)
Total											
Full	5,317,370	35.4	(29.5)	807,214	49.1	(3.6)	15.18	36.7	7,223,753	42.0	(33.7)
Reduced	9,711,809	64.6	3.8	835,614	50.9	40.0	8.60	34.9	9,959,674	58.0	3.3
Grand Total	15,029,179	100.0	(11.1)	1,642,828	100.0	14.6	10.93	28.8	17,183,427	100.0	(16.3)

Source: Air Transport Association of America.

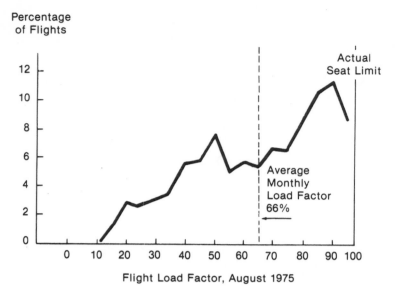

(a) Distribution of Load Factors

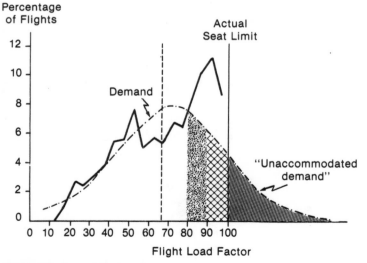

(b) Distribution of Demand

Source: Air Transport Association, ''The Significance of Airline Passenger Load Factor''
(August 1980).

Figure 5-8. Distribution of Load Factors and Demand, Chicago-Denver
Route

Table 5-9
Distribution of Load Factors by Day of Week (Chicago-Denver Route, August 1975)

Day	Average Load Factor (%)
Sunday	72
Monday	68
Tuesday	60
Wednesday	59
Thursday	65
Friday	68
Saturday	68
Average	66

Source: Air Transport Association, "The Significance of Airline Passenger Load Factor" (August 1980).

load-factor-service-inconvenience problem through the introduction of *capacity-controlled fares*, that is, fares offered for an overall percentage of the total capacity on a given route. The percentage of seats is, of course, adjusted on specific flights in terms of the normal-fare demand. This method is an improvement over the traditional off-peak pricing policy, which was an inflexible policy, given the fact that the timing of peak varied by route

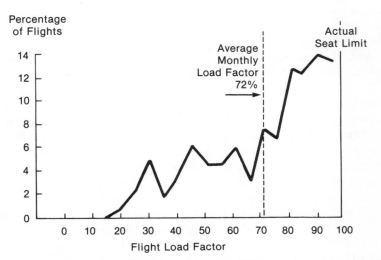

Source: Air Transport Association, "The Significance of Airline Passenger Load Factor" (August 1980).

Figure 5-9. Distribution of Load Factors on Sunday Flights, Chicago-Denver Route

and by direction. The capacity-controlled fares, on the other hand, provide full advantage of off-peak pricing schemes but retain the control as to the specific seats available at discount fares.

Finally, it is also important to note that while an improvement in the average load factor during the last decade has improved efficiency and reduced the cost per passenger, the declining fares, combined with the increasing costs, have raised the break-even load factors. Table 5-10 shows the trend in actual and break-even load factors since the first quarter of 1971 on a quarterly and twelve-month basis. The break-even costs are computed at a level where 100 percent of the fixed costs are recouped. Therefore, on a twelve-month basis, while the average load factor during the first six months of 1980 has been over 60 percent, comparable to peak-month load factor only a few years ago, the break-even load factor has increased even further, resulting in a negative spread, and consequently, industry-wide losses.

Mergers

Since deregulation merger activity in the U.S. airline industry has increased to a new level and four mergers have been consummated: Pan American-National, North Central-Southern (to form Republic), Republic-Hughes Air West, and Flying Tiger-Seaboard. Proposals have also been made to merge Continental with Western, Wien Air with Alaska Airlines, and Air Florida with Air California. In addition, an attempt was made by Texas International to take over TWA, by Eastern to buy National, and now by Eastern to merge with Braniff.

The first applicants on the scene were Continental and Western, seeking approval to merge only a month before the passage of the Airline Deregulation Act of 1978. The theory was that in the deregulated environment the resulting carrier would be in a position to compete more effectively with the large trunk carriers. The application was turned down by the CAB in July 1979. The deregulation had not been in place for any significant time and the CAB was of the opinion that the merged carrier would overly dominate the operations in the western part of the country. Moreover, according to the CAB, competition between the merged carrier and United in western markets would have produced ineffective price competition.

Two years later, in September 1980, the two carriers filed again for approval to merge their operations. The second time around, the probability of a favorable decision is much higher. First, the CAB has had two years to monitor the economic behavior of the industry in the deregulated environment. Second, new carriers have entered the western markets, both existing carriers as well as totally new carriers. Third, Denver (the major hub for the

Table 5-10
Break-Even Load Factor (Trunks and Local-Service Carriers)

	Quarterly			Twelve Months Ended		
	Actual	Break-Even	Spread	Actual	Break-Even	Spread
First quarter, 1971	45.9	51.0	−5.1	—	—	—
Second quarter, 1971	50.2	49.5	0.7	—	—	—
Third quarter, 1971	52.5	47.3	5.2	—	—	—
Fourth quarter, 1971	49.5	49.3	0.2	—	—	—
First quarter, 1972	50.1	51.6	−1.5	50.6	49.4	1.2
Second quarter, 1972	53.8	51.7	2.2	51.5	50.0	1.5
Third quarter, 1972	60.3	54.8	5.5	53.5	51.9	1.6
Fourth quarter, 1972	52.8	52.0	0.8	54.3	52.6	1.7
First quarter, 1973	50.6	52.0	−1.4	54.4	52.7	1.7
Second quarter, 1973	53.8	51.3	2.5	54.4	52.5	1.8
Third quarter, 1973	55.1	50.3	4.8	53.1	51.4	1.8
Fourth quarter, 1973	54.3	53.8	0.5	53.5	51.8	1.7
First quarter, 1974	57.2	57.1	0.2	55.1	53.0	2.1
Second quarter, 1974	58.2	53.3	4.8	56.1	53.4	2.7
Third quarter, 1974	58.0	52.7	5.2	56.9	54.1	2.9
Fourth quarter, 1974	50.8	52.0	−1.3	56.0	53.7	2.3
First quarter, 1975	50.5	53.9	−3.4	54.4	53.1	1.3
Second quarter, 1975	53.7	53.2	0.5	53.3	53.0	0.3
Third quarter, 1975	58.2	56.0	2.2	53.4	53.9	−0.5
Fourth quarter, 1975	56.1	57.7	−1.6	54.7	55.2	−0.5
First quarter, 1976	54.0	56.7	−2.8	55.5	55.9	−0.4
Second quarter, 1976	57.8	54.0	3.8	56.6	56.1	0.5
Third quarter, 1976	59.8	54.1	5.6	57.0	55.5	1.5
Fourth quarter, 1976	54.3	53.4	0.9	56.6	54.5	2.0
First quarter, 1977	54.2	54.5	−0.2	56.6	54.1	2.5
Second quarter, 1977	56.8	53.3	3.5	56.3	53.9	2.5
Third quarter, 1977	59.9	54.1	5.8	56.4	53.9	2.6
Fourth quarter, 1977	56.5	54.4	2.1	56.9	54.1	2.8
First quarter, 1978	58.4	57.1	1.2	57.9	54.8	3.2
Second quarter, 1978	63.8	57.8	6.0	59.7	55.9	3.8
Third quarter, 1978	67.3	58.7	8.6	61.7	57.1	4.5
Fourth quarter, 1978	58.5	57.2	1.3	62.1	57.8	4.3
First quarter, 1979	60.5	60.6	−0.1	62.5	58.6	3.9
Second quarter, 1979	69.0	65.9	3.1	63.8	60.6	3.2
Third quarter, 1979	66.1	64.8	1.4	63.5	62.1	1.4
Fourth quarter, 1979	57.8	59.7	−1.9	63.3	62.8	0.5
First quarter, 1980	57.2	60.4	−3.2	62.4	62.9	−0.4
Second quarter, 1980	60.0	61.6	−1.7	60.4	61.8	−1.4

Source: Air Transport Association of America.

resulting carrier) is now served by many more trunk and local-service carriers. Finally, in the deregulated environment it is conceivable that the CAB may consider only the standard tests applicable under the Clayton and Sherman antitrust laws as opposed to the public-interest criteria; after all, if the policy is to totally deregulate the industry, then the public convenience and necessity criteria are no longer meaningful. On the other hand, it should be pointed out that the Department of Justice and the Bureau of Consumer Protection do not favor the proposed merger.

Among the four mergers that have been consummated since deregulation of the industry, the acquisition of National by Pan American has the most interesting history. The deregulated environment provided sufficient threats and opportunities for four carriers to show a serious interest in acquiring all or part of National, which had a fleet of fifty-five modern aircraft, very little debt outstanding, and a reasonably strong market identity across the sunbelt portion of the country.

Pan American had discussed the merger proposal with National as far back as May 1977. On learning that Texas International had acquired 9.2 percent of National's stock at about $17 per share, Pan American applied for CAB permission to increase its ownership of National's stock from 4.8 percent to 25 percent. The offer was made at $35 per share with the condition that the acquired stock would be placed into a trust. A tentative agreement was reached at $41 per share and National requested the CAB to block further purchase of stock by Texas International. Before the proxy material had been sent to National's stockholders, Eastern offered to buy the stock at $50 per share. Finally, Air Florida entered the scene by offering to buy four of National's DC-10 aircraft, along with National's international routes from Miami to London, Paris, Frankfurt, and Tel Aviv.

The motives behind Texas International's attempt to acquire National are open to question. One view is that the small airline wanted to expand its southwest route system into the U.S. east coast and southern-tier routes. This justification would have been reasonable had the fleet of the two airlines been compatible and if Texas International had sufficient financial resources and strength to take on a carrier much larger than itself. The other speculation is that the merger proposal was a purely financial strategy and that Texas International had in fact no intention of merging. National's stock was undervalued and Texas International's interest in National would undoubtedly raise other carriers' interest in National, thus increasing considerably the value of the stock.

In the case of Pan American, the primary motivation was the acquisition of a domestic system to feed its international system. Historically, Pan American picked up passengers transported by domestic carriers from internal U.S. cities to the major gateways. However, recent route decisions by the CAB provided the traditionally domestic carriers with authority for direct service from internal domestic points to international points. Examples include Delta's service from Atlanta to London, Northwest's service from Minnesota to Scandinavia, and National's expansion of international service out of Miami. On the Pacific, Pan American was given added competition from Continental and potential competition from United that had been awarded a route to Tokyo. Although Pan American had been given some domestic "fill-up" rights, these rights could not be used to develop an effectively marketable domestic system. The acquisition of National would link effectively the routes of the two carriers at important points such as New York, Miami, Houston, Los Angeles, and San Francisco. Moreover, considering that National's peak activity is during the winter months and Pan American's during the summer months, a merger between the two would reduce the severity of the seasonality problem and improve the utilization of the combined fleet.

As in the case of Texas International, Eastern's motives for the merger proposal are also open to question. Some industry observers consider Eastern's bid of $50 per share for the National stock to be a "spoiler" strategy—one that was meant to slow down Pan American's progress. Some analysts considered Eastern's move to be purely defensive. Others considered Eastern's merger proposal to be a means to acquire aircraft at a very reasonable cost, to protect its Florida routes, and to gain entry into the London-Miami market. As for the anticompetitive aspects, Eastern pointed out that it competed effectively with National in only two markets, New York-Florida and Washington, D.C.-Florida. And, since any airline could choose to enter any market after deregulation, the anticompetitive arguments against the merger were no longer applicable. In fact, Eastern was even willing to make the merger contingent on the certification of another airline on routes where it was assumed that competition would be eliminated. The CAB was also of the opinion that because of the slot shortages at La Guardia and National, new carriers would not be in a position to compete effectively with the carrier resulting from the Eastern-National merger. However, Eastern was willing to consolidate flights from New York and Washington to Miami to alleviate congestion, particularly at the capacity-constrained airports of La Guardia and National. Such a move would in fact free up some slots for competitors to move into.

Air Florida's proposal added a new twist to the entire case. This carrier proposed to buy four DC-10 aircraft from National's fleet as well as National's international routes out of Miami. Air Florida was in favor of Pan American acquiring National's domestic routes and the remaining aircraft. And since the CAB was concerned about the reduction of competition on the Atlantic in the Pan American-National proposal, Air Florida's proposal would in fact strengthen Pan American's case. As for the Eastern-National merger, Air Florida objected violently on the grounds that it would erode its Florida traffic since Eastern competed with Air Florida on almost three quarters of Air Flordia's routes.

In the final analysis, the CAB approved the Pan American-National proposal, providing Pan American with a domestic system and Texas International with a substantial profit for its National stock. However, it is debatable as to whether National's traffic feed is having any significant impact on Pan American's North Atlantic and Pacific routes, given the geographic location of National's routes relative to the routes of Pan American.

Merger activity has clearly increased in the deregulated environment. Prior to deregulation an important, but by no means only, reason for carrier acquisition was the traffic rights of the acquired carrier. Other reasons included the acquisition of a more-or-less viable but a functioning system, a fleet of suitable aircraft, and an integration of the route system of the acquired carrier with the system of the acquiring carrier. These reasons are just as valid under deregulation as they were under regulation. Therefore, while the route franchise no longer has any value, it should not be assumed that massive route expansion can provide the same benefits as a merger. There are at least two major reasons. First, through merger one is also acquiring the market identity, schedule pattern, sales force, and the operational infrastructure of the acquired carrier. Second, entry in a market through route expansion, as opposed to acquisition, could fragment the market sufficiently to produce inadequate traffic for one or more carriers in the market. For these reasons, as well as the conviction of some carriers that only large carriers will survive deregulation, there is a distinct possibility that there will be less trunk and local-service carriers in the future.

Market Fragmentation

Airline deregulation in the United States and its limited implementation in some international markets has had a significant impact on passenger traffic flows on major routes. The on-board passenger loads on major routes have been reduced with the introduction of a more and more direct service. This fragmentation of passenger traffic has already had and will continue to have significant influence on airline economics with respect to dilution of yield, frequency, size of aircraft, and load factor.

Fragmentation of traffic has been experienced in both U.S. domestic and international on both short- and long-haul routes. Direct service between Newark, New Jersey and Oakland, California is an example of long-haul domestic markets. Previously most of the true O&D Newark-Oakland traffic was transported over the JFK-SFO segment or at least the EWR-SFO segment.

The fragmentation of transatlantic traffic has been even more noticeable because of the increase in the number of U.S. gateways and carriers (both U.S. and foreign flag). Figure 5-10 shows that the number of gateways has more than doubled and the number of U.S. international car-

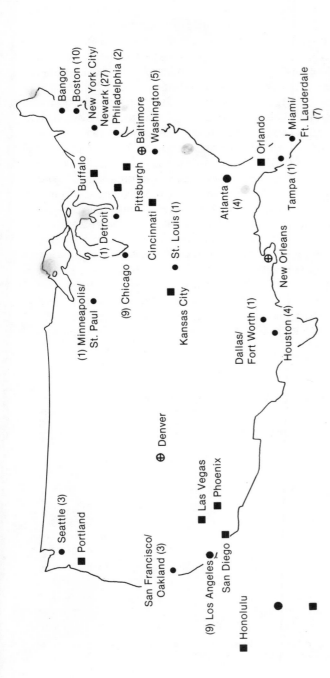

Source: Lockheed-California Company, "Gateway Fragmentation Analysis: The Transatlantic Market," Report no. EATF 2975 (September 1980).

Note: ● Current
⊕ New
■ Future (Wild card)
( ) Number of Airlines

Figure 5-10. Increase in Number of Gateways and Carriers to Europe (August 1980 Official Airline Guide)

riers has more than tripled. During the sixties, more than three-quarters of the passengers between the United States and Europe moved through the New York gateway. Although New York's share of the total transatlantic traffic has been declining for some time, the proliferation of gateways as a result of international deregulation has further reduced New York's share of total traffic. New gateways such as Dallas, Minneapolis/St. Paul, and Atlanta now account for a respectable share of the transatlantic traffic relative to other traditional gateways such as Chicago, Boston, Los Angeles, Miami, Washington, Seattle, and San Francisco (see table 5-11).

In addition to the proliferation of gateways, there has been an increase in the number of carriers, both U.S. and foreign flag. Traditionally, the North Atlantic market has been served by three U.S. combination carriers: National, Pan American, and TWA. Now there are ten. The new entrants are Air Florida, Braniff, Capitol, Delta, Northwest, Transamerica, and World. And the carrier proliferation has added to the market-segmentation problem. Consider, for example, the case of the Florida-Euorpe market (figure 5-11). In the sixties, passengers from the Miami area could either flow through New York or take multistop service via the Bahamas. In 1972, British Airways and National offered direct service between Miami and London. In 1978, direct service was added to Amsterdam, Frankfurt, and Paris. Previously a portion of the traffic to these three cities went through London. In addition, National was authorized to serve Amsterdam and

Table 5-11
U.S.-Europe Passenger Percent Distribution by Gateway

	1975	1979
New York/Newark	61.1	56.3
Chicago	8.9	7.2
Boston	7.4	7.1
Los Angeles	5.2	5.8
Miami	2.4	4.4
Washington/Baltimore	3.8	3.6
Seattle	2.5	2.2
San Francisco	0.5	2.2
Houston	1.6	1.4
Dallas	0.1	1.6
Atlanta	0.1	1.8
Detroit	1.2	0.8
Philadelphia	1.4	1.3
Bangor	1.7	2.4
Minneapolis	—	0.6
Other	2.1	1.3
	100.0	100.0

Source: Lockheed-California Company, "Gateway Fragmentation Analysis: The Transatlantic Market." Report no. EATF 2975 (September 1980).

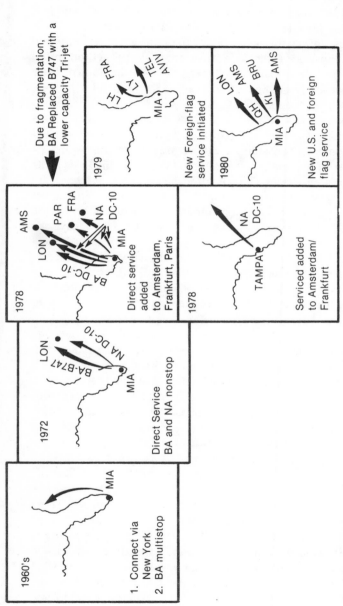

Figure 5-11. Fragmentation Example: Transatlantic (Florida-Europe)

Source: Lockheed-California Company, "Gateway Fragmentation Analysis: The Transatlantic Market." Report no. EATF 2975 (September 1980).

Note: BA - British Airways
       NA - National Airlines
       LH - Lufthansa
       LY - El Al
       KL - KLM Royal Dutch Airlines
       QH - Air Florida
       GK - Laker

Frankfurt directly from Tampa. In 1979, two foreign-flag carriers (Lufthansa and El Al) began to serve the Miami-Frankfurt and Miami-Tel Aviv markets. Finally, in 1980, direct service was introduced to Brussels and two additional carriers (Air Florida and KLM) entered the market.

Given the trend in market fragmentation, the premise for *international deregulation* (that is, lower air fares) is inconsistent with the method (more carriers and gateways) of deregulation. Whereas the introduction of lower fares warrants the use of high-capacity aircraft (with high load factor), market fragmentation calls for the use of smaller aircraft with higher direct operating costs per available seat-mile. The existence of "giveaway" fares in markets with new direct service is a temporary phenomena, established for promotional purposes. Eventually, a carrier must either raise fares or leave the market. Braniff was authorized to serve Europe on the basis of its promises to implement lower fares. Shortly after the initiation of lower-fare service, the carrier filed for considerably higher fares. World offered lower fares in the Boston-London market for one month only. And on the Pacific routes low fares and high operating costs have forced Braniff to leave the market.

The change in structure of the traffic flow has diluted yield for the carrier responsible for the transatlantic portion of the trip. Figure 5-12 shows average passenger yield for U.S. domestic, intra-Europe, and transatlantic markets during 1978. It is clear that as the connecting distance is increased (at either or both ends of the trip), the dilution due to prorate is also increased. Marginal transatlantic yield is the revenue received for connecting distance and intra-Europe and U.S. domestic yields are revenues paid out in prorates. As shown in table 5-12, the dilution due to prorate can be as much as 20 percent for connecting distances of 600 miles. One reasonable way of reducing the impact of prorate dilution is to offer direct service to secondary U.S. or European gateways. However, the advantage of improvement in yield must then be traded against higher direct operating costs per seat-mile, resulting from the use of smaller aircraft.

In the near future, market fragmentation is likely to increase as new U.S. and foreign-flag carriers exercise their new authorities. The U.S.-U.K. agreement alone calls for two additional cities each during 1981, and one each in 1982, 1983, and 1984. There is a strong possibility of more carriers from the Mideast and Africa offering direct service to the United States, leading to further market fragmentation. The result in the near future is likely to be a diversification of routes, service, and fare combinations. On the other hand, there are some factors that could reverse the trend in market fragmentation. First, the unfair policies and practices of some of the foreign airlines and their governments could reach a level that would force the U.S. government to slow down or even reverse its open-skies policy. Second, continued escalation of fuel prices could slow down the market

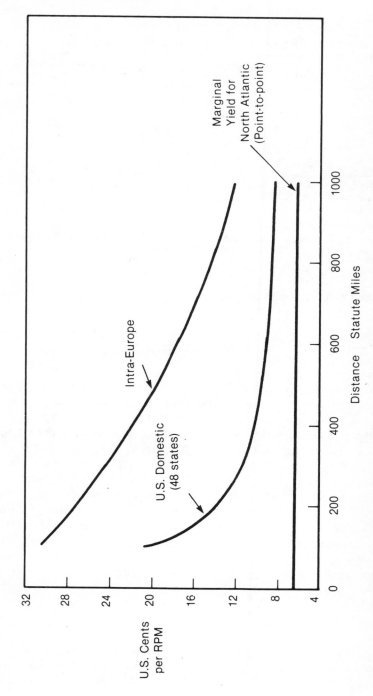

Source: Lockheed-California Company, "Gateway Fragmentation Analysis: The Transatlantic Market." Report no. EATF 2975 (September 1980).

Figure 5-12. Yields versus Distance: U.S. Domestic, Intra-Europe, and North Atlantic (1978)

Table 5-12
Effect of Connecting Distance on Yield: Viable Prorates (1978)

Connecting Distance[a] (ST. MI.)	Transatlantic Yield[b] (¢/RPM)	Percent Dilution Due to Prorate[c]
0	6.50	0
100	5.93	8.8
200	5.65	13.1
300	5.45	16.2
400	5.31	18.3
500	5.23	19.5
600	5.18	20.3

Source: Lockheed-California Company, "Gateway Fragmentation Analysis: The Transatlantic Market." Report no. EATF 2975 (September 1980).

[a]15 percent circuitry.

[b]Point-to-point yield: 6.5¢/mi.

[c]Prorates 50 percent European, 50 percent Domestic; European prorates at average, Intra-Europe yield, domestic prorate at average forty-eight state yield (F) distance.

fragmentation trend through the use of larger and more fuel-efficient aircraft.

Summary

During recent years, the economic behavior of the airline industry has changed considerably as a result of the more relaxed regulatory environment and the significant increase in operating costs. The substantial increase in the price of fuel, in particular, has brought about a change in airline scheduling and network planning. All carriers have begun the fleet, route, and fare rationalization process. In international operations, liberalization policies of the U.S. government have resulted in the proliferation of gateways and carriers, resulting, consequently, in market fragmentation. The U.S. procompetitive policy, implemented during a time of high fuel costs, has produced a dilemma for the industry: low fares and high fuel costs warrant the use of high density wide-body aircraft but market fragmentation warrants the use of smaller long-haul aircraft which, given the currently available fleet, are not economically viable.

Notes

1. P.J. Bakes, Jr., "As Fast as the Law Allows," in *Corporate Planning Under Deregulation: The Case of the Airlines*, Proceedings of a conference held at Northwestern University, 11-12 June 1979.

2. R.S. Maurer, "Deregulation—The Sword of Damocles or the Golden Fleece" (Presentation made at the annual meeting of the Travel Research Association in Savannah, Georgia, 17 June 1980).

3. Merrill Lynch, Pierce, Fenner and Smith, Inc., *Aviation Log*, vol. 3, no. 15 (22 October 1980).

4. M.H. Schlansky, "Restructuring of the Airline Industry Under Deregulation: The Domestic Route Network" (Presentation made at the 59th Annual Meeting of the Transportation Research Board in Washington, D.C., 22 January 1980).

5. J.C. Meehan, *Observations on the Impact of Deregulation*, Report no. FEA/2946 (Lockheed-California Company, August 1980).

6. British Airways, "Appendices to Comments of British Airways in Response to Order 77-7-4," *North Atlantic Fares Investigation* (Docket 27918), (19 October 1977), p. 11.

7. M.A. Brenner, *Some Observations on the First Half Year of Passenger Deregulation*, MIT-FTL Report no. R79-7 (July 1979).

8. Air Transport Association of America, *The Significance of Airline Passenger Load Factors* (August 1980).

6 Marketing Planning

Deregulation, increasing consumerism, high inflation rates, and spiraling fuel costs have altered the environment, and these forces of change could intensify during the 1980s. The financial survival of an airline could depend on how well it adapts to the new environment by finding creative methods of harmonizing company profits and passenger and shipper satisfaction.

The New Marketplace

Because of the overriding importance of marketing threats and opportunities, it is imperative that an analysis be made of the marketplace to identify trends that affect the airline industry as well as individual airlines. An analysis of passenger and shipper behavior and major operating characteristics in each market segment is necessary before alternative strategies can be examined and the optimal strategy selected and implemented to meet desired corporate objectives.

The marketplace in the 1980s has changed considerably from that of earlier decades. First, regulation of the U.S. domestic airline industry has been relaxed considerably, and there are strong pressures to implement similar changes in the international arena. No longer are routes, rates, and competition in domestic markets totally under the control of the CAB. An airline can offer service on almost any route and charge any rate within a wide zone. Within the next three years, the remaining controls and constraints are to be eliminated. The relaxed economic regulations and the possibility of a completely unregulated environment, are totally alien to the airline industry. The airline marketing planner must therefore adapt to this changed environment. However, since the jury is still out on the net benefits of deregulation, the long-term strategies selected should be flexible in case Congress decides to revert to some form of regulation.

The second change in the marketplace is the result of an economy altered by the existence of high inflation rates, unemployment, and interest rates. All of these factors have slowed growth in real incomes and altered the buying habits of passengers and shippers. Although there has been an increase in the number of two-income families, the discretionary traveler appears to be, even more than in the past, willing to accept much lower quality in air-transportation service in exchange for lower fares. High interest rates are changing consumer savings and debt patterns and, consequently, spending patterns. High energy costs have not only increased the costs of all goods and services but have influenced the trade-off between air and automobile travel.

The third change in the marketplace has been caused by the evolving demographic environment. This includes population growth rates, geographical shifts in population, distribution of age groups, higher education levels, and, in some countries such as the United States, increased numbers of nonfamily households.

The fourth change relates to changing life styles and consumer values, attitudes, and norms. Examination of these trends will provide useful information on consumer needs and the optimal responses by the airline industry.

There is an accelerated rate of technological progress, which also affects the marketplace. Technological developments influence not only the demand for air-transportation services but also the cost of producing and marketing air-transportation services. Consider the pace of technological developments in just two industries: computers and communications. More intensive use of computer technology could, for example, lower direct and indirect operating costs and alter channels of distribution. Advancements in communications technology will undoubtedly increase the use of picture phones and electronic photocopying, both of which will influence demand for air-transportation services (passenger and airfreight).

Environmental analysis in these five areas, particularly with respect to regulatory and economic changes, will identify marketing threats and opportunities. It is the task of the marketing planner to make management aware of these trends so that appropriate strategies can be developed and implemented.

The Role of Marketing

In a firm that is truly marketing oriented, all functions revolve around the customer. After all, without customers, there would be no firm. Such organizations view marketing's function not only as indispensible but as integrative. The marketing enthusiasts claim that identification and satisfaction of customer needs is the key to success, and the task of marketing is to attract customers through promises and hold customers by delivering satisfaction. Since the delivery of such satisfaction is planned, produced, priced, distributed, and delivered by departments other than marketing, the latter should therefore be viewed as an integrative function. For an airline, then, the role of marketing is to understand the needs of passengers and shippers and help management adapt to the continuously changing needs of passengers and shippers in a competitively viable manner. Moreover, marketing must identify the airline's weaknesses and strengths, as well as potential competitive challenges and opportunities, and then pinpoint strategies that will allow the airline to evolve from a passive to an adaptive, and ultimately a creative, organization.

Marketing can fulfill this role through strategic planning, which can do far more than predict and prepare an airline for the future; it can, in some ways, make the future happen. There are two types of variables: uncontrollable and controllable. *Uncontrollable variables* are those such as the state of the economy, the price of fuel, and the level and type of competition. *Controllable variables* are those such as the elements of *marketing mix* (service, price, promotion, and distribution). The task of strategic market planning is to set creative, strategically controllable variables to adapt to the environment containing uncontrollable variables in a manner that harmonizes airline objectives and resources with the marketplace opportunities. The creative aspects of the harmonization process are essential, since the two types of variables are interrelated, and it is not possible to model consumer behavior in any precise manner.

The strategic-marketing-planning process must support and fulfill the overall corporate objectives, strategies, policies, and plans. Within the context of these corporate objectives, the marketing planner can begin the development and implementation of a market plan.

The first phase in the strategic-marketing-planning process is to conduct a situation analysis that essentially describes the current situation with respect to customers, competitors, market characteristics, and general trends. Customer analysis is normally performed through the use of surveys. All major airlines (and, since 1973, IATA) have been conducting their own corporate in-flight surveys to collect information on trip purpose and frequency, fare type, and demographic and socioeconomic characteristics such as age, sex, occupation, income, education, residence, and marital status. Crosstabulations of passenger composition, behavior, and attitude data can provide significant input into service planning, advertising campaigns, media and channel selection, and market-share analysis. In addition to the use of surveys (in-flight or on-ground interviews) that provide information on a specific individual, useful information can also be obtained from sales, reservations, and travel agents. The latter source provides information on the collective purchase behavior of passengers; information that can play a vital role in the analysis of an airline's image and, ultimately, its success in the marketplace. Typically such information would fall into the categories of advertising recall, reservations data, passenger compliments and complaints, innovative and competitive fares, sales by outlet, and points of ticket sale. Feedback from travel agents on how they and passengers perceive different airlines and different service features can be invaluable.

Having analyzed the customers, the next step is to analyze one's competitors. Such an analysis will help an airline understand its own weaknesses and strengths relative to its existing and potential competitors. The object in the analysis of competitors is to evaluate their strategy, their performance, and their weaknesses and strengths—past, current, and potential. A competitor's strategy can be evaluated by examining its traffic growth, revenue growth, change in yield, change in market share relative to seat share, change in average load factor, and change in profits. The analysis of strength and weakness involves an examination of the quality of services offered by a competitor, channels of distribution, fleet characteristics with respect to age and operating costs, general cost structure, network integration, financial capabilities, and management of human resources. This analysis will ultimately be used to project possible competitive reactions and scenarios.

After examining competition, the next step should be to analyze characteristics of the market, all routes, segment by segment. Market analysis relates to the demand as well as supply characteristics. On the demand side, the important characteristics are the size of the market and its rate of growth, the nature and degree of concentration, customer composition, seasonality, and directionality. The analysis relating to customer composition should attempt to disaggregate passengers and shippers by their price elasticity of demand. On the supply side, information should be analyzed with respect to structure, performance, and conduct. In this respect cost structure and cost behavior are of particular interest.

The next step in the situation analysis is an examination of general environmental trends. Besides an analysis of the social changes mentioned already, an attempt should be made to assess (to the extent possible) changes in the economic, political, regulatory, and technological environment. The economic changes would relate to the general state of the economy as well as the major components of the gross national product that may influence future transportation patterns and behavior. The changes in the political environment may have significant influence on foreign investment and relations and, in turn, foreign travel of passengers and goods. Regulatory changes, such as those implemented by the United States in domestic markets and those proposed for the international markets, could have a dramatic impact on travel in individual markets. Finally, technological changes with respect to aircraft, computers, automation, and advanced communications would have both positive and negative impacts on air travel. Greater automation of ground services would, for example, facilitate travel and therefore have a positive impact. Further advances in communications technology, on the other hand, may provide alternative means of satisfying the needs of the business traveler and so may represent a negative impact. An assessment of the general environmental trends will provide valuable insight into market planning for the future.

The final step in situation analysis is for an airline to make an assessment of itself. The analysis thus far would have provided an airline with an assessment of the available opportunities. An assessment of itself and its competitors, however, will provide an airline with the necessary information to determine if in fact it is in a position to be able to take advantage of the opportunities identified.[1] Self-assessment should be made in a manner similar to the one used to analyze competition.

The second phase of marketing planning is to formulate and study alternative strategies and select an optimal strategy that will achieve the stated corporate and marketing objectives. The formulation of an overall marketing strategy requires a thorough examination of each of the marketing-mix elements. In addition to analyzing each marketing-mix element separately, it is necessary to examine any potential interaction among the elements. A large number of analytical techniques, methods, and models have been developed to help the marketer analyze and select the optimal strategy. These include, for example, multivariate statistics, pricing models, advertising models, and inventory-control models.

The third phase in marketing planning is the development and implementation of monitoring, evaluation, and control systems to assess, on an ongoing basis, the progress of the marketing plan. More specifically, the object would be to monitor the results to determine if passenger and shipper needs are being fulfilled, corporate objectives being achieved, and market opportunities exploited in a competitively viable manner. There are basically four types of controls that can be implemented to review the progress of the marketing plan: annual-plan control, profitability control, efficiency control, and strategic control.[2] *Annual-plan control* examines performance against a specific plan. *Profitability control* measures the financial performance of each service. *Efficiency control* checks the impact of various marketing expenditures such as advertising. *Strategic control* evaluates the effectiveness of the overall marketing plan in terms of available opportunities.

Marketing-Mix Variables and Strategy

Marketing mix is a set of controllable variables whose level an airline can set to influence individual target market segments. Traditionally, these marketing-decision variables have been classified into four groups: product, price, promotion, and distribution. The level of these variables can be changed to develop and evaluate alternate marketing-mix strategies. Determination of the optimal marketing mix depends on the objective of the airline at any given time.

Product

The *product mix* of a firm is usually discussed in terms of its width, depth, and consistency.[3] The width of the product-mix concerns the number of different product lines within an airline. Typically, these would include passenger, charter, and freight operations. The depth of the product mix concerns the number of items offered by an airline within each product line. In scheduled passenger transportation, it could either include the number of routes served or, for any given route, the number of services (first class, economy, standby, budget, and so forth) offered. The consistency of the product mix concerns the relationship among the various product lines in their end use, production requirement, or distribution channels. In the case of an airline, consistency would refer to the relationship between passenger and freight transportation or part-charter flights. Given that market requirements and preferences, competition, environment, and individual airline strengths and weaknesses are changing continuously, it is the responsibility of marketing management to continuously evaluate the current product mix in light of existing and future opportunities and constraints.

This responsibility for determining the needs and wants of a carrier's existing and potential passengers is usually carried out through segmentation, a process that involves disaggregation of information, followed by reassembly and, ultimately, synthesis. In the case of an airline, for example, it is necessary to analyze passengers and shippers because all of them do not have the same needs with respect to the services offered.

The total market of passenger travel may be segmented into business travelers and nonbusiness travelers; the latter then can be further subdivided into vacation travelers and visitors of friends and relatives. All groups can be divided into male or female categories and into frequent and infrequent travelers. Although there is no unique form of market segmentation, it is emphasized that while the method of segmentation should relate to the research objectives, the needs of passengers and shippers should be interpreted broadly and should go beyond the boundaries of service characteristics. The broader interpretation of various segment needs is necessary because market groups can be characterized either by differences in benefits sought through the service or by the characteristics of customers within the group. For example, one could say that business travelers tend to be interested in departure and arrival times.

There is no doubt that much of the information received through segmentation has played an important role in the identification of potential markets and strategies to serve different needs of different passengers. However, there are at least four areas in which improvements can be made in customer analysis and segmentation.

First, there is usually too much emphasis on data collection and not enough emphasis on analysis, and ultimately on actionable recommendations. For example, it is simply not enough to find out that passengers liked a certain service feature or even that X percent liked the feature. The more important questions are: How many additional passengers were attracted to this airline by the introduction of this service feature? How many passengers would switch airlines if this feature were discontinued? Similarly, while many surveys conducted in the past were informative in pointing out problems with service, they did not probe deep enough to indicate if the problem was serious enough for the passenger to select a competitor in the future.

Second, despite its overall usefulness, the vast quantities of demographic information collected is still not sufficient to determine, within a certain demographic and socioeconomic profile, why certain people travel and why others do not. It has been suggested that answers to such questions can only be obtained by going beyond demographic analysis and into psychographic analysis.[4] For example, it has also been suggested that fare innovation investigations should be related to demographic and psychographic information. In the past some attempts have been made to utilize attitudinal segmentation research to improve market analysis and planning. The airline industry is, however, far behind other industries in this area of market research.

Life-style segmentation is one example of psychographic or attitudinal market research. Air Canada's market research shows the life-style groups for nonbusiness travelers to be: (1) extravagant consumers, (2) nature people, (3) playsters; and (4) cautious homebodies. The carrier then divides the vacation destinations into six groups: peace and quiet; aesthetic appreciation; hot climate; grand hotel; inexpensive activity; and relatives and friends.[5] The object is to crosstabulate general life-style groups and ideal vacation types to estimate leisure-travel potential.

Third, much more attention needs to be paid to nontravelers. Analyzing existing passengers is simply not enough; they have already purchased their tickets and are already on board when they are surveyed. What about potential passengers on the ground? Given the fact that a significant percent of the world population has never flown, it is questionable whether the industry has yet reached maturity. From the viewpoint of the traditional, idealized "product life cycle," at what stage (development, growth, maturity, or decline) is the airline industry? This question cannot be answered without more knowledge about nontravelers. For example, it is necessary to know the points at which various segments of the nontravelers approach air travel. Moreover, research needs to be directed at identifying the hurdles (at each point) faced by nontravelers.

Fourth, it is necessary for market researchers to establish a theory about the way a given segment of the population behaves before the statistical data are analyzed. In other words, it would be more appropriate to initially hypothesize the theory about a given market's dynamics, and then test it with empirical data, than proceed in the reverse order.

Market research can provide valuable information to improve service planning. The business traveler is primarily interested in convenient and on-time schedules, prompt and accurate reservation service, prompt and efficient airport processing, and comfortable in-flight accommodations where he or she can work and rest.[6] This information, combined with other attributes such as lower sensitivity to price and trip duration, more flexible schedules, and less advance notice of the decision to travel, can help a marketer determine his marketing-mix strategy. For example, since frequency is important on business routes, scheduled capacity should be offered with smaller aircraft. At the airports, special check-in lines and express baggage submission and retrieval systems should be developed. A number of airlines have already established multiclass seating configuration and in-flight service. Although most of these services have already been implemented, there are other areas in which service can be improved for the business traveler. Door-to-door service, along the lines of Federal Express, is just one example; valet parking is another.[7]

Market research can also improve the understanding of potential passengers. Consider, for example, the role market research has played in the establishment of British Airways Family Reunion Clubs to generate and expand visiting-friends-relatives traffic.[8] From research conducted in the United Kingdom, the airline learned about the existence of a significant market to the United States, Canada, Australia, and South Africa consisting of visits to relatives in these countries. Moreover, many individuals in this category thought that they could not afford to travel by air for a visit and that in any case the travel arrangements would be too complex. Extensive market research was conducted to analyze these potential customers with respect to size of market, type of relatives in destination countries, age group, and concerns about making a trip. Based on the results, clubs were established (with minimal membership costs) to provide a sense of belonging, distribute promotional literature and information on travel savings plans, and encourage the desire to travel. Special arrangements were made with the infrastructure industries to produce low-cost packages. Advertising stressed reassurance and care. And, according to British Airways, the generative effect was overwhelming.

In planning for the future, it is clear that there will be dramatic changes in attitudes and demographic profiles of the various populations. These changes will undoubtedly have a significant influence on the marketing of air-transportation services. According to one researcher, the travel variables of the 1980s for the U.S. population will be: (1) deterioration of work ethic;

(2) demand for leisure time; (3) young multi-earner families; (4) a more affluent population; (5) time restrictions; and (6) higher incomes in the blue-collar sector.[9] The airline industry, therefore, will have to become sensitive to the needs of different types of travelers (for example, women executives). And the working husband and wife, while more affluent, will be constrained by time, requiring short but well-planned vacations. This decade will undoubtedly present new challenges for the airline marketing executive.

It is evident from recent developments that, in the future, marketing management will play an even more significant role in product planning. For example, the share of pleasure travel has been increasing at a rapid rate and the needs and wants of the pleasure traveler are considerably different from those of the business traveler. Thus, the emphasis in airline marketing would have to reflect this trend. On the other hand, the airlines cannot afford to overlook the real profit base: the full-fare economy passenger on business travel.

Let us examine improvements in the product, that is, service offered with special attention to activities on the ground. In the future, automatic check-in and boarding systems could be developed that would substantially change the operations inside the airline terminal. An arriving passenger could step up to a display console at various points at the airport, request information on flights to his destination (or specify his airline and flight) confirm his reservation, insert his credit card for ticketing, and receive a boarding card as a receipt. The boarding card may also contain instructions for gate and seating. Baggage could be checked into a conveyor system for delivery to the gate. At the gate, automatic gate displays and turnstiles could control the boarding process, reducing the number of gate attendants required. Insertion of the boarding card can allow confirmed passengers (and authorized standbys) to board. Late-arriving passengers could be informed if they are accepted for the flight when checking in with the dispersed consoles. If the passengers are too late, the consoles could suggest to them the next best flight(s) and also make a reservation.

Such an automated system will be an improvement on the design of future airline-terminal buildings. While the present check-in counters are not likely to be totally eliminated because of the need to handle first-time travelers or special problems, the automated system will handle the bulk of repeat travelers and reduce the floor area required to handle the higher traffic volumes of future years. An automated system will also encourage the establishment of remote check-in facilities at suburban and city-center locations, where an airport-access vehicle could be synchronized with aircraft departures. Such vehicles can bypass the terminal building and deliver passengers directly to the aircraft, passing through an automatic turnstile to record the passenger manifest and confirm boarding.

Generally, up to this time, airlines have used computers as storage and retrieval devices for the reservations systems and more recently for automatic ticketing. However, from current trends in the industry, it appears that computer technology can play an important role in either reducing the cost of producing or improving the level of existing services. The real job of product planning in the future will be to develop true product-price combinations such that passengers pay only for the services they receive and in turn receive only the services they pay for.

Price

In the marketing of air-transportation services, price is probably the most important element in the marketing mix. In setting a price for one of its products (services) an airline must pay attention to a number of factors: (1) company objectives; (2) cost of production; (3) market demand; (4) competition; and (5) external parties. Successful pricing decisions involve taking account of not only these five factors but also the other three elements of the marketing mix (product, promotion, and distribution). The importance of pricing policies should be evident from the fact that it is the only element in the marketing mix that generates sales revenue; the other three elements generate costs. Unfortunately, despite its importance, it cannot be claimed that the airline industry has scored well in its pricing decisions. Moreover, not all the blame can be placed on the existence of government regulations. Some airlines worshipped cost-oriented pricing philosophy with little attention paid to the demand aspects; some were so demand oriented that they overlooked the cost of production; a few overlooked the advantage of the changing market environment; and some were so competition oriented that they lost sight of all other pricing-mix and marketing-mix elements.

In establishing the prices for its services, the objectives of top management must first be clearly stated, understood, and accepted. The objectives can take on of many forms: maximization of profit, sales, or market share, or sometimes promotion. For profit maximization, economists have developed models where price is established by the interaction between demand and cost functions. These models have severe limitations in that they do not take into account competition, government regulations, or other marketing-mix variables. Moreover, they assume that it is possible to estimate accurately both demand and cost functions. The other common objective is to set price to maximize market share. In this case, the theoretical chain of events would be: an airline buys excess capacity and sets price below competition to gain market share; initially there may be a loss, but it is hypothesized that unit costs will decrease as traffic builds up; the latter event would not only allow further price reductions, but it could also produce profit. Again, this is only theory. In the real world, price reduction may or may not stimulate a proportionate increase in traffic; unit costs may or may not decrease sufficiently to accommodate further reductions in price or the existence of profit; and finally, the theory has no validity if competition matches the price, as is likely to be case in the airline industry.

The second point relates to those airlines who like to establish prices based on the cost of production, including an adequate return on investment. Until the Airline Deregulation Act of 1978, this practice was advocated by the CAB. The only problem with this approach is that either the airline or the CAB was required to estimate the level of traffic to establish a price; but the price level itself is an important determinant of passenger traffic. Furthermore, certain cost-allocation criteria are arbitrary.

The third factor concerns airlines who in the past have espoused the use of demand-oriented pricing practices. These airlines maintain that price should be related to the passenger's perception of the value of service offered. Then if this level of demand is not sufficient to recover costs and provide an adequate return, service should not be offered. The only problem with this theory is that one needs to have an accurate estimate of the market's perception of alternative forms of service offered and the value attached to each form of service. Moreover, the value attached to a particular service is not constant.

Differential pricing is a closely related aspect of demand-oriented pricing. The idea here is to sell virtually the same service to two different passengers at two different prices where the prices may not necessarily reflect a proportional difference in marginal costs. In the airline industry differential pricing practices have been used on the basis of service form, place, and time. Unfortunately, these pricing policies have not always been effective. In order for differential pricing to work a certain number of conditions must exist. First, various segments of the population must have different price elasticities of demand. Second, these segments must be identifiable. Third, sufficient conditions must be implemented to stop or at least minimize dilution (switching services). Fourth, a competitor should not be able to undersell the airline to the segment being asked to pay the higher price. Fifth, an intermediary should not be able to acquire the service at a low price and sell it at a price lower than that charged by the airline. Sixth, differential pricing practices should keep resentment among different categories of passengers to a minimum. And seventh, the process of market segmentation and policy should be cost effective. Since all these assumptions do not hold for all carriers in the industry, differential pricing has not worked out successfully for all carriers. In theory, it should have worked fairly well since domestically the industry was regulated by the CAB, and internationally the airlines had agreed to charge prices coordinated through the IATA multilateral forum. Drive for an increase in market share, however, led a number of airlines to cheat on either their own rules or those of other airlines.

The fourth factor to keep in mind in establishing pricing policies is competition. A number of airlines maintain a policy of competition-oriented pricing. They will match prices charged by competitors even though their costs or demand has not changed. In a highly competitive market environment with virtual product homogeneity, or in situations of oligopoly, there is no choice but to establish competition-oriented pricing policies. In such situations the only way out is to differentiate the product. But in the airline industry, passengers are either not informed of differences in service or they do not place significant value on these differences. Consider, for example, the differences in service between World Airways and United Airlines on the Boston-San Francisco route. Comparison of United's Super Saver Fare with World's Standard Fare shows that for a few dollars more, the United passenger is provided with nonstop flights with lower density seating configuration, not to mention the availability of back-up aircraft in case of equipment failure, discounts for children, and access to United's reservations system and route structure from virtually any point in the United States.

The fifth factor to be considered in pricing policies is the input from other parties. This will include input from infrastructure industries such as hotels and tourist boards, from travel agents and tour operators, and, perhaps most important of all, from government agencies. Despite deregulation of the airline industry in the United States, the rest of the world still considers the industry a public utility. In general, governments endeavor to encourage pricing policies that insure the economic stability of their airlines, produce the lowest fare available to the public, require the lowest level of subsidy, and guarantee adequate maintenance of service on politically and socially desirable routes at reasonable fares.

In establishing reasonable pricing policies it is important to consider not only these five factors but also the other three elements of marketing mix. It is also necessary to take account of all interactions among these factors. Consider, for example, the complexities of product-line pricing, an issue which brings into focus not only the interrelated cost structure but also interrelated demand characteristics. In addition to comprehensive cost analysis, airlines will have to perform extensive market research to determine the underlying reasons travelers (and travel agents) choose airline seats. Airlines will have to learn more about how passengers choose one service feature (aircraft type, nonstop service, and so forth) over another and how they trade off service features against price. Market research, combined with techniques of operations research, will be needed to determine the demand for these various services and price options.

In the future, one can anticipate an increase in the number of fares offered. Even now the industry is using its new freedom in pricing by going to peak-off-peak pricing, traditional discount fares, and individual market sales. But the proliferation of fares requires effective seat management. Consider the different types of fares that can be offered: nonrefundable; transferable tickets; ticket exchanges; tickets sold on consignment, auction, and Dutch auctions. With this level of sophistication, capacity control of the different fares is absolutely necessary to maximize profit of any given flight, that is, space will have to be controlled overall and also by fare type. Furthermore, this will have to be done not by simply assigning a certain percentage of overall seats for a specific fare level but by forecasting demand for specific markets by fare type, in real time, as a flight becomes more and more fully booked. The carriers that will be successful will be those that accurately project demand and properly allocate cost to individual flights.[10]

Since carriers will have the option to get in and out of markets rapidly, more accurate profit forecasts will be required, including forecasts of competitive responses. Consequently, increased resources will have to be expended on planning and forecasting since the costs of incorrect decisions will become even higher. Thus, the impact of alternative pricing policies on revenues, cost, demand, and supply of seats will become even more important in the future as the public is given more service options. Only those airlines that implement carefully analyzed pricing policies will survive and grow.

Distribution

Once the product-line and pricing policies have been established, the next element of marketing mix is *distribution*: methods of getting the product to the customer. The traditional airline distribution system has had five elements: the carrier's sales outlets, other carriers' sales outlets, travel agents and tour operators, corporate travel departments, and the government. The airline sales outlets include ticket counters at airports, reservations by phone followed by tickets by mail, and city ticket offices that can be on-line or off-line. Tickets sold by travel agents require a commission paid by the airline which, until recently, was regulated by the CAB for domestic carriers. And, in turn, the travel agents were required to meet certain minimal standards with respect to qualification, financial operations, and normal business practices.

For the industry as a whole, the city ticket office (CTO) outlet has been stable in the last ten years, although for individual carriers the activity through this channel has fluctuated. The use of CTOs provides the most control and reduces the dependence on other channels such as the travel agent. However, the decision on the number of ticket offices in any given city must be evaluated very carefully. The factors to be included in the decision are:

the cost of the CTO; overall corporate policy; total service offered to and from the city; market share; the size, composition, and characteristics of the population; and the relationship with the travel agents. Delta is an example of a carrier relying heavily on this channel of distribution and USAir represents a carrier with the least number of CTOs per station among the major U.S. carriers.

The costs and benefits of each channel of distribution vary significantly from carrier to carrier. Approximately half of the domestic passenger tickets and three-fourths of the international tickets are sold by travel agents. These intermediaries can play an important role in three respects. First, an airline cannot possibly maintain sales offices in every town across the country, let alone the entire world. Second, the travel agent can sell complementary services such as hotel space and ground transportation. Third, a travel agent can provide useful information and assistance in travel arrangements, particularly those involving travel documents, different currencies, and different languages. These advantages, however, are not free. There are commissions to pay, and the carrier can lose control over the services offered for sale. Once agreed upon, any one of the hundreds of thousands of travel agents can issue a valid ticket on a carrier, and the carrier has an obligation to honor that ticket. And on routes served by competitive carriers, there is no guarantee that a given travel agent will select a particular carrier.

The loss of control is a very important aspect of the decision to use travel agents. Given the range of services offered by each airline, a travel agent can choose to sell one service more aggressively than another. The agent might concentrate on business travelers since more selling effort is needed in attracting the pleasure traveler. Moreover, the total commission earned will undoubtedly be large. Or, the travel agent may promise service not offered on the flight in question, placing the airline in the position of either honoring the agent's promise or explaining the discrepancy. Also the airline is at the mercy of the travel agent for fast and accurate cancellation information. An airline's own sales outlets do not have any of these disadvantages, but they are expensive and limited with respect to the size of the market they can reach.

After deregulation, the CAB began to investigate the competitive aspects of marketing airline services and concluded that the fixed percentage commission for travel agents represented an anticompetitive policy, one that was not in the public interest. The CAB instead expressed interest in, for example, net fares. However, both segments of the industry (carriers and agents) expressed some doubts about the concept. Carriers pointed out that since passengers would not be able to bargain at the airport or city ticket offices, the concept would provide an unfair advantage to the travel agents. The association of the travel agents also expressed some doubt, contending that the concept may increase competition at the retail level to harm smaller members of the industry. Since the net-fares concept was found to be unattractive, various airlines proposed alternative commission schedules, the most controversial being United's first offer to pay a flat fee of $8.50 for each ticket sold by an agent. For obvious reasons, this proposal was rejected immediately by the agents, at which time United replaced it with one containing a sliding scale. Given the diversity of views and the market control enjoyed by the agents, both sides are exercising great caution in deviating too far from the traditional commission rates.

While the airlines have been examining their relationship with the travel agents, a number of new ideas have been proposed to increase the channels of distribution. These include self-ticketing machines, Ticketron, banks, and bulk-fare contractors. The first two methods are self-explanatory. Self-ticketing machines have caught the interest of PSA and Eastern, and World Airways is interested in Ticketron. As to banks, the commission rate could be lowered since this would be an ancillary service provided by the banks, as well as the fact that public access to the airlines would be increased substantially. The bulk-fare concept requires an independent contractor to purchase tickets at bulk rates which will be disposed of at fares determined by the contractor. While the potential for large profits exists for the contractor, there is also the risk of being left with a large inventory after the scheduled flight time.

The selection of an optimal distribution system will vary from airline to airline and depend on passenger characteristics and composition, services offered, competition, and number of intermediaries. Important passengers' characteristics are geographic dispersion and purchasing patterns (for example, frequency of purchase). Service characteristics relate to different types of service offered and degree of emphasis placed by the airline on each type of service. The competitive characteristics are obvious. If an airline's competitors use travel agents to sell their services then that particular airline is also forced to use this channel to distribute its services. Important characteristics relating to intermediaries are their cost structure and aptitude for performing many functions, such as promotional packaging of tours. All these factors play an important role in the selection of an optimal distribution system.

In the future, each airline must evaluate the cost effectiveness of each alternative channel of distribution using the following criteria: economics, control, adaptability, cooperation, conflict, and competition. Such an evaluation should be made in light of the airline's marketing resources and corporate policies, on the one hand, and market opportunities and constraints, on the other hand.

Promotion

It has been stated that the most important element of marketing mix is pricing. However, a good product, correctly priced and distributed, will not sell by itself; it has to be promoted effectively. In 1979, the eleven U.S. trunk carriers spent close to $3 billion or 13 percent of their total operating revenue promoting and selling their services. Promotion and sales expenses include expenditures for advertising, publicity, reservations, and travel agents' commissions. As shown in table 6-1, the U.S. trunk carriers spend approximately 11 percent of the total operating revenue on reservations and sales. This percentage varies among the carriers; in 1979, the percentage for American was 10.0, and for National, 13.3. In addition, advertising took 1.4 percent and publicity took 0.3 percent of the total revenue.

Once the management appropriates a certain amount for promotion and sales, it is the function of the marketing manager to distribute this total amount into various categories. Table 6-1 shows the relative amount of funds spent in advertising by the trunk carriers. The advertising budget is usually some percentage of the total operating revenue. It is a discretionary cost incurred to increase or maintain revenues for an airline and is subject to competitive circumstances and managerial policy.

The decision to use a set percentage of revenue on advertising has a certain appeal. It can provide an idea of what the airline can afford and encourage marketing executives to think about the cost in terms of revenue and profit. It can also be a method to keep parity with competition. However, this method does have a disadvantage in that it tends to allocate funds in relationship to their availability as opposed to allocating funds to exploit a marketing opportunity or reduce the perception of a weakness. In the future, it may be more appropriate to set advertising budgets based on the fulfillment of a certain objective. This method would first require the establishment of an advertising objective, followed by the determination of tasks to be performed to fulfill the stated objective, and ultimately the computation of expenses needed to perform the tasks.

There has never been a clear rationale behind the distribution of the advertising expenditure by market or by medium. It appears to be a function of the competitive circumstances and managerial policy. Coverage and community are, presumably, the criteria in selecting media. The cost per thousand persons reached can be used as one criterion for selecting a medium. For example, in 1979, U.S. and foreign airlines paid $71,062 and $22,116 per page for advertising in *Time* and *Business Week* magazines, respectively.[11] Let us assume that the estimated readership is 10 million persons for *Time* and 2 million for *Business Week*. The cost per thousand persons reached is then about $7 for *Time* and $11 for *Business Week*. Although such a method is simple, it does not place any value on the composition of readership (that is, exposure value).

The measurement of advertising effectiveness, particularly the relationship between advertising and sales, is a complex task. Researchers in the past have developed sophisticated multiple-regression models to determine

Table 6-1
Advertising, Publicity, and Reservation and Sales Expense (1979)

Carrier	Total Operating Revenue (000)	Advertising (000)	Advertising Percent of Revenue	Publicity (000)	Publicity Percent of Revenue	Reservation of Sales (000)	Reservation of Sales Percent of Revenue
American	3,252,532	42,093	1.3	7,170	0.2	325,234	10.0
Braniff	1,337,784	12,423	0.9	4,112	0.3	140,689	10.5
Continental	922,337	22,310	2.4	4,161	0.5	95,590	10.4
Delta	2,672,068	34,557	1.3	4,337	0.2	304,768	11.4
Eastern	2,881,526	40,232	1.4	9,828	0.3	306,456	10.6
National	692,941	15,864	2.3	2,602	0.4	91,940	13.3
Northwest	1,296,906	12,815	1.0	1,444	0.1	155,082	12.0
Pan American	2,573,943	34,875	1.4	3,578	0.1	315,236	12.2
Trans World	2,891,904	45,205	1.6	3,307	0.1	328,915	11.4
United	3,224,100	52,494	1.6	13,249	0.4	337,011	10.5
Western	932,119	13,354	1.4	3,895	0.4	103,198	11.1
Total	22,678,160	326,222	1.4	57,683	0.3	2,504,119	11.0

Source: Air Transport Association of America and the Civil Aeronautics Board.

the short- and long-term impact of advertising on sales. Some researchers have used simultaneous equations to account for the direction of causality to determine the optimal level of advertising. Others have used distributed lags to account for the long-term effects of advertising. Dhalla, for example, views advertising as a capital investment with sales revenue generated like a stream over time.[12] Although all of these models provide some useful insights into the sales-advertising relationship, there are still numerous fundamental problems that have not been solved. For example, leaving aside all statistical problems, there is not even an agreement on the unit of measurement for advertising. Dollars are not adequate units of measurement because of the creativity factor.[13] Nevertheless, businesses, including airlines, continue to advertise their products and services, hoping to increase sales or profits but never being certain of the precise returns on investment.

Strategic Planning Models

It is evident that future market planning for an airline will become more complex, yet more imperative. Now more than ever there is a need for the implementation of more formal planning methods. Although *strategic market planning* is not a new activity in major industries, what is new is the degree of its formalization.[14] It is the development and implementation of formal systems that will help determine the strategic direction for airlines planning their operations for the 1980s. Formal planning systems, developed primarily from computer-based information, should ideally be interwoven into the entire process of management decision making and they should be tailored to the unique characteristics of each airline. If these systems are harmonized with the existing planning environment in an airline, they are likely to aid the development of effective plans and serve corporate needs by being responsive to corporate objectives.

Decision Support Systems

The key to future airline marketing planning is through the use of decision-support systems (DSS). Such a system can be used by an airline to examine market opportunities and evaluate the airline itself to determine if it is able to take advantage of the opportunity identified. The technology needed to develop comprehensive DSS is available, given the advances in hardware, programming, communications, and computer-network technology. The essential element needed in the implementation of DSS is the willingness on the part of management to adopt the use of available technology for decision making. It is important to keep in mind that DSS should be developed and implemented specifically to facilitate decision processes. This is different than using electronic data processing (EDP) systems merely to make clerical-transaction processing more efficient. Second, DSS should support not automate decision making. It is also important that DSS respond quickly to the changing needs of decision makers.[15] In fact, while a DSS encompasses the normal functions of EDP (automatic storage and retrieval of data resulting in lower costs, higher accuracy, and faster access to data), it also improves and expedites the processes by which managers make decisions. American Airlines' Analytic Information Management System (AAIMS) is an example of a good EDP system for data analysis and report generation. However, as a DSS it is of very limited value.

One example of a DSS is the Competitive Airline Strategy Simulation (CASS) developed at the Flight Transportation Laboratory at the Massachusetts Institute of Technology and at Flight Transportation Associates, Inc., to address complex planning problems facing an airline.[16] It is a package of computer programs that can assist management in the evaluation of the operational and financial consquences of various scenarios and alternative decisions in a convenient and timely manner. The system is capable of analyzing alternatives at any level of the three-cycle planning process: the corporate level at which top management and decision makers develop overall strategy and goals; the functional level at which each department expresses its resource requirements and objectives while complying with the overall strategy; and in the budgeting or implementation level at which detailed plans of operation and finance are decided. Both long- and short-term questions can be addressed by running the simulation for any desired period. Consider, for example, the use of such a system to examine the following issues at each of the three-cycle planning levels of an airline:

What are the long-term consequences of shifting toward a hub-and-spoke pattern?

What are the significant short- and long-term financial consequences of a decision to enter a highly competitive market?

How can unexpected fuel shortages be dealt with promptly and cost effectively?

Airline management can participate in the simulation at any level of the three-cycle planning process (see Figure 6-1).[17] The system can be used to improve the structure and consistency of the planning process throughout various departments and levels of the airline. As a result, understanding and

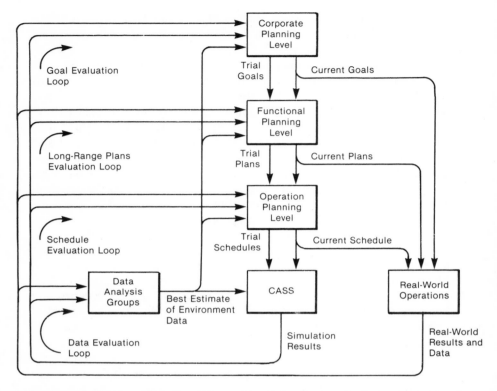

Flight Transportation Associates, Inc., "Competitive Airline Strategy Simulation: A Decision Support System for Airline Planning" (Cambridge, Mass.: July 1980).

Figure 6-1. Integration of Simulation Activity with Airline Planning Activities

communication between organizational units can be enhanced by using a common reference point for evaluating each department's plans. Resolution of conflicts at any stage of the planning process can be expedited through a rapid evaluation of proposed compromises.

Based on the gaming approach, the CASS system requires a number of *players* (called game participants) to drive, with the decisions, numerical models of the other components of the system. The system permits the major aspects of an airlines's operating environment to be specified by the user who provides information on markets, routes, aircraft, and the business environment. In addition, for the airline being evaluated and for each competitor, decisions must be made with respect to routing and scheduling, connections, fares, cost allocations, equipment procurement and disbursement, and financial transactions.

A flow diagram of the generalized structure of CASS is shown in figure 6-2. Each participant (or team of participants) plays the role of an individual airline. Decisions and proprietary information are exchanged directly between an individual participant and his private computer file. System-wide data, such as would be publicly available from the CAB and other sources, is made available by the simulation to each participant. The *exogenous participant* or technical monitor enforces restrictions and makes qualitative judgments concerning the specified scenario.

Once a scenario is in place and all operational and financial management decisions have been entered, CASS simulates the consequences of the inputs under the given scenario for any assumed time period. The simulation uses scenario and management inputs together with a series of state-of-the-art mathematical models for demand simulation, market-share determination, and cost determination. Finally, the results of the simulation are organized and reported in familiar formats and statistical summaries such as: CAB table 10 traffic data, on-line traffic statistics, cost and revenue breakdowns, complete financial accounting statements, and system summary statistics. Input reports are also produced, such as complete schedule listings in OAG format and complete station activity listings. Appropriate outputs are distributed to the technical monitor and game participants so that they may evaluate the consequences of their decisions and prepare inputs for the next simulation period.

CASS is just one example of an advanced DSS that can be used in corporate and market planning. It is the development and implementation of such systems that will improve the planning process to take advantage of market opportunities.

Portfolio Analysis

Portfolio analysis is a technique that can be used to select and chart a competitive operating strategy for an airline, having taken account of competitors' positions. The technique is based on the development of a growth-share matrix, illustrated in figure 6-3.[18] The vertical axis is market growth and the horizontal axis is relative share of the market, that is, share of airline divided by share of the largest competitor. Each route of an airline is represented by a circle, and it is the position and size of the circle that is important in analyzing and formulating a marketing strategy.

There are four basic areas to consider in figure 6-3. *Cash cows* are routes that lie in the lower left-hand quadrant. They represent mature markets (low growth) in which the airline has a dominant share. It is assumed that routes in this quadrant provide a net positive cash flow to the airlines,

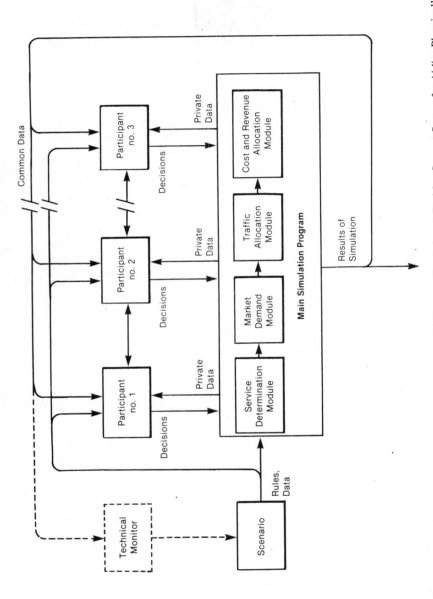

Figure 6-2. Generalized Simulation Structure

Source: Flight Transportation Associates, Inc., "Competitive Airline Strategy Simulation: A Decision Support System for Airline Planning" (Cambridge, Mass.: July 1980).

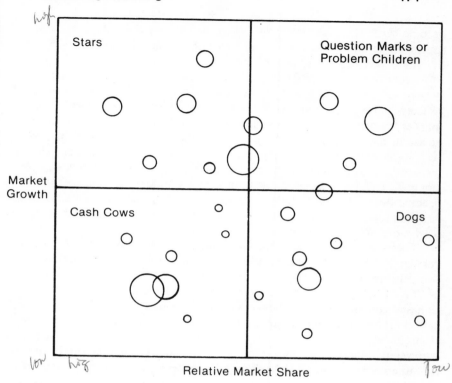

Stars

Question Marks or
Problem Children

Market
Growth

Cash Cows

Dogs

low   hig

Relative Market Share

low

Figure 6-3. Growth-Share Matrix

cash that may be reinvested, paid out in dividends, or used to pay off debt. A cash-cow route is, therefore, a current cash producing asset of an airline.

Routes that lie in the upper left-hand quadrant are called *stars*. They represent a high growth market in which the airline has a dominant position. However, these routes may or may not be self-sufficient in cash flow. But as the market matures and reinvestment and costs of maintaining share decrease, the star routes should transform into cash cows. The stars therefore, can be seen as future net cash producers for an airline.

Routes in the upper right quadrant are known as *question marks* or *problem children*, representing low share of fast-growing markets. These routes translate into low profitability and cash flow. Because the market is growing rapidly, such routes require substantial amounts of investment to maintain market share and even more to gain market share. While high market growth appears attractive on the surface, such routes do require investment to contribute to a strong network. If the investment is not made during the growth phase to transform these routes into stars, they ultimately become *dogs*: net cash sinks. By this classification, then, dogs are mature routes where an airline has a small share of the market. Even maintaining this share may require additional capital.

According to this scheme, the location of the routes on the chart is indicative of the current health of the network portfolio; movement over time reflects market dynamics and market strategy planning. One long-term market strategy would be to use cash generated by the cows to finance an increase in market share for the problem children in which an airline has a reasonable competitive position. And, if successful, such a strategy should transform a problem child into a star and eventually into a cash cow. Problem children with weak competitive positions should be dropped before they become dogs. If they do become dogs, they should be maintained only so long as they contribute to cash flow and do not tie up capital that could be used more effectively elsewhere.

There is no one strategy that is optimal for all airlines. It depends on the current location of the circles, cost position, airline's resources relative to its competitors, other routes, and actions and reactions of competitors. An airline should plot such charts over a period of time to determine the direction and rate of travel of any given circle. Serious strategy planners should also chart the position of their competitors to evaluate their weaknesses and strengths. Close attention should be paid to large circles, particularly those with relative share near unity. Finally, growth-share matrices should also be examined for a future time horizon as if present policies were maintained.

As with any technique, there are assumptions and weaknesses. In the case of portfolio analysis, there are three basic assumptions: First, all routes have a life cycle. Second, production costs decrease with an increase in sales. Third, important determinants of profit are market share and investment intensity, that is, the ratio of investment to sales. The value of the technique, therefore, rests on the validity of these assumptions. Moreover, for a given route, portfolio analysis focuses only on three factors: market growth, market share, and the size of the market. However, there are many other factors that may be important: barriers to entry, seasonality, load factors, customer composition and the related price elasticity of demand, promotion, management capability, and the value of a route as a member of the entire network. But despite these weaknesses the technique shows a real potential for strategic market planning.

Summary

The role of marketing is to help an airline understand and adapt to the continuously changing marketing environment. Effective market research is the mechanism to assess market threats and opportunities and analyze the airline's strengths and weaknesses in order to determine if and how threats can be contained and opportunities exploited. However, for market research to provide effective information, it will be necessary to spend more time on analysis of information than its collection, go beyond the demographic and into psychographic analysis, and pay more attention to the segment of the population that has never flown.

The product mix of an airline is changing rapidly in the new environment. For effective product planning in the future, it will be necessary to develop true product-price combinations such that passengers pay only for the services they receive and in turn receive only the services they pay for. Price decisions should reflect company objectives, production costs, market demand, competition, and the input from external parties. Once the product line and pricing policies have been established, the next element of marketing-mix is distribution. Here the traditional channels need to be evaluated with respect to their cost effectiveness and new channels examined in the same manner.

New legislation, state of the economy, increased fuel costs, and increased consumerism have all made the task of strategic market planning increasingly more difficult, yet more imperative. This situation warrants the development and implementation of more formal decision-support systems.

Notes

1. D.F. Abell and J.S. Hammond, *Strategic Market Planning: Problems and Analytical Approaches* (Englewood Cliffs, N.J.: Prentice-Hall, 1979), p. 62.

2. P. Kotler, *Marketing Management: Analysis, Planning, and Control*, 4th ed. (Englewood Cliffs, N.J.: Prentice-Hall, 1980), p. 629.

3. Ibid., p. 354.

4. A.B. Magary, "What can Travel Research Do?," *Understanding More About the Passenger*, Air Transport Research Symposium organized by the IATA Industry Research Division and held in Dublin, 25-26 May 1978.

5. W. Garrett, "Management Confidence in Action-Oriented Research," *Understanding More About the Passenger*, Air Transport Research Symposium organized by the IATA Industry Research Division and held in Dublin, 25-26 May 1978.

6. J.A. Walles, "Serving the Business Traveller," *The Airline Product in the 1980s—New Concept of Service*, Air Transport Research Symposium organized by the IATA Industry Research Division and held in Malta, 30 November to 1 December 1978.

7. M.I. Grove, "The Growing Age of Specialization in Air Transportation," SAE Paper no. 800754, 20-22 May 1980.

8. M. Brooks, "Clubs are Trumps," *Understanding More About the Passenger*, Air Transport Research Symposium organized by the IATA Industry Research Division and held in Dublin, 25-26 May 1978.

9. K.G. Narodick, "The Travel Market of the 80s: How Will We Respond?," *A Decade of Achievement*, Proceedings of the Tenth Annual Conference of the Travel Research Association (University of Utah, October 1979), p. 189.

10. R.A. Ausrotas et al., "The Shape of the Future" (Paper delivered at the Honeywell Seminar on *New Directions in Airline Industry Automation*, Phoenix, Arizona, 21 January 1980).

11. J.S. Murphy, "How Airlines Advertise in 28 Magazines," *Airline Executive*, vol. 4, no. 6 (June 1980):16.

12. N.K. Dhalla, "Assessing the Long-Term Value of Advertising," *Harvard Business Review* (January-February 1978):87-95.

13. G.D. Hughes, *Marketing Management: A Planning Approach* (Reading, Mass: Addison-Wesley, 1978), p. 368.

14. P. Lorange, and R.F. Vancil, *Strategic Planning Systems* (Englewood Cliffs, N.J.: Prentice-Hall, 1977).

15. S.L. Alter, *Decision Support Systems: Current Practice and Continuing Challenges* (Reading, Mass.: Addison-Wesley, 1980).

16. A.L. Elias, "The Development of an Operational Game for the U.S. Domestic Airline Industry," M.I.T. FTL Report R78-5, February 1979.

17. "Competitive Airline Strategy Simulation: A Decision Support System for Airline Planning" (Cambridge, Mass.: Flight Transportation Associates, Inc., July 1980).

18. Boston Consulting Group, "The Product Portfolio," Perspective no. 66, 1970.

7

Financial Analysis and Performance

As of 1979, according to the Air Transport Association, the U.S. scheduled airline industry is expected to spend $90 billion during the next ten years on flight and ground equipment. Assuming that these figures are reasonable estimates of the carriers' needs for funds, it is of some interest to examine the possible sources of these funds in view of the industry's earnings and rate of return on investment in recent years. This chapter describes the different ways the industry has met its financial requirements in the last three decades to provide some insight as to how the industry may finance its future requirements. It also provides the reader with some insight into the theoretical concepts of financial management—concepts that may aid the financial planning process at an airline operating in the deregulated environment.

Historical Financing-Decision Analysis

The following industry analysis is performed through an examination of the financial policies and practices concerning the acquisition of corporate capital during the last thirty years. The industry considered includes the total system operations of the domestic trunk carriers plus Pan American. The industry analysis is followed by a brief survey of the financing decisions of four individual airlines to show the diversity of individual airline policies and practices.

The early 1950s represented a period of strong financial stability achieving operating ratios around 90 percent, leaving 10 percent of the operating revenue for interest charges, taxes, and profit. The earning power relative to the fixed interest charges was extremely favorable, as evident from an examination of the interest coverage ratio. The long-term financial risk was fairly low, as indicated by the ratio of long-term debt to stockholder equity, and financial leverage measured as the ratio of long-term debt to total assets was quite reasonable. During this period the industry met its capital requirements through internal sources, basically depreciation and earnings.

In planning for the jet aircraft during the mid-fifties, the carriers committed themselves to almost $2 billion for flight equipment and the associated ground equipment, a considerable amount of capital to be raised through pure equity. In any case, the rate of return on investment had dwindled to about 3 percent. Consequently, a large portion of the requirements had to be met through external debt. Because of the airlines' high interest coverage ratios, insurance companies began to show interest in negotiating long-term debt with them and provided a little over 40 percent of the funds required.[1]

During the first half of the sixties, financial requirements were met through internal sources, due basically to the high profits earned during this period. Almost 40 percent of the funds came from depreciation and about 20 percent from net earnings (see table 7-1). Profitability was important in this period not only as an internal source of funds but also because of its leverage on the availability of debt financing. The contribution of internal financing can also be measured by the new investment as a percent of net internal funds. The value of this ratio stood at 171.1 percent in the period from 1961 to 1966. This implies that only 71 cents were acquired from external funds for every internal dollar. (A 100 percent figure would mean that the industry would be financed totally by internal funds.)

During the second half of the sixties, the industry placed orders amounting to $10 billion for the larger wide-body equipment, a commitment made soon after the industry had realized substantial profits. However, toward the end of this decade the financial position of the industry began to deteriorate, as seen from high operating ratios, fluctuating and uncertain earnings, high inflation, and declining airline stock prices. Capital in the form of debt or equity was not as readily available as in the previous decade, and the industry began to investigate different and more expensive instruments of financing its capital requirements, including subordinated convertible debenture financing, bank financing, and lease financing. During the 1966 to 1971 period, for every dollar generated internally, $1.72 was raised externally.

The industry's financial position at the end of 1970 was extremely poor as a result of the slowdown in the economy, excess capacity, and substantial increase in operating costs. With the interest coverage ratio at 0.2, the operating ratio at 99.4 percent, the highly leveraged position of the industry resulted in substantial losses. Consequently, during the first half of the seventies, most of the capital requirements of the industry were met through depreciation and increase in current liabilities. Depreciation alone financed more than half of the new investment. During the period 1971 to 1974, only 66.5 cents were raised externally for every dollar raised internally; the ratio of new investment to net internal funds decreased from 186.6 percent in 1972 to 133.4 percent in 1974.

The industry made a turnaround in 1971 as a result of the drastic cost-cutting measures initiated by the carriers (capacity control and a reduction in labor force), and the improvement in operating revenue (traffic growth plus increase in yield). However, operating costs began to rise again after

Table 7-1
Airline Industry Asset and Investment Management Analysis
(millions)

Year	Total Assets[a]	Internal Funds — Deprec- iation	Internal Funds — Interest	Internal Funds — Pretax Income	Internal Funds — Total[b]	Internal Funds — Total Percent of Assets	Percent Tax Rate	Net Income	Dividends	Net Internal Funds	New Investment — Amount	New Investment — Percent of Assets	New Investment — Percent of Internal Funds	Debt and Leases	Capitalization — Equity	Capitalization — Total	Debt Percent of Total
1960	$3,014.5	$272.3	$53.8	$75.6	$401.5	13.32	45.8	$41.0	$26.9	$286.2	$721.0	23.92	251.9	$1,447.2	$892.0	$2,339.2	61.9
1961	3,350.8	359.0	82.2	0	446.5	13.33	—	(22.8)	22.6	313.6	631.4	18.84	201.3	1,693.8	881.5	2,522.8	67.1
1962	3,482.7	360.6	92.0	76.7	540.4	15.52	49.0	39.1	23.0	376.7	383.2	11.02	101.9	1,694.8	908.3	2,603.1	65.1
1963	3,532.9	351.4	89.3	208.1	660.2	18.69	54.3	95.0	25.8	420.6	447.9	12.68	106.5	1,535.2	1,007.1	2,542.3	60.4
1964	4,010.6	344.2	87.1	370.9	818.9	20.42	44.5	205.7	38.1	511.8	945.3	23.57	184.7	1,676.9	1,226.1	2,903.0	57.8
1965	4,858.3	389.3	95.0	548.1	1,056.9	21.75	39.5	331.6	47.7	673.2	1,160.8	23.89	172.4	1,922.9	1,648.6	3,571.5	53.8
1966	6,343.8	446.5	118.2	645.4	1,243.7	19.60	39.8	388.4	70.7	764.2	1,762.2	27.79	230.6	2,699.6	2,146.5	4,846.0	55.7
1967	8,035.2	543.7	162.5	638.4	1,385.8	17.25	36.3	406.5	86.0	864.2	2,246.9	27.96	260.0	3,549.8	2,676.2	6,226.0	57.0
1968	9,332.9	635.2	212.2	423.1	1,345.5	14.42	37.1	266.3	95.8	805.7	2,699.7	28.93	335.1	4,374.9	2,863.1	7,237.6	60.4
1969	10,630.3	778.0	284.9	231.1	1,451.2	13.65	37.5	175.6	82.8	870.8	2,423.1	22.79	278.3	5,372.2	3,062.5	8,434.7	63.7
1970	11,553.2	875.2	325.5	(109.5)	1,266.0	10.96	21.8	(85.6)	60.8	728.8	2,527.3	21.88	346.8	6,545.0	2,962.9	9,507.9	68.8
1971	11,721.8	896.7	337.7	23.0	1,492.6	12.73	—	24.6	32.0	889.3	1,428.3	12.18	160.6	6,147.6	3,443.7	9,591.3	64.1
1972	12,592.8	947.7	318.2	231.5	1,734.1	13.77	25.9	171.5	27.5	1,091.7	2,037.1	16.18	186.6	6,457.0	3,673.0	10,130.0	63.7
1973	13,487.7	1,025.8	383.2	272.1	1,951.2	14.47	44.8	150.3	29.5	1,146.6	2,133.7	15.82	186.1	6,818.0	3,783.4	10,601.4	64.3
1974	14,968.4	1,154.9	519.8	484.0	2,316.2	15.47	49.3	245.6	52.6	1,347.9	1,798.6	12.02	133.4	7,729.4	3,893.3	11,622.7	66.5
1975	15,291.5	1,178.6	499.5	(119.3)	1,715.6	11.22	3.7	(114.9)	52.3	1,011.4	1,536.5	10.05	151.9	7,690.3	3,694.2	11,384.5	67.6
1976	15,653.6	1,234.9	502.5	451.9	2,338.3	14.94	35.8	290.3	51.1	1,474.1	1,129.3	7.21	76.6	7,304.3	4,032.2	11,336.5	64.4
1977	16,943.6	1,351.7	528.2	726.8	2,628.3	15.51	25.1	544.3	78.0	1,818.0	1,951.5	11.52	107.3	6,585.6	4,842.3	11,427.8	57.6
1978	18,537.5	1,434.0	522.4	1,264.0	3,256.1	17.57	17.9	1,037.6	117.7	2,353.9	2,981.3	16.08	126.7	6,229.4	6,050.1	12,279.5	50.7

Source: Merrill Lynch, Pierce, Fenner and Smith, Inc., "U.S. Trunk Airlines: Converting Dollars Into Seats," Institutional Report (New York: August 1979), p. 27. Reprinted with permission.

[a]Total assets include all assets consolidated by individual companies, not just airline assets. For 1977 and 1978, the capitalized value of leases is fully reflected; from 1969 through 1976 leases are included where the individual companies have restated their balance sheets. Internal funds include depreciation, aircraft leasing charges (not shown), interest, and pretax income. External funds include net change in debt and accounts payable, the book value from the sale of equipment, new equity sold, and deferred taxes. New investment includes capital expenditures, the value of aircraft leased, the net change in receivables and inventories and other investments.

[b]Including aircraft leasing charges not shown.

1973 because of the increased price of fuel. The recession during 1973 and 1975 produced a significant impact on the growth of passenger traffic. And the accompanied increase in operating costs resulted in a financial loss for the industry. Beginning in 1976, however, the financial picture of the industry began to improve significantly in each of the three succeeding years. The industry profited from the improvement in the economy; the airlines increased the quantity of discount fares, leading to an increase in load factor and profits; and, profits increased since the discount-fare traffic was carried at marginal costs on existing capacity. The result of increased profitability during 1976 and 1978 allowed the industry to finance most of its capital requirements internally. The ratio of new investments to net internal funds was only 111.3 percent, during the three-year period from 1976 to 1978.

Individual carriers, however, have pursued quite diverse policies and practices. There has never really been a shortage of capital available, relative to the industry's earning power, to meet its requirements. However, a number of companies had invested at a rate well above their earning potential; Pan Am, Eastern, and TWA would be included in this group, with their new investment as a percent of net internal funds close to or above 200 percent. For these carriers an overinvestment (relative to their earning power) resulted in high fixed interest charges and lease charges which in turn reduced the net profits. For example, Pan Am (for the period 1960 to 1978) had total interest obligations amounting to $786.6 million compared to a cumulative pretax income of only $260.5 million (see table 7-2). Other carriers, such as Delta and Northwest, kept their new investment proportional to their earning power, allowing only sufficient borrowing to maintain a healthy debt-equity ratio. For Delta, for the period 1960 to 1978, total interest obligations amounted to $258.9 million compared to a cumulative pretax income of $1,447.9 million (see table 7-3). The investment policy of carriers such as Delta has, therefore, been closely related to their financial ability rather than market growth or new types of aircraft available.[2]

Future Capital Requirements

In a recent study, the Air Transport Association of America has estimated the financial requirements of the U.S. airline industry to be $122 billion from 1979 to 1989. This amount is made up of $90 billion for equipment, $19 billion for debt service and repayment, $11 billion for dividends, and $2 billion for working capital. The questions are: What is the basis for the estimate of fleet equipment? What sources will the industry use to meet these mammoth capital requirements? Is there a shortage of sufficient external funds to support the needed investment of the next decade? These questions are answered here. The information regarding the capital requirements is drawn from the study published by the ATA.[3]

Table 7-2
Pan American World Airways Asset and Investment Management Analysis
(millions)

Year	Total Assets[a]	Internal Funds Deprec-iation	Interest	Pretax Income	Total[a]	Total Percent of Assets	Percent Tax Rate	Net Income	Dividends	Net Internal Funds	New Investment Amount	Percent of Assets	Percent of Net Internal Funds	Debt and Leases	Capitalization Equity	Total	Debt Percent of Total
1960	$585.7	$50.2	$12.4	$14.1	$76.7	13.10	49.6	$ 7.1	$5.3	$52.0	$138.9	23.72	267.1	$317.3	$138.4	$455.7	69.6
1961	573.1	59.1	16.4	12.4	87.9	15.34	33.1	8.3	5.3	62.1	14.6	2.55	23.5	290.9	140.7	431.6	67.4
1962	564.0	58.3	15.5	30.8	104.6	18.55	51.3	15.0	5.3	68.0	76.4	13.54	112.4	261.2	151.0	412.2	63.4
1963	552.7	56.3	12.8	68.2	137.3	24.84	50.7	33.6	7.2	82.7	47.5	8.59	57.4	183.1	174.1	357.2	51.3
1964	663.1	54.1	12.0	58.1	124.2	18.73	36.1	37.1	6.3	84.9	190.5	28.72	224.4	246.1	221.9	468.0	52.6
1965	777.7	60.9	15.0	78.3	154.2	19.83	39.6	47.3	8.6	99.6	161.3	20.74	161.9	295.6	275.2	570.8	51.8
1966	1,039.4	70.3	18.0	128.8	217.1	20.89	33.2	86.0	9.3	147.0	301.8	29.03	205.3	428.9	379.2	808.1	53.1
1967	1,279.1	88.3	22.3	92.0	202.6	15.84	33.3	61.4	11.5	138.2	316.1	24.71	228.7	576.5	442.4	1,018.9	56.6
1968	1,458.8	104.5	33.4	64.4	205.9	14.11	23.5	49.2	13.5	140.2	356.0	24.40	253.9	669.0	482.5	1,151.5	58.1
1969	1,626.3	106.2	41.3	(44.8)	110.1	6.77	41.1	(26.4)	6.8	73.0	341.0	20.97	467.1	877.3	446.8	1,324.1	66.3
1970	1,836.0	121.2	55.1	(66.1)	127.9	6.97	27.5	(47.9)	0	73.3	562.2	30.62	767.0	1,295.7	405.7	1,701.4	76.2
1971	1,829.0	115.4	59.5	(62.5)	145.5	7.96	24.5	(47.2)	0	68.2	224.8	12.29	329.6	1,259.4	423.6	1,683.0	74.8
1972	1,785.5	134.0	57.2	(51.3)	175.0	9.80	43.1	(29.2)	0	104.8	104.3	5.84	99.5	1,285.3	390.6	1,675.9	76.7
1973	1,683.7	126.5	59.0	(37.6)	185.1	10.99	42.2	(21.8)	0	104.7	28.3	1.68	27.0	1,175.5	367.4	1,542.9	76.2
1974	1,469.3	124.3	51.4	(135.0)	80.7	5.49	37.1	(84.9)	0	39.4	203.1	13.82	515.5	1,139.1	260.2	1,399.3	81.4
1975	1,629.4	124.2	52.8	(54.2)	165.5	10.16	15.0	(46.1)	0	78.1	56.0	3.44	71.7	1,069.5	214.6	1,284.1	83.3
1976	1,771.8	133.9	76.5	(14.5)	251.0	14.17	9.7	(13.1)	0	120.8	171.5	10.24	142.0	1,092.3	315.5	1,407.8	77.6
1977	1,896.6	152.9	92.2	51.2	304.9	16.08	12.1	45.0	0	197.9	254.6	13.42	128.7	1,094.7	360.5	1,455.2	75.2
1978	2,048.3	172.2	83.8	128.2	397.5	19.41	7.3	118.8	0	291.0	399.4	19.50	137.3	857.1	647.9	1,505.0	57.0

Source: Merrill Lynch, Pierce, Fenner and Smith, Inc., "U.S. Trunk Airlines: Converting Dollars Into Seats," Institutional Report (New York: August 1979), p. 46. Reprinted with permission.
[a]Includes aircraft leasing not shown.

Table 7-3
Delta Air Lines Asset and Investment Management Analysis
(millions)

Year	Total Assets[a]	Internal Funds									New Investment			Debt and Leases	Capitalization		
		Depreciation	Interest	Pretax Income	Total[a]	Total Percent of Assets	Percent Tax Rate	Net Income	Dividends	Net Internal Funds	Amount	Percent of Assets	Percent of Net Internal Funds		Equity	Total	Debt Percent of Total
1960	$121.9	$11.8	$1.5	$5.4	$18.7	15.34	48.1	$2.8	$1.3	$13.3	$31.0	25.43	233.1	$52.9	$38.9	$91.8	57.6
1961	134.9	15.2	2.9	9.0	27.1	20.09	47.8	4.7	1.3	18.6	25.9	19.20	139.2	52.5	41.1	93.6	56.1
1962	158.1	17.7	2.9	12.2	32.8	20.75	42.6	7.0	1.5	23.2	42.7	27.01	184.1	57.3	53.6	110.9	51.7
1963	181.4	19.8	3.6	29.3	52.7	29.05	52.9	13.8	2.6	31.0	37.2	20.51	120.0	57.0	64.9	121.9	46.8
1964	194.2	19.9	3.1	32.2	55.2	28.42	51.2	15.7	3.6	32.0	37.3	19.21	116.6	47.5	77.0	124.5	38.2
1965	231.3	22.2	3.0	42.5	67.7	29.27	45.9	23.0	4.8	40.4	47.7	20.62	118.1	51.4	95.2	146.6	35.1
1966	314.5	26.3	3.7	64.2	94.2	29.95	46.1	34.6	6.1	54.8	82.3	26.17	150.2	88.4	123.7	212.1	41.7
1967	369.4	30.8	5.2	90.0	126.9	34.35	45.9	49.2	6.4	73.6	108.1	29.26	146.9	86.3	166.5	252.8	34.1
1968	468.2	40.7	7.0	65.6	113.3	24.20	45.0	36.1	7.7	69.1	141.9	30.31	205.4	132.4	195.0	327.0	40.5
1969	634.3	56.9	12.6	73.4	142.9	22.53	46.6	39.2	7.7	88.4	214.3	33.79	242.4	214.9	226.5	441.4	48.7
1970	692.0	69.9	20.3	78.3	168.5	24.35	43.2	44.5	7.7	106.7	127.8	18.47	119.8	206.6	263.4	470.0	44.0
1971	744.5	77.6	15.9	42.2	135.7	18.23	28.9	30.0	9.6	98.0	135.7	18.23	138.5	188.9	283.8	472.7	40.0
1972	780.7	83.0	13.0	56.0	155.6	19.93	24.6	42.2	9.6	115.6	81.8	10.48	70.8	167.2	317.5	484.7	34.5
1973	907.9	84.9	15.8	116.2	234.3	24.81	43.2	66.0	9.9	141.0	156.9	17.28	111.3	168.0	364.6	532.6	31.5
1974	1,195.3	99.9	28.3	161.3	317.9	26.60	43.8	90.6	11.9	178.6	454.6	38.03	254.5	345.1	443.8	788.9	43.7
1975	1,380.1	128.4	37.4	79.8	268.0	19.42	35.0	51.9	11.9	168.4	300.9	21.80	178.7	390.4	483.8	874.2	44.7
1976	1,467.5	150.2	34.6	109.5	306.3	20.87	35.9	70.2	11.9	208.5	230.2	15.69	110.4	351.0	542.1	893.1	39.3
1977	1,491.8	166.2	26.0	155.0	353.6	23.70	40.4	92.4	13.9	244.7	265.9	17.82	108.7	237.5	620.6	858.1	27.7
1978	1,646.7	168.2	22.1	224.8	422.6	25.66	41.7	131.1	14.9	284.4	270.9	16.45	95.3	167.3	736.8	904.1	18.5

Source: Merrill Lynch, Pierce, Fenner and Smith, Inc., "U.S. Trunk Airlines: Converting Dollars Into Seats," Institutional Report (New York: August 1979), p. 42.
[a]Includes aircraft leasing not shown.

The capital needs of the industry are based on the need to replace aircraft and the need to acquire additional aircraft to accommodate the growth in passenger and cargo traffic. The fleet replacement part of the capital requirements are based on an aircraft service life of eighteen years and amount to $29.1 billion through 1989. The cumulative capital requirements for new equipment to meet traffic growth amount to $60.4 billion. The assumptions are: average annual traffic growth of 7 percent for passenger RPMs and 9 percent for cargo RTMs; average annual load factor of 63 percent for passengers and 65 percent for cargo; aircraft utilization of 9.5 block hours per day; an increase in aircraft seating density of 2 percent over 1978; and an aircraft annual inflation rate of 7 percent (see figure 7-1). Figure 7-2 shows the sensitivity of capital requirements to alternative sets of assumptions. Thus, depending on the assumptions, capital requirements for fleet can vary from $70 billion to $113 billion.

Most of the assumptions seem quite reasonable except for the annual aircraft cost inflation rate of 7 percent. Even at this rate, the average cost per seat of $114,000 in 1979 will rise to $211,000 by 1989. However, it is quite possible that inflation in the United States and aircraft cost could average closer to 10 percent. Moreover, even if the inflation rate did not reach this level during the decade, the aircraft-cost inflation rate could still be relatively high, given the demand for and the cost of high technology in future aircraft. On the other hand, a high rate of aircraft-cost inflation should not be a significant concern if the productivity and efficiency of future aircraft is increased substantially.

The second question relates to the sources of the entire $122 billion. The ATA estimated net income to provide $45 billion (36.9 percent); depreciation to provide $34 billion (27.9 percent); and new debt and equity to provide the remaining $43 billion (35.2 percent). The key factor determining the ability and needs of the carriers to raise the necessary funds will be the future profitability, which will not only be a significant source of internal financing but also will exert substantial influence in attracting external funds. As seen from the historical analysis, the airlines represent a high-risk industry. Earnings fluctuate considerably, operating ratios are high, and the industry is highly susceptible to the business cycle. Furthermore the industry is highly competitive and subject to rapid technological change. It is difficult, therefore, to forecast correctly the extent and timing of future profitability, particularly in the deregulated environment.

As an example of the high-risk characteristics of the airline industry, consider the impact of high operating ratio on profitability. In a recent paper, Gritta demonstrates the relationship between operating ratio and profit variability by equation 7.1.[4]

$$\text{Percent change in profit for a 1.0 percent change in revenue} = \frac{1.0\% \,(1-t)}{1 - O.R.} \qquad (7.1)$$

where t = the carrier's tax rate, and
  O.R. = operating ratio.

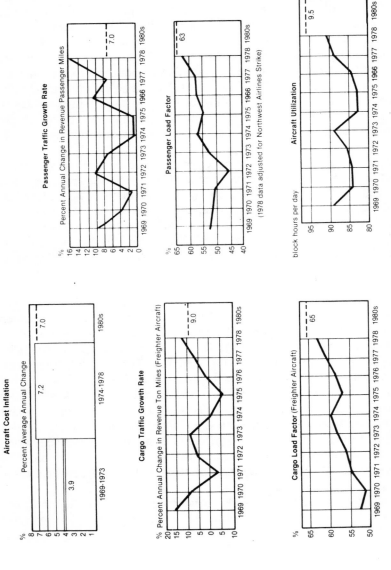

Figure 7-1. ATA Assumptions for the Capital Requirements' Study

Source: Air Transport Association, "Airline Capital Requirements in the 1980s: $90 Billion by '90" (September 1979).

Assumptions	Base Study	Alternate Assumptions									
Annual growth rate											
Passenger RPMs	7%	5%	9%									
Cargo RTMs	9%	7%	11%									
Load Factor											
Passenger A/C	63%			61%	65%							
Cargo A/C	65%			63%	67%							
Aircraft service life											
Passenger	18 Yr					16 Yr	20 Yr					
Cargo	18 Yr					16 Yr	20 Yr					
Inflation rate											
Passenger A/C	7%							6%	8%			
Cargo A/C	7%							6%	8%			
Utilization											
Passenger A/C	9.5 hr/day									9 hr/day	10 hr/day
Cargo A/C											
Seating density											
Passenger A/C	+2%									+2%	+2%
Capital Requirements (billions)	$90	$70	$113	$93	$87	$96	$82	$83	$96	$95	$83

Source: Air Transport Association, "Airline Capital Requirements in the 1980s: $90 Billion by 90 (September 1979).

Figure 7-2. Summary of Capital Requirements: For Alternate Assumptions (1979-1989)

Consider a carrier with an operating ratio of 0.90 and a tax rate of 48 percent; a 1 percent change in revenue will be accompanied by a 5.2 percent change in profit. Therefore, it is imperative that carriers in the future should attempt to control their operating ratio, at least with respect to elements that are under management control. For example, carriers should no longer acquire capacity under competitive pressures alone.

The difficulty in forecasting lies in the inability to forecast accurately the operating costs, traffic growth, trends in yield, and the operating load factors. Within operating costs, the single largest uncertainty is the price of fuel. In other areas where the labor costs are expected to increase, carriers will have to maximize their cost-control efforts in areas that are subject to management discretion. Current forecasts of average annual passenger traffic growth are 5 to 7 percent through 1989. The upward trend in yields is expected to continue through fare increases, which are necessary to offset increasing labor and fuel prices. Thus despite the losses during 1980, reasonable earnings for the next five years are expected, even though for many carriers they will not reach the average annual corporate return on investment of 13 to 15 percent required to meet the forecast capital requirements.

For an understanding of airline financial performance in the future, Greenslet at Merrill Lynch suggests an interesting form of the profit equation.[5] The basic parameters in the equation are capacity, cost per ATM, yield per RTM, and traffic measured in RTMs (see table 7-4). The object is to compute the point spread between break-even traffic and actual traffic. The break-even traffic is equal to the change in capacity plus the change in the unit capacity costs, minus yield per RTM. For the period 1958 to 1978, table 7-4 shows the amount of traffic growth required to achieve break even in the profit equation. The benefit in using such an equation is indicated by the fact that it can capture the interaction among individual elements. As a result, the focus is no longer on the expected traffic growth; rather, it is on the spread between break even and actual traffic. For example, it makes little difference whether a given spread is accompanied by high or low traffic

Table 7-4
The Profit Equation
(percentage change in key variables)

	Capacity (ATMs)	+	Cost per ATM	−	Yield per RTM	=	Break-Even Traffic	−	Traffic in RTMs	=	Spread (Points)[a]
1958[b]	2.7	+	1.4	−	3.4	=	0.7	−	2.6	=	1.9
1959	13.6		3.1		1.1		15.6		15.6		0
1960	13.0		(0.7)		3.0		9.3		6.6		(2.7)
1961	11.9		(3.7)		(0.7)		8.9		5.4		(3.5)
1962	14.5		(7.4)		(0.9)		8.0		12.4		4.4
1963	15.1		(6.5)		(2.6)		11.2		13.4		2.2
1964	17.3		(7.7)		(3.3)		12.9		17.1		4.2
1965	20.6		(5.7)		(5.4)		20.3		23.5		3.2
1966	17.1		(1.9)		(8.5)		23.7		24.1		0.4
1967[c]	32.9		(5.3)		(6.2)		33.8		29.6		(4.2)
1968	21.5		(3.5)		(2.1)		20.1		15.3		(4.8)
1969	13.8		1.0		3.7		11.1		8.3		(2.8)
1970	3.8		6.2		3.6		6.4		1.3		(5.1)
1971	7.1		(1.5)		4.3		1.3		3.8		2.5
1972	2.6		6.0		1.9		6.7		8.9		2.2
1973	5.9		6.1		5.9		6.1		5.3		(0.8)
1974	(5.5)		20.8		15.2		0.1		(0.6)		(0.5)
1975	0.5		7.3		5.2		2.6		(1.7)		(4.3)
1976	4.6		5.8		4.6		5.8		9.5		3.7
1977	5.7		7.2		6.4		6.5		6.8		0.3
1978	2.3		8.8		1.5		9.6		11.6		2.0

Source: Merrill Lynch, Pierce, Fenner and Smith, Inc. *Aviation Log* vol. 2, no. 20 (17 December 1979):4. Reprinted with permission.

[a]The spread is shown with the sign inverse to the way the formula is written: that is, a 0.7 break-even minus actual traffic of 2.6 equals minus 1.9, but it is shown as a plus because actual traffic exceeds break-even.

[b]From 1958 through 1966, data are for domestic trunks and international passenger cargo carriers.

[c]From 1967 to 1977, data are for trunk airlines-system operations.

growth; the important factor is the size of the spread. Such a concept can provide quite a different outlook on future expectations. For example, as long as a carrier shows a favorable spread, it may not be important whether the actual traffic growth is high or low or even zero.

The third question is the possible shortage of sufficient external funds to support the needed investment. Taken as an industry, and not by individual carrier, the financial community does not believe that there has been in the past, or will be in the future, a shortage of new investment. The extent of external funds depends, of course, on the relative earning power of the industry. As such, some carriers, such as Delta and Northwest, will continue to represent attractive investment opportunities because of their low debt, high profitability, and investment policies that are closely tailored to their financial ability. On the other hand, weak carriers such as Braniff, Eastern, Pan Am, and until recently TWA, with relatively high debt burdens, could experience a shortage of investment capital needed to maintain their relative market positions. Under such circumstances it may be necessary for the weak carriers to reduce their relative market share and invest at a rate commensurate with their earnings. Therefore, the availability of sufficient capital to some carriers and not to others could change drastically the operating structure of the airline industry, as investors become more sensitive to leverage and capital structures due to uncertain economic, regulatory, and market behavior environments.

Since airline stocks are generally considered short-term trading vehicles, equity financing should increase with improved earnings. It is difficult, however, to forecast the extent of this source, since it would depend on the financial position of the industry. Again, carriers that have shown a relatively low level of business and financial risk should have no problems in attracting equity capital. Delta and Northwest are certainly examples of investment grade; these two carriers are the only ones that have continually paid dividends, even through the recent recession periods.

Leasing as a source of equipment financing should continue to be popular as long as the investment tax credit is in existence and the tax laws do not change enough to alter its attractiveness to the lessors. (Information on the capitalization of financing leases can be found in the Financial Accounting Standards Board's *Statement of Financial Accounting Standards No. 13*.) However, since the lessor is normally in a junior position relative to the senior lenders, he is particularly interested in the future profitability of the airline. In recent years the improvement in profitability of the airline industry has reduced the amount of funds derived from this source, since the airlines can take advantage of the tax benefit themselves. In addition, the high market values for used aircraft have also reduced the use of this source, since the risk is greater that the airline may be forced to purchase at a high price at the end of the lease period. However, the continuation of favorable tax laws and the low level of earnings could increase the use of aircraft leasing as a source of financing investments.

Financial Management

Financial management at an airline is concerned with the solution of an optimal combination of three decisions: the investment decision, the financing decision, and the dividend decision. The *investment decision* relates to the allocation of capital to investments, such as aircraft and routes, which will provide financial benefits in the future. The *financing decision* focuses on the optimal financing mix (capital structure) for the airline. Finally, the *dividend decision* relates to that part of the airline's earnings paid out to the shareholders. Needless to say, all three decisions are interrelated and it is the function of airline financial management to determine the optimal combination of these three decisions. Although there are many criteria on which the performance of financial management can be measured, for the purposes of this discussion, the objective is to maximize the value of the airline for its shareholders or owners.

Capital Investment

Capital investment involves the estimation and evaluation of cash flows for a proposed investment such as the purchase of an aircraft or a fleet of aircraft. These cash flows are then used in conjunction with an acceptance criterion to evaluate the investment under consideration or to choose, in the case of multiple proposals, the most financially beneficial investment. Experienced financial officers also monitor the investment continuously to evaluate the outcome of their ultimate decision.

The key to the success of the investment decision lies in the estimation of the relevant cash flows. Consequently, the degree of confidence that can be placed in the outcome of the decision process depends on the degree of confidence with respect to the estimated cash flows. Cash flows and net income are projected on an after-tax and incremental basis, that is, the difference between the cash flows of an airline with and without the investment project (for example, the aircraft). All cash inflows and outflows must be considered (for example, salvage value of the aircraft, maintenance costs, depreciation, interest charges, investment tax credit, and income taxes).

Although there are a number of methods available for evaluating the investment decision, a widely used method is one known as the net-present-value method. In this case all cash flows are discounted to present values using the required rate of return. The investment is made if the present value of cash inflows is equal to or greater than the present value of cash outflows. Sometimes the investment project may be contingent or dependent on another project. In such cases the two must be considered jointly. For example, the decision to go into a new market may be contingent on purchasing or leasing another aircraft. Similarly, the decision to acquire a fleet or new aircraft may be contingent on the acquisition of the necessary infrastructure facilities, such as maintenance and pilot-training facilities.

There are a number of points that should be kept in mind in using this method for evaluating investment decisions. There is a degree of risk involved in any investment which may alter the business-risk complexion and, therefore, the valuation of the airline. Risk can be measured by the standard deviation of the probability distribution of possible net-present values. Moreover, cash flows over time can be dependent, in which case it may become necessary to use conditional probability distributions. If the investments involve sequential decisions over time, it may be appropriate to use decision-tree analysis. It is also necessary to take account of inflation in estimating cash flows.

The computation of discount rate is another controversial issue. One generally accepted criterion is to use the overall cost of capital for the airline. However, the measurement of this rate is a difficult task. It involves computing the cost of various components of the airline's capital structure. Typically, these include the costs of various forms of debt, stock, and retained earnings. In addition, once the individual component costs have been estimated, it is necessary to weight these components according to some criterion to obtain the weighted-average cost of capital. One approach is to use the proportions corresponding to the existing capital structure.

There are a number of controversial issues relating to the computation and use of the weighted-average cost of capital as a proxy for the discount rate. First of all, there is no unique way of computing the cost of the individual components making up the airline's capital structure. It is debatable whether the costs of individual components should be based on historical data or on the marginal costs of the proposed financing scheme. It is not clear whether the weighting scheme should be based on historical data or on proposed methods of financing. Finally, no matter how it is computed, there is an issue as to whether the discount rate should be based on the weighted-average cost of capital in the first place. This issue arises because the use of this criterion assumes that the airline's investments are homogeneous with respect to risk and that the investment project under consideration contains risk identical to all other existing investments.

Financing Decision

The second decision relating to the evaluation of an investment proposal is the decision on the alternative means available to raise capital. It should be pointed out that the financing decision is not altogether independent of the investment decision. The general view is that a firm can lower its overall cost of capital and increase its market value by careful use of leverage. However, the increasing use of leverage increases the overall risk, causing lenders to demand higher interest rates. Therefore, beyond a certain point, the cost of capital begins to increase. This point, then, represents the optimal cost of capital. Although we will not go into the argument here, there is another theory that claims that, in the absence of corporate income taxes, the cost of capital is independent of the capital structure of a firm.[6]

There are a number of methods available for determining the optimal capital structure. One method is an analysis of the relationship between earnings before interest and taxes (EBIT) and net earnings. For alternative methods of financing, this method provides information about the differential impact on earnings per share. Another method would be to analyze cash flows carefully to determine the ability of the firm to service fixed charges, which would include principal and interest payments on debt, lease payments, and dividends on preferred stock. The two methods, in combination, should provide reasonable guidelines to evaluate the capital-structure decision.

Dividend Decision

The third major decision faced by the financial management of an airlines is the decision on dividend policy. The dividend decision plays an important role in the overall financial decision for two reasons: the amount and timing of dividends will influence the market price of stock and, consequently, the level of equity financing available. Also, earnings not paid out as dividends will influence the magnitude of retained earnings and thus the amount of financing available internally.

The key issues are whether the investors have a preference for dividends and the relationship between the firm's return on its long-term investments and its cost of capital. If, for example, the dividends do not influence the value of common stock, then dividends can be retained as long as they can be invested to provide return that is greater than the cost of capital. If, on the other hand, dividends are important to the stockholders in that they prefer current dividend to capital gains, then the dividend-payout ratio can be determined by the balance between the difference in cost between retained earnings and new equity financing. It should be pointed out that these criteria are only guidelines; there are many other factors that can influence the firm's dividend policy. From the viewpoint of the investor, the trade-off between dividends and capital gains is a function of his need for current income, the amount of transaction costs, and the differential tax rates (investor versus firm). From the viewpoint of the firm, dividend policy may also be influenced by the desire to maintain stability of dividends, the liquidity of the firm, the ability of the firm to borrow, institutional restrictions, timing of investment opportunities, and the impact of inflation on the replacement of assets.[7]

Historically, the dividend policy has not been a major factor in the airlines' financial management decisions.[8] For example, between 1969 and 1978, the U.S. scheduled airlines paid out only 26.8 percent of their net income in dividends compared to 44.7 percent for the U.S. industry.[9] It is possible that the low dividend rate may have been the result of the capital-intensive nature of the industry or the belief that airline stocks were not purchased for long-term income. However, with deregulation of the industry, it is possible that the airline industry may be required to pay dividends comparable to other U.S. industries if it is to compete effectively in the market for equity investment.

Summary

This chapter attempted to highlight the financial managerial practices in the airline industry with a focus on how the industry has financed its capital requirements in the past thirty years. Profitability has always been the key factor in determining the ability of the airlines to finance their capital requirements. This factor is not only a significant source of internal financing but it can also exert substantial influence in attracting external funds. In the future, profitability will undoubtedly play a more significant role in meeting the capital requirements of the industry given the deregulated environment, and given the size of the capital requirements ($122 billion in the next ten years). The survivors in the industry will be the airlines that not only control costs and tailor capacity acquisition to financial ability, but also attempt to find an optimal solution to the balance among the investment decision, the financing decision, and the dividend decision.

Notes

1. N.K. Taneja, *The Commercial Airline Industry: Managerial Practices and Regulatory Policies* (Lexington, Mass.: Lexington Books, D.C. Heath and Co., 1976), ch. 5.

2. Merrill Lynch, Pierce, Fenner and Smith, Inc., "U.S. Trunk Airlines: Converting Dollars Into Seats," Institution Report (Washington, D.C.: August 1979), p. 4.

3. Air Transport Association of America, "Airline Capital Requirements in the 1980s: $90 Billion by '90" (Washington, D.C.: September 1979), p. 4.

4. R.D. Gritta, "The Significance of the Operating Ratio in Air Transportation," Proceedings of the Tenth Annual Meeting of the *Transportation Research Forum,* vol. 20, no. 1 29-31 October, 1979), p. 178.

5. E.S. Greenslet, "The Airline Profit Equation Revisited," *Aviation Log,* published by Merrill Lynch, Pierce, Fenner & Smith, Inc., vol. 2, no. 20 (17 December, 1979).

6. J.S. Van Horne, *Financial Management and Policy,* 4th ed. (Englewood Cliffs, N.J.: Prentice-Hall, 1977), ch. 9.

7. Ibid., ch. 11.

8. E.S. Greenslet, "The Airline Industry—An Analysis of Asset and Investment Management 1959 to 1990" (New York: Shields Model Roland 4 May, 1977), p. 3.

9. Air Transport Association, "Airline Capital Requirements," p. 4.

8 Fleet Planning

Deregulation of the U.S. domestic airline industry, aircraft noise regulations, international route proliferation, and the spiraling price of aviation fuel are all having a profound influence on carrier equipment actions with respect to purchases and options, retirements and reengining, and configuration changes. This chapter reviews the carriers' near-term priorities in planning their fleet, the fleet planning processes, and the role of the manufacturers in the airlines' equipment decision-making process.

Aircraft Selection Criteria

The decision to procure new aircraft has historically been based on an expected growth in traffic; a new route authority; the desire to increase capacity, frequency, or market share; or the desire or need to replace some of the existing aircraft for reasons of efficiency. Among the major categories of factors usually considered, technical performance, financial costs, and economic costs have played a major role in the final choice of the aircraft. The influence of each category and many factors within each category vary from carrier to carrier. Furthermore, it is often necessary to make trade-offs between the various factors. It is very rare that an aircraft will score high on each of these considerations simultaneously. In recent years, however, airline management priorities, and consequently trade-offs, have changed to reflect the changes in the marketplace.

Technical Factors

In the past, technical performance has always been very important, and the parameters usually considered are cruise performance, aircraft configuration, maintenance, runway requirements, and noise performance. The analysis for cruise performance is usually performed on payload-range diagrams, which show the relationship between payload (number of passengers and cargo) and the distance the aircraft can fly. For each aircraft there is a maximum payload that can be carried up to a specific range. Beyond this the payload must be reduced to accommodate more fuel. Finally there is the maximum distance that the aircraft can fly, and the

191

altitude is important for routes involving mountains and in consideration of airways congestion.

The common parameters considered with respect to aircraft configuration are: type of engine (including fuel burn), seating, maximum takeoff gross weight, maximum landing weight, maximum zero-fuel weight, fuel capacity, operator's empty weight, containers and pallets, bulk volume, and total volume. The problem in comparing alternative aircraft available is quite complex since each aircraft can have multiple configuration options. For example, there are numerous engine options available in any given thrust category. In the 40,000 to 50,000 pound thrust class, for example, the available options are: GE CF6-6D2, GE CF6-45 and -45B, P&W JT9D-7A and -7F, RR RB211-22B, and RR RB211-524B. Given the importance of fuel economy, it is easy to see the significance of the choice of the power plant. Similarly, numerous choices are available for interior configurations. The typical seating arrangement for a DC-10-30 can, for example, vary from 284 (mixed class) to 320 (charter class). However, charter configuration entails lower galley service, which reduces the capacity for lower deck LD-3s from 26 to 14 and total cargo volume from about 4,600 cubic feet to about 3,000 cubic feet.

Maintenance considerations relate to spare parts, fleet compatibility, product support, technical record, and, of course, costs. The most important comparison, however, is that of total maintenance costs. Figures 8-1a and b show, for example, a comparison of the maintenance cost trends during the service life of six aircraft. It is important to note that maintenance expense is influenced by a number of factors which should all be taken into account if meaningful aircraft comparisons are to be made. These include, for example, differences between stage lengths and the amounts paid for outside services. In addition to maintenance costs, one must consider dispatch reliability and product support. With respect to the latter point, it might be important for a small carrier, operating outside of the mainstream, to consider the proximity of other operators of aircraft from the viewpoint of potential advantages in spares pooling, backup support, and airport and ground support commonality.

The other areas of technical performance relate to runway requirements and noise performance. Runway requirements can play a significant role in the selection of an aircraft for airlines operating out of airports situated at considerable height above sea level and in extremely hot climates. There may also be external constraints such as mountains, cliffs, and water. Aircraft noise regulations continue to change airline priorities with respect to equipment decisions. The ICAO states now require their carriers to meet FAR and ICAO Stage III noise limitations by 1988. However, the decision to meet these regulations is complicated by the existence of a number of other factors such as outstanding depreciation, the market for used aircraft, and,

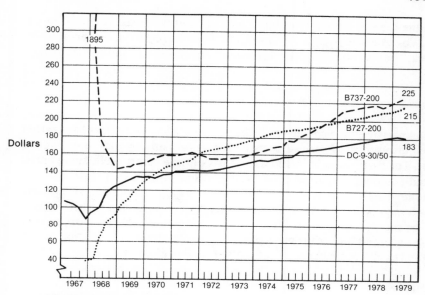

(a) Standard-body Aircraft

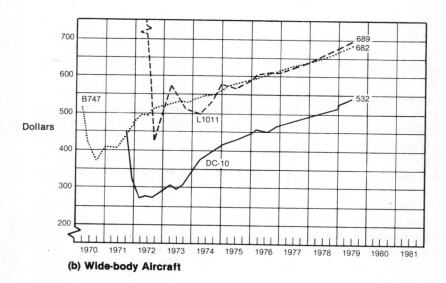

(b) Wide-body Aircraft

Source: Douglas Aircraft Company,'' Total Maintenance Cost Comparisons,'' Reports MIC 79-005 and 79-019 (May 1980).

Figure 8-1. Total Reported Maintenance Costs: U.S. Trunkline, Cumulative Dollars per Revenue Flight Hour

as in the case of the United States, existing and proposed financial incentives. For example, the earlier incentives favored retrofit over replacement whereas the recent bills favor replacement over retrofit and reengining.

Financial and Economic Costs

Having narrowed the choice on the basis of technical factors, consideration is then given to the financial costs of acquisition and operation (economic costs). The financial cost includes the costs of the aircraft itself, spare parts, ground equipment, maintenance, training, and, last but not least, the cost of money itself. Thus it is quite possible that while the actual price of one aircraft may be less than another, the total price, including all other factors, may be more. For example, one manufacturer may charge more money "up-front" and higher progress payments, while the choice of another aircraft may call for higher start-up costs. It is therefore essential to examine the cumulative capital investment requirements over a well-defined planning horizon.

The cost of money refers to the alternative financial arrangements available. If there are any trade-ins, then the purchase price offered for those must also be taken into consideration. This aspect brings into focus the price of used aircraft. Finally, consideration must also be given to the existing tax benefits, such as the investment tax credit, if the decision is one between new and used aircraft. Having taken all of these financial factors into consideration, the aircraft must provide a return that is higher than the airline's hurdle rate.

The analysis of economic costs is, perhaps, the most complex task within the whole evaluation process. This involves an analysis of aircraft productivity, revenue potential, and direct operating costs. And all three factors, in turn, relate to the route structure, traffic flow and composition, existing traffic volumes, future potential growth, seating density, load factor, and utilization. While direct operating cost per seat-mile is an important factor, it should be used with caution in evaluating alternative aircraft. First, there is no single direct operating cost per available seat-mile. For a given aircraft, it varies with range. Thus if this parameter were used, the comparison should be made for a particular range or trip (see figure 8-2). Second, choosing an aircraft on the basis of very low value of direct operating costs per seat-mile is not very useful if the seats cannot be filled with paying passengers. High capacity aircraft show lower direct operating costs per seat-mile. However, they require greater passenger loads to break even. These aircraft, therefore, tend to find greater application in high-density markets. In any case the lower direct operating costs must be compared to high initial investment costs.

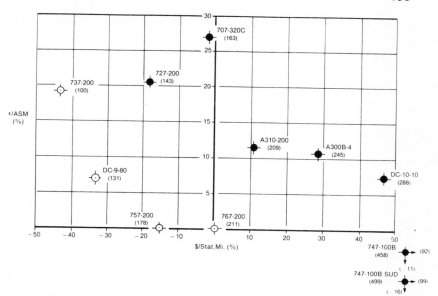

Source: Boeing Commercial Airplane Company.

Note: Mixed Class Seating; Fuel at $1.00/gallon; Stage Length = 1,000 Nmi.

-⧲- 3-man crew

-✦- 2-man crew

Figure 8-2. Relative DOC: 767-200 Baseline (U.S. Domestic Rules)

One component of direct operating costs that has been receiving substantial attention in recent years is the cost of fuel. In light of recent fuel shortages and significant increases in the price of fuel, a number of airline managers are focusing on specific fuel consumption, in particular, and fuel efficiency, in general. In 1973, at 12 cents per gallon, fuel represented 21 percent of the direct operating costs; the other two categories were labor (42 .percent) and capital (37 percent). In 1979, at 80 cents per gallon, fuel represented 52 percent of the direct operating costs; the other two categories had declined to 29 percent for labor and 19 percent for capital. Figure 8-3 shows the significant elements of the direct operating costs for U.S. trunk carriers. The importance of fuel efficiency is evident in this figure. As in the case of total direct operating costs, fuel efficiency should be compared on a per-seat or per-trip basis (see figure 8-4).

Table 8-1 shows the direct operating costs for existing aircraft in the trunk carriers' fleet in 1979. It is clear that on a per-seat basis, the operating costs for the B-707 and the B-727-100 are extremely high. While the fuel-cost component is high for these aircraft relative to the wide-body aircraft,

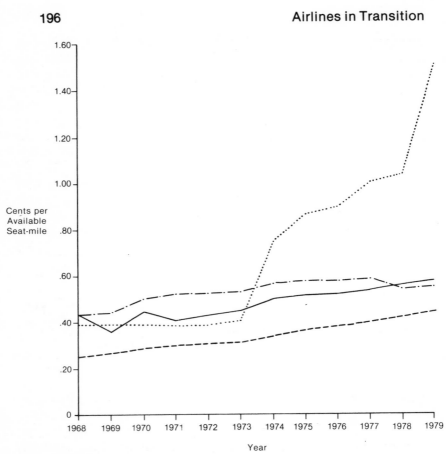

Source: CAB Form 41, Schedule P5.
Note: . . . . Fuel (Acc. 5145.1)
　　——————— Maintenance (direct and indirect, Acc. 5299)
　　— — — — Crew (Acc. 5123 + 5124)
　　——— . ——— All Other (depreciation, rentals, insurance, obsolescence, and so on)

Figure 8-3. Direct Operating Cost Elements: U.S. Trunk Airlines, Total
　　　　　　　Services

one must not overlook the labor-cost component. For some carriers such as
United and Western and for some aircraft such as the B-737, the labor cost
is high, given the requirements of a three-person crew. For these carriers,
the B-737 shows poor economics despite its reasonably good fuel performance. And in the current environment the importance of good aircraft
economics cannot be emphasized enough, given that the fare in the
marketplace tends to be set by the operator of the lowest-cost equipment.
Unfortunately, a large percentage of the existing fleet is old (see table 8-2)
with poor aircraft economics.

At this point in the evaluation procedure it is necessary to perform a profitability analysis. The usual procedure is to investigate an aircraft with respect to the total airline system, that is, over a wide range of length of hauls, taking into account the carrier's indirect operating costs as well as the effective fare structure. One method is to combine the break-even-load diagrams with the payload-range diagrams for various aircraft to produce *profitability-load diagrams.*[1] Figure 8-5 shows the general shape and characteristics of such diagrams. For any given route AB, the profitability-load diagram shows the profit that can be made using different aircraft available. If the shaded areas do not overlap, the decision is fairly simple. But if the areas do overlap, as shown in the figure, then, all other things being equal, the aircraft selected should be the one where the point of intersection of traffic on route and trip distance lies close to the upper boundary of the payload-range limits. For the route AB shown in figure 8-5, the

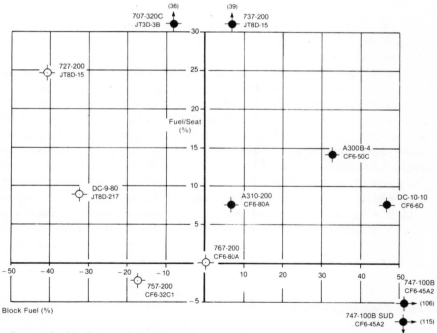

Source: Boeing Commercial Airplane Company.

Note: Mixed Class Seating; Stage Length = 1,000 Nmi.

◆ 3-man crew
⟠ 2-man crew

Figure 8-4. Relative Fuel Burn: 767-200 Baseline (U.S. Domestic Rules)

Table 8-1
Aircraft Direct Operating Costs, 1979: U.S. Trunk Airlines-System Operations
(dollars per block hour)

	Labor	Fuel	All Other	Total $	Average Seats	Block Hour Cost per Seat		
						Total	Labor	Fuel
707-100	$416.59	$890.98	$626.23	$1,933.80	135	$14.32	$3.09	$6.60
707-300	547.24	1,088.62	736.50	2,372.36	175	13.56	3.13	6.22
727-100	362.17	695.21	390.82	1,448.20	105	13.79	3.45	6.62
727-200	353.90	752.68	389.18	1,495.76	134	11.16	2.64	5.62
DC-9-30	287.19	483.22	289.94	1,060.35	92	11.53	3.12	5.25
737	417.78	463.34	418.33	1,299.45	102	12.74	4.10	4.54
747	586.18	2,172.76	1,454.85	4,213.79	390	10.80	1.50	5.57
DC-10	535.18	1,264.46	1,117.21	2,916.85	270	10.80	1.98	4.68
L-1011	484.53	1,364.21	1,219.33	3,068.07	285	10.77	1.70	4.77
A-300	496.33	1,024.63	766.72	2,287.68	240	9.53	2.07	4.27

Source: Merrill Lynch, Pierce, Fenner and Smith, Inc. *Aviation Log*, vol. 3, no. 15 (22 October 1980):2.
Reprinted with permission.

medium, long-range aircraft should be selected over the large, long-range aircraft. However, one should not overlook the potential growth in market that can increase traffic load.

The preceding discussion emphasizes the need for flexibility. The aircraft under investigation should not only be flexible in its own missions, it should also be flexible from the perspective of growth and shrinkage potential. In the deregulated environment of the United States, while the carriers are rationalizing their route structure and matching more carefully their aircraft to particular routes, there is still a critical need for flexibility on the part of the small operator. This need for flexibility is even more important for operators outside the United States. A small airline, for example, might fly a passenger-freight combination service in one direction, and use the aircraft in a high-density configuration in the reverse direction to accommodate charter traffic. The aircraft selected also should be flexible to accommodate gross weight and range changes in its design during the production life cycle.[2]

Fleet-Planning Process

With the Airline Deregulation Act of 1978 opening up market entry and exit, the aircraft-selection and fleet-planning process has become an even more critical management planning function. Moreover, since the aircraft-selection and fleet-planning process is highly integrated with many other activities in an airline, the first part of this section provides an overview of the overall airline corporate planning process to highlight the role of aircraft selection and fleet planning. Corporate planning within an airline, like any other organization, requires the identification and analysis of alternative corporate strategies and the development of plans for many different levels or activities that are all closely integrated.

Speyer, in his master's thesis, describes the airline corporate planning process as a continuous information-exchange process among three planning levels: corporate-strategy planning, corporate-resource planning, and implementation planning.[3] These interactive levels are in order of decreasing hierarchy (see figure 8-6). At the highest level corporate-strategy planning focuses on the formulation and updating of corporate objectives and policies. The second inner ring in Speyer's web diagram represents corporate-resource planning and focuses on the development of coordinated plans for the acquisition, use, and disposal of four basic airline resources: finance, market, routes, and aircraft. The third ring in the diagram relates to the execution of the specific actions by the operating and field groups in an airline. The various areas within this level (finance, marketing, route, aircraft, and operational) receive information from their corresponding areas at the resource level and then implement the plans for the acquisition or disposal of the required resources in a timely manner. Speyer's web diagram also shows a fourth, outer ring that depicts the actual operations or activities of an airline. These include, for example, the day-to-day scheduling function and cost and traffic forecasting. It is not clear whether these activities are a formal part of the corporate-planning process; they do, however, provide input to all levels of the planning process. Speyer's description of the airline corporate-planning process follows the general corporate-strategic-planning process. Lorange and Vancil's theory on corporate planning, for example, can be summarized by their snake diagram, which depicts three formal planning cycles (business, functional, and budget planning) cascading across the three organizational levels (corporate, divisional, and functional level).[4] Speyer's first three rings correspond to Lorange and Vancil's three cycles, respectively.

Fleet-planning function is an important part of resource planning within the general framework of airline corporate planning. There is strong interaction between fleet planning and strategic planning (first ring) and implementation planning (third ring), on the one hand, and between fleet planning and the three other elements of resource planning (finance, marketing, and route), on the other hand. The degree of interaction among the rings and among the elements within a ring depends on the size of the airline, corporate structure, financial stability, and the chief executive. Moreover, there is usually interaction between the fleet planning group at the airline and the external community. This would include not only the airframe and the engine manufacturer but also airports and the financial com-

Table 8-2
Aircraft Age

Aircraft Distributed by Year of Acquisition

	4 E.W.	3 E.W.					4 E.N.			3 E.N.		2 E.N.				
Year	B-747	Total	DC-10	L1011	Total	B-720	B-707	DC-8	DC8/60	B-727	Total	B-737	DC-9	BAC111	Other	Other
1959					10		4	6								10
1960					5		5									5
1961					1			1							3	4
1962					21		19	2								21
1963					3		3			6						9
1964					11		6	5		71					4	86
1965					13		10	3		43	5		5		7	68
1966					32	1	24	7		63	8		21	5	6	109
1967					60		46		14	61	25	1		3	17	163
1968					65		33	6	26	110	124	53		4	6	305
1969	2				49		27		22	84	86	47	5	3	8	229
1970	54				2		2			26	13	3	10		2	97
1971	20	13	13							5	6	6	6		1	45
1972	2	58	44	14						31	19	2	8	3		110
1973	5	52	26	26	4			4		58	10	4	14	10		129
1974		44	19	25						39	18	6	19	2	4	105
1975	4	22	16	6						52	27	6	7		2	107
1976	8	6	1	5	5			5		43	13	2	20		4	79
1977	5	4		4	2				2	55	22	13	19		4	92
1978	3	11	5	6	4		3		1	109	32	21	20		17	173
1979	11	13	7	6	1				1	83	41				8	160
Total	114	223	131	92	288	1	182	39	66	939	449	164	255	30	93	2,106

ASM's Distributed by Year of Aircraft Acquisition

Year	Total
1959	1,471
1960	974
1961	258
1962	3,933
1963	1,518
1964	12,977
1965	9,610
1966	17,267
1967	25,886
1968	45,041
1969	34,678
1970	42,032
1971	19,280
1972	27,998
1973	33,225
1974	24,949
1975	21,877
1976	16,602
1977	17,124
1978	27,846
1979	30,767
Total	415,314

Source: Air Transport Association of America.

E = Engine
W = Wide-body
N = Narrow-body

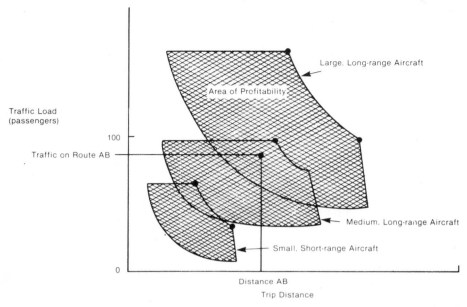

Source: Robert W. Simpson, *Technology for Design of Transport Aircraft*, Lecture Notes, M.I.T. (July 1972), p. 44.

Figure 8-5. Profitability-Load Diagrams

munity. The interaction with the aircraft manufacturer is particularly strong given that the manufacturer is usually attempting to compromise the design to meet the requirements of numerous domestic and international airlines.

Airline corporate planning in the past was a relatively straightforward exercise since one-half of the profit equation was controlled by the Civil Aeronautics Board. Routes and rates, and therefore revenue, were tightly controlled by the government. The only avenues open for airline management were to control costs and select optimum aircraft. However, with added route and pricing freedom, it is a new ball game. Not only has aircraft selection and fleet planning become a more important element of the planning process at an airline, but it has become a much more integral part of overall corporate planning. Its success in the future, therefore is not only dependent on the sophistication of the analysis within the process itself but also on the interaction among the four components of resource planning and on the other three planning levels.

Given the resources of an airline, a forecast of the market environment and the carrier's corporate plan, the process of fleet planning provides management with a timetable of fleet acquisitions and phase-outs for a

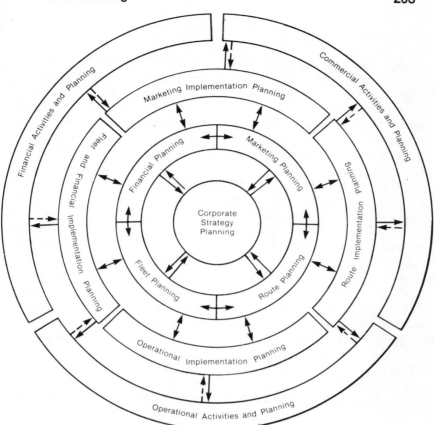

Source: J.J.W. Speyer, "Planning Processes in U.S. Airlines," Master's thesis (M.I.T., September 1978), p. 37. Reprinted with permission.

First ring: Corporate strategy planning
Second ring: Corporate resource planning
Third ring: Implementation planning
Fourth ring: Operations activities and planning

Figure 8-6. Functional Planning Framework for an Airline

given planning horizon. Historically, the fleet-planning process has been carried out by hand. Each time management changed its corporate strategy, the fleet-planning process was undertaken to produce a fleet plan to implement the new strategy. For a given planning horizon, management would produce traffic forecasts and market-share analysis followed by a detailed analysis of the operating schedule. Next, individual segment analysis would be undertaken with respect to performance and aircraft-related costs. Finally, detailed financial analysis would be performed, followed by an operating plan for the planning horizon. In the last fifteen years, computer models have been developed which, given a set of inputs such as passenger and cargo traffic, route structure, existing fleet, financial and economic costs, and tariffs, can determine future fleet requirements over a planning horizon. Moreover, the output of fleet-planning models can be used to analyze and plan for other activities such as maintenance, crew and staff requirements. The analytical formulation of the model provides management with an opportunity to assess the impact of alternative policy actions and, alternatively, set up assumptions such as traffic flows, financial structure, and operating costs.

The Airline Deregulation Act of 1978 has provided a new dimension to the airline fleet-planning process and models. Since the basic inputs to the fleet-planning models are route structure, traffic, yields, and costs and since all of these are changing rapidly in the industry, it is important that the models be extremely sensitive to these factors. If the momentum gained in the use of fleet-planning models in the airline corporate-planning process is to continue, then it will be necessary for these models to incorporate all marketing, economic, financial, regulatory, and technological variables to examine alternative scenarios of the future by varying these variables in the system. In other words, the planner should be able to manipulate each of these variables separately, or in some combination, to determine the optimal strategy with respect to fleet planning.

The benefits of the use of a comprehensive fleet-planning model increase as the complexity of the environment in the marketplace increases. While no fleet-planning model can be expected to predict the future, its use can help management cope more effectively with risk and uncertainty. However, high payoffs from the use of a fleet-planning model can only be achieved if the model has been custom designed to meet the specific planning requirements and successfully integrated into the overall corporate-planning process.

The Manufacturer's Perspective

The fleet-planning exercises undertaken by an aircraft manufacturer are even more complex than those undertaken by an airline. Consider the trade-offs that an airline must make in selecting the most appropriate fleet of aircraft. Yet the manufacturer must consider not only all those factors for a given airline but also the needs and requirements of many other domestic and international airlines to determine the optimal design. Moreover, each manufacturer must consider not only his own existing and planned aircraft but also those under production or development at his competitors' plants. Unless a manufacturer can combine the requirements of a sufficient number of airlines to reach a reasonable level of production run, the research, development, test, and evaluation costs for a new aircraft are likely to be prohibitively high and quite possibly well beyond the investment capability of any one manufacturer. For a totally new design, it could be beyond the financial capability of all manufacturers combined.

The fleet-planning process at the manufacturer level is more macro in nature. Most manufacturers produce a forecast of open-lift and capacity gap requirements such as those shown in figures 8-7a and b. These requirements can either be forecast directly by forecasting total world traffic and load-factors, or by aggregating the forecasts of individual carriers. The methodology used by the Boeing Airplane Company is shown in flow-chart form in figure 8-8. There are alternative methods. Douglas Aircraft

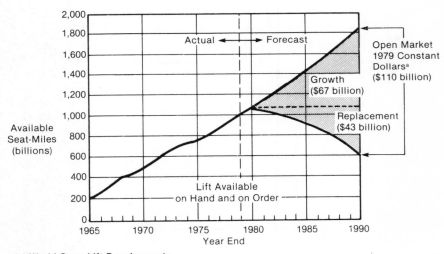

(a) **World Open-Lift Requirements**

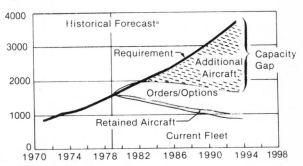

(b) **Capacity Demand and Supply Forecast**
   All-Services, World

Source: (a) Boeing Commercial Airplane Company, "Dimensions of Airline Growth." (March 1980) p. 68. (b) Douglas Aircraft Company, "Outlook for Commercial Aircraft." Report no. CL-802-5559A (Long Beach, Calif.: June 1980), p. 28.

[a]1979 non-U.S. ASKs are estimated.

Figure 8-7. World Open-Lift Requirements and Capacity Demand and Supply Forecast

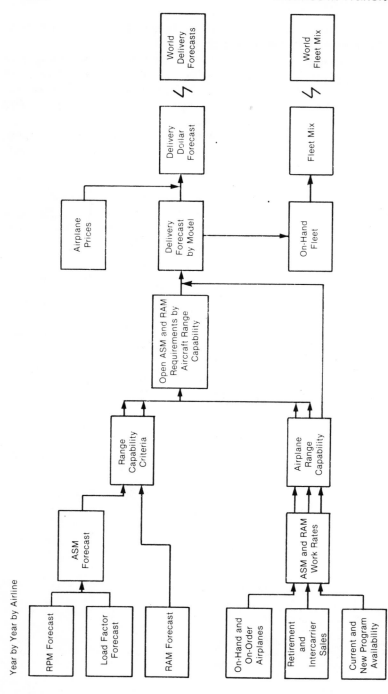

Source: Boeing Commercial Airplane Company, "Dimensions of Airline Growth" (March 1980) p. 64.

Figure 8-8. Airplane Forecast Methodology

Company, for example, forecasts world traffic divided into nineteen inter- and intraregional flows and one region representing domestic service.[6] Next, projections are made for the market share of each airline in each region based on historical data and expected changes in the future. An individual carrier's traffic is then obtained by aggregating its activity in each region. Next, each airline's traffic is converted into capacity requirements through the application of load-factor forecasts. Finally, the capacity gap is determined by projecting and deducting from the total capacity required, capacity available in the future from aircraft on hand and on order.

Once the total open-lift or capacity gap requirements have been forecast, the next step is to convert these requirements into generic types of aircraft (table 8-3) and market shares for each manufacturer. The worldwide aircraft requirements are divided approximately equally by small, medium, and long lengths of haul in terms of dollar values. In terms of number of aircraft, however, the share of the small aircraft category is much larger.

Once the generic aircraft categories have been identified, the aircraft design decision depends on the payload-range diagrams. This decision calls for an examination of the different requirements of individual airlines. For any given airline these in turn depend on: existing fleet, route structure, competition, and volume and composition of traffic. Take, for example, the elements of existing fleet and route structure. In looking for a

Table 8-3
Airplanes for the Next Two Decades

Category	Current and Committed	Possible Additions
Short range	737-200 DC-9-30/80 747SR BAC-111/F-28	757-100 JET/ATMR/YXX F-29
Medium range	727-200 A300-2/4 A310 DC-10-10 L-1011 767-200 757-200	A300 stretch DC-10 derivative L-1011-400 767 stretch
Long range	707-320C DC-10-30/40 747-100/200 747SP L-1011-500	777 747 derivative A300-11 707-700 DC-10 derivative
Freighter	747F/C DC-10C/F	A300F/C 767 F/C

Source: Boeing Commercial Airplane Company.

new aircraft to replace the B-727, United was interested in a medium-size and medium-range aircraft with two engines. American, however, was more interested in an aircraft with transcontinental range, over-the-water capability, and three engines. It would be impossible to satisfy both carriers with a single aircraft. The solution to this problem becomes almost impossible when all other airlines are brought into consideration. The only rational and cost-effective solution is to develop and offer a family of aircraft. The result, in the case of Boeing, was the 757, the 767 and, potentially, the 777.

The aircraft sizing problem has been accentuated under deregulation; the size, payload, and range requirements have become more specific. Most carriers in the United States have recently been rationalizing their route structures. The larger carriers have been dropping routes where traffic did not warrant the size of aircraft available in their fleet. Some of the smaller carriers, on the other hand, have been picking up some longer-haul routes to improve their efficiency (load factor and utilization) and exploiting to a greater extent the new marketing opportunity.

The specificity of individual airline requirements represents a dilemma for both the airline and the manufacturer. There is a move in the direction of standardization in the industry, a motivation resulting from the desire to improve efficiency. Put simply, it causes airline planners to go after the mass market with low fares and large aircraft. However, the more innovative and market-oriented researchers in the industry are pointing to the need for specialization and product differentiation to distinguish and satisfy discrete market segments.[7] The dilemma, therefore, heightens and brings into focus the intricacies of interaction among three elements of airline planning: fleet planning, route planning, and pricing planning. This dilemma will undoubtedly present the manufacturers with a real challenge, one that could easily test the survivability of some manufacturers.

Even after the manufacturer has identified the optimum sizing parameters of the proposed aircraft, the problem is not yet solved. It is also necessary to forecast the ability of individual airlines to purchase the aircraft. The relationship between aircraft orders and airline profitability has been established reasonably well (see figure 8-9). Although from the manufacturer's viewpoint airline profitability is a key to the development and production of a proposed aircraft, forecasting this parameter is an even more complex task than forecasting and amalgamating individual airline requirements.

Individual carrier requirements and financial capabilities must now be reconciled with the requirements and investment capabilities of the manufacturer to determine whether to start a new program or improve the existing equipment. New aircraft programs are generally not cost effective unless: (1) existing aircraft face technical, economic, or regulatory ob-

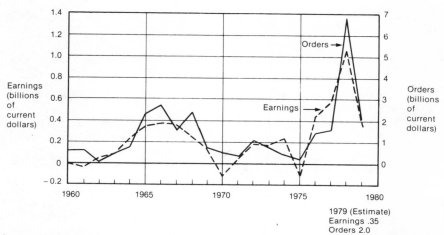

Source: Boeing Commercial Airplane Company, "Current Market Outlook" (February 1980).
Figure 8-9. U.S. Trunk Airline Earnings and New Equipment Orders

solescence; (2) the improvements required cannot be economically incorporated into the existing aircraft; or (3) the new program offers sufficient competitive advantage to offset the financial risks of both the airline and the manufacturer.[8] In the past, airlines placed their priorities on speed and performance. Now the focus is on efficiency, not only in performance but in design and production. There is no question that efficiency can be improved significantly through advances in aerodynamics, structures, systems, propulsion, and flight management (see figure 8-10), but one must trade off increased efficiency against the higher operating costs resulting from higher priced aircraft. On the other hand, continuous improvements to an existing aircraft to keep it competitive can be expensive. Consider the case of the B-727: figure 8-11a shows the orders received since 1965. Clearly the orders received in 1972 and 1976 were predicated on the improvements incorporated into the existing aircraft (see figure 8-11b). The gross weight of the aircraft has increased by 37 percent, thrust by 31 percent, and fuel capacity by 62 percent. But the cost of these improvements has not been insignificant (figure 8-11c). In the changing economic and regulatory environment, improvements in equipment are imperative; the issue is one of improvements to existing equipment versus totally new programs.

In the area of extremely small stage lengths (about 100 miles) there is a need for new aircraft that are both fuel efficient and comfortable. Such aircraft would meet the needs of commuter carriers in the United States to serve markets that are being abandoned by the trunk and local-service carriers. At the present time, these markets are being served with small turboprop-powered aircraft which, despite their old technological base, still

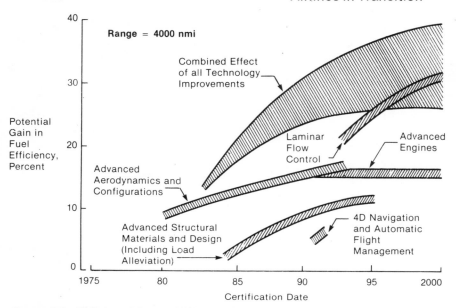

Source: John E. Steiner, "Commercial Transport Aircraft Trends: Present and Future." Lecture given at M.I.T. (10 October 1980), p. 10.

Figure 8-10. Technology Improvement

produce reasonable economics in short-haul operations relative to the use of existing jet aircraft. The on-going research at NASA in this area shows that through the use of advanced technology, short-haul aircraft can be developed that will offer a great improvement in fuel efficiency and passenger acceptance with respect to safety, comfort, and noise level.

Finally, from a manufacturer's viewpoint, government regulation has not been reduced but has actually proliferated. Consider, for example, the regulations with respect to design, production, certification, and even sale of aircraft.[9] These regulations cover a broad spectrum of concerns ranging from safety and clean environment to foreign policy.

Summary

Aircraft selection and the fleet-planning process is an integral part of overall airline corporate planning. The deregulated environment has added a new dimension to the process. Among the many factors considered in selecting aircraft, technical performance, financial and economic costs, and flexibility play a major role in the final decision. However, aircraft noise requirements and the escalating price of fuel have changed airline priorities.

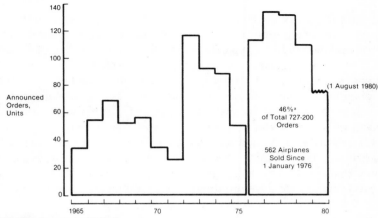

(a) 727-200 Announced Orders

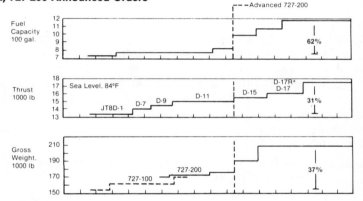

ªAt 77°F.

(b) 727 Development

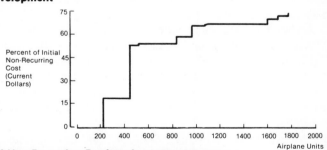

**(c) Cost of Non-Recurring Produce Improvements as a
Percent of Initial Nonrecurring Cost, 727 Program**

Source: John E. Steiner, "Commercial Transport Aircraft Trends: Present and Future." Lecture given at M.I.T. (10 October 1980), p. 14.

Figure 8-11. Boeing 727: Product Improvements

Given the complexity of the marketplace, the use of fleet-planning models has increased. These models can help management cope more effectively with risk and uncertainty. Typically, when given the resources of an airline, and a forecast of the market environment, a fleet-planning model can provide management with a timetable of fleet acquisitions and phase-outs for a given planning horizon. The output of the fleet-planning model (aircraft requirements) can be used to analyze and plan for other activities such as financial, crew, and maintenance requirements. Fleet-planning models can be developed either at a microlevel for an airline, or at the macrolevel for a manufacturer. The planning process at the manufacturer level is far more complex than the airline level, given the need to amalgamate individual airline requirements to develop, finance and produce a marketable product.

Notes

1. R.W. Simpson, "Technology for Design of Transport Aircraft," Lecture notes for Massachusetts Institute of Technology courses, Flight Transportation Laboratory (Cambridge, Mass.: M.I.T., July 1972).

2. E.H. Boullioun, "Earnings and Quality of Service," in *Corporate Planning Under Deregulation: The Case of the Airlines* (Evanston, Ill.: Northwestern University, 11-12 June 1979).

3. J.J.W. Speyer, "Planning Processes in U.S. Airlines" (Master's thesis, M.I.T., 1978).

4. P. Lorange, and R.F. Vancil, *Strategic Planning Systems* (Englewood Cliffs, N.J.: Prentice-Hall, 1977).

5. R.W. Simpson, *Scheduling and Routing Models for Airline Systems*, FTL Report R68-3 (Cambridge, Mass.: M.I.T., December 1969); McDonnell Douglas Aircraft Company, *Computer Applications for Airline Progress and Profit*, Report Number 800-1159 (September 1969); N.S. Clerman, "An Airline Fleet Planning Model" (Master's thesis, M.I.T., August 1969); H. Faulkner, "An Airline Fleet Planning Model with Financial Constraints" (Master's thesis, M.I.T., June 1970); M. Pollack, "Some Elements of the Airline Fleet Planning Problem," *Transportation Research*, II (1977)301-310; and D.F.X. Mathaisel, "Air Transport Fleet Planning: Network Aggregation and Cell Theory" (Ph.D. thesis, M.I.T. December 1980).

6. Douglas Aircraft Company, *Outlook for Commercial Aircraft*, Report No. CL-802-5559A (Long Beach, Calif: June 1980).

7. M.I. Grove, "The Growing Age of Specialization in Air Transportation," SAE Technical Paper 800754, May 20-22, 1980.

8. J.E. Steiner, "Commercial Transport Aircraft Trends: Present and Future," Lecture given at M.I.T. on October 10, 1980, p. 13.

9. E.H. Boullioun, *Corporate Planning*, p. 32.

9   Airfreight

Despite the advantage of aircraft speed, airfreight has captured an insignificant share of the total freight movements. The justifications often include the existence of regulatory constraints, lack of dedicated freighters, and the cost handicap for the air mode. However, given that a large percentage of shippers are more service- than price-sensitive, it is not unreasonable to assume that more flexible and innovative marketing can produce profitable growth for the industry. This chapter reviews the airfreight market, and examines current and future potential.

Market Perspective

In 1979 it is estimated that the world air-cargo market amounted to more than 24 billion revenue ton-miles, 2 billion ton-miles of which were transported by the USSR operations. Leaving out the USSR operations and the mail, the world airfreight traffic amounted to a little more than 20 billion revenue ton-miles. Less than half of this traffic was transported in all-cargo aircraft and a little more than half in aircraft in combination service. Only a third of the total airfreight was transported by the U.S. carriers whose share has been declining continuously; it has been reduced from 60 percent in 1960 to 33 percent in 1979. Since the mid-sixties the rate of growth of the non-U.S. carriers has exceeded by far the rate experienced by the U.S. carriers. The overall size of the world air-cargo market in 1979 and its growth during the last two decades are shown in figure 9-1 and table 9-1.

In 1979 air-cargo revenue ton-miles of the U.S. carriers were divided into 59 percent U.S. domestic and 41 percent U.S. international; the division with respect to all-cargo services and combination services represented 54 percent and 46 percent, respectively. During the sixties, the U.S. carriers experienced an annual growth rate in airfreight of 20.7 percent during the first half of the decade and 10.6 percent during the second half. But since 1970 the annual growth has been averaging a little more than 5 percent. In general, U.S. international operations outperformed U.S. domestic operations. In 1960 the split among scheduled freight and express, nonscheduled freight, and mail for U.S. carriers was 56.2 percent, 23.8 percent, and 20.0 percent, respectively. In 1979 these three components accounted for 75.3

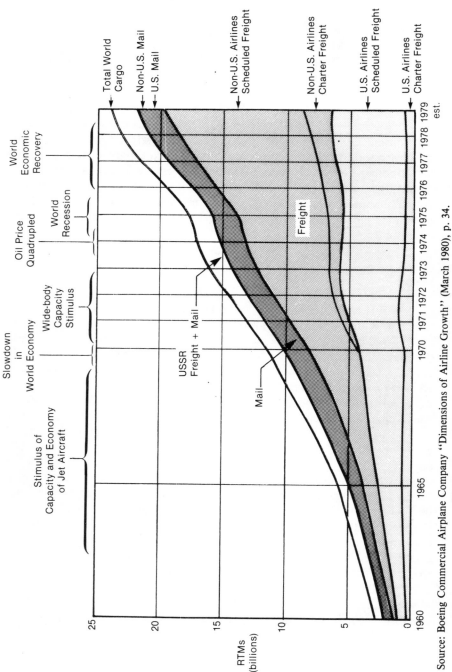

Figure 9-1. Historical Profile of Cargo Revenue Ton-Miles

Source: Boeing Commercial Airplane Company "Dimensions of Airline Growth," (March 1980), p. 34.

Table 9-1
Composition of World Air Cargo in 1979

	RTMs (billions)	Percent of Total World Cargo	
Scheduled freight			
U.S. airlines	5.97	24.7	
Non-U.S. airlines	11.40	47.1	
Total			71.8
Charter Freight			
U.S. airlines	0.74	3.1	
Non-U.S. airlines	2.06	8.5	
Total			11.6
Mail			
U.S. airlines	1.22	5.0	
Non-U.S. airlines	0.79	3.3	
Total			8.3
USSR (freight and mail)	2.02	8.3	
Total		8.3	
Total world cargo	24.20		100.0

Average Annual Growth Rates
(percent)

	1960-1965	1965-1970	1970-1975	1975-1979
Scheduled freight				
U.S. airlines	20.9	14.0	6.5	5.7
Non-U.S. airlines	16.1	20.0	14.2	12.5
Total	18.6	16.8	10.7	9.9
Charter freight				
U.S. airlines	20.2	−0.2	−2.4	3.1
Non-U.S. airlines	—	—	28.8	11.8
Total	—	—	2.0	9.1
Total freight				
U.S. airlines	20.7	10.6	5.1	5.4
Non-U.S. airlines	16.1	20.0	18.6	12.4
Total	18.9	14.4	8.7	9.8
Mail				
U.S. airlines	14.6	24.6	−5.7	2.4
Non-U.S. airlines	9.1	9.0	6.7	8.8
Total	12.5	20.1	−2.5	4.7
USSR (freight and mail)	18.9	7.0	7.0	3.4
Grand total	17.9	14.2	9.6	8.7

Source: Boeing Commercial Airplane Company "Dimensions of Airline Growth" (March 1980), p. 35.
Note: Weighted average total.

percent, 9.4 percent, and 15.3 percent, respectively. The share of the air-freight traffic transported in nonscheduled operations in general has been declining since 1972.

Since the mid-sixties the non-U.S. airlines have continuously outper-formed U.S. airlines in annual average growth. As a result their share of the total air-cargo traffic has increased significantly, from 34.6 percent in 1960 to 58.9 percent in 1979. Although among the non-U.S. airlines, the largest share of the traffic is transported by the scheduled services of the airlines of Europe, significant increase in air-cargo traffic has been experienced during the last decade by the scheduled operations of carriers in the Middle East, Asia, and the Pacific. Their gain in traffic has been achieved at the expense of a loss in share by carriers in the western hemisphere and the USSR. Moreover, air-cargo traffic carried by nonscheduled operators has been increasing steadily since 1971. By 1979 their share of the total non-U.S. carrier traffic has reached a respectable 12.6 percent.

During 1978, scheduled airfreight traffic accounted for 78 percent of total world air cargo, excluding the USSR traffic. In absolute terms this traffic amounted to 16.4 billion revenue ton-miles. The U.S. domestic operations account for 21 percent of the total market, followed closely by the traffic carried on the North Atlantic and the transpacific routes, 19.0 percent and 13.0 percent, respectively (see table 9-2). During the sixties, the world scheduled airfreight traffic grew at an average annual rate of almost 20 percent; the highest annual average growth was recorded on the transpacific routes (41 percent) and the lowest in the U.S. domestic market (16 percent). The North Atlantic and Europe-Far East routes experienced an average annual growth of 23 percent and 19 percent, respectively. During the seventies the average annual rate for world scheduled airfreight growth dropped down to 10 percent. As before, the transpacific and the Europe-Far East routes continued to experience growth rates well above the average, 15 percent and 17 percent, respectively. On the other hand, U.S.

Table 9-2
1978 Scheduled Airfreight Breakdown by Market

U.S. Domestic	21
North Atlantic	19
Transpacific	13
Europe Far East and Australia	11
Europe-Africa	7
Europe-Latin America	5
North America-Latin America	4
Intra-Europe	3
Europe-Middle East	3
Intra-Far East and Australia	2
Other international	4
Other domestic	8
Total	100

Source: Boeing Commercial Airplane Company, "Dimensions of Airline Growth" (March 1980), p. 37.
Note: Excludes USSR traffic.

domestic and transatlantic routes have begun to show characteristics of mature markets, with average annual growth rates of 5 percent and 7 percent, respectively.

Total world scheduled airfreight growth during the last two decades has been influenced by the introduction of standard-body jet aircraft during the sixties, slowdown in world economies during the late sixties and early seventies, the stimulus provided by wide-body aircraft during the early seventies, the increased price of oil during 1973 and 1974, the world recession during 1974, world economic recovery, further increases in the price of oil, and the deregulation movement. In addition to this list, there are many other factors that have influenced the growth in airfreight traffic. The Boeing Company separates all these factors into stimulants and constraints.[1] Each group is then further subdivided into four areas: economic, cost, service, and marketing (see figure 9-2)

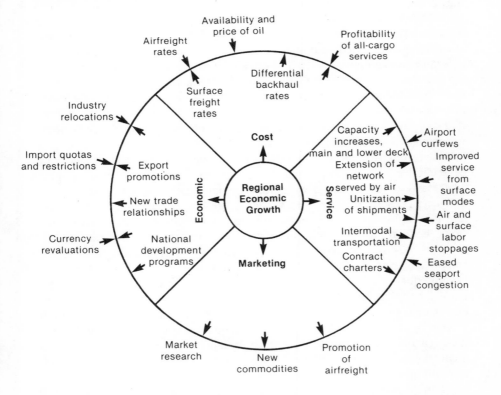

Source: Boeing Commercial Airplane Company, "Dimensions of Airline Growth" (March 1980), p. 40.

Figure 9-2. Forces and Constraints on Airfreight Growth

With the use of analytical models, combined with a qualitative assessment of each factor according to its impact on world airfreight, Boeing has forecast the following growth rates over the next fifteen years. The forecast calls for the total world air-cargo average annual growth to be between 5.5 and 8.0 percent from 1980 to 1985, between 4.9 and 7.3 percent from 1985 and 1990, and between 4.3 and 6.7 percent from 1990 to 1995.[2] The growth rate for the U.S. carriers (both domestic and international) is forecast to be lower than the rates for non-U.S. carriers.

U.S. Domestic Deregulation

In the United States, the Flying Tiger Line and Federal Express were at the forefront of the deregulation movement from the beginning. The industry had a history of unprofitable or marginally profitable domestic all-cargo service and Flying Tiger had repeatedly petitioned the CAB for new route authority (primarily in the growing regions of Alaska and the sunbelt) and the elimination of artificial restraints and controls. For example, service by direct air carriers was restricted to certain cities plus a twenty-five-mile pickup and delivery zone. Substitute service by truck was limited to points that were included in a carrier's route certificate. As to the rate structure, it was not economical for carriers to offer service in the short- and medium-haul markets. Indirect carriers, on the other hand, enjoyed unlimited geographic coverage and substantial tariff flexibility. The CAB's economic regulations had therefore impeded the operations of a carrier such as Flying Tiger from offering the full complement of the service features to the shipping public. The features included: (1) widespread geographic coverage; (2) overnight delivery; (3) shipment size and weight flexibility; (4) door-to-door service; and (5) single-carrier responsibility.[3] Similarly under existing CAB regulations, Federal Express could not operate jet aircraft the size of the B-727.

The inability of the industry to generate reasonable profit on its freighter operations had resulted in a substantial deterioration in the quantity and quality of services offered. Continental, Delta, and Eastern, for example, had eliminated their scheduled freighter service in the mid-1970s, and American and United were beginning to reduce their nighttime freighter service to reduce their financial losses. The increased price of fuel forced these carriers to eliminate or reduce freighter service in the small- and medium-haul markets. The more fuel-efficient aircraft, on the other hand, were inappropriate for these markets.

The Air Cargo Deregulation Bill was signed by President Carter on 9 November 1977 opening competition in the domestic market by eliminating the CAB's control over market entry and exit and curtailing sharply its jurisdiction over rates. As of 9 November 1978 entry was open to any U.S.

citizen who, according to the CAB, was fit, willing, and able to offer domestic all-cargo service and all requirements to file tariffs were eliminated. As of July 1980, the CAB had certificated 97 all-cargo 418 carriers, including supplemental carriers, air-taxi operators, and airfreight forwarders. These carriers offer a mix of service attributes depending on the size of the package and the desired time frame.

Advocates for deregulation of the industry with respect to passenger carriers had claimed that deregulation would produce lower passenger fares. No such claims were made by proponents of deregulation of the aircargo industry. It was generally claimed that before deregulation there was a high quality of passenger service and high prices to go with such quality. In the airfreight industry, rates were low and so was the quality of service provided. Even the CAB's *Domestic Air Freight Rate Investigation* concluded that average prices were almost 40 percent below average costs. Deregulation of the industry was therefore not expected to produce a round of price cutting. On the contrary, rates on the average were expected to increase and they did. But deregulation was expected to result in a wide range of service and price options, and it did.

Since deregulation, the structure of the industry has changed substantially. A number of carriers (some formerly supplemental carriers, some freight forwarders, and some air-taxi operators before deregulation) have inaugurated scheduled airfreight service. The most significant change that has taken place is the increase in the number of airfreight forwarders and the introduction of extensive freighter service by four of these forwarders. In 1976, there were 366 certificated U.S. airfreight forwarders. As of July 1980, this number had increased to 1,284. And four of these forwarders (Airborne, Air Express International, Emery, and Profit-by-Air) operate 50 percent more freighters and serve twice the number of cities served by the scheduled carriers.[4] (Most of the aircraft operated by this group are leased from the other 418 operators.) However, two points should be kept in mind: an increase in freighter service does not necessarily imply an increase in capacity, and forwarders are still very much dependent on direct carriers for long-haul capacity.

Current information on the financial operations of airfreight forwarders is not readily available. For the year ending December 1978, the top twenty U.S. airfreight forwarders reported an operating profit of almost $100 million and a net income of almost $60 million. Operating revenues for the period were $1.5 billion (see table 9-3) and operating expenses were $1.4 billion. About half of the total operating expenses represented air transportation purchased from air carriers for the movement of airfreight. U.S. domestic operations produced approximately two-thirds of the system operating revenue and operating expenses.

It is interesting to note that the freight forwarders are able to offer

Table 9-3
Operating Revenue of Top-Twenty Forwarders, (1978)
(millions of dollars)

Forwarder	1978
1. Airborne Freight	188
2. Air Express International	153
3. Amerford International	50
4. Associated Air Freight	28
5. Behring International	15
6. Bor-Air Freight	23
7. Burlington Northern	155
8. CF Air Freight	42
9. Circle Air Freight	55
10. DHL	15
11. Emery Air Freight	405
12. Five Star	14
13. Imperial Air Freight	16
14. International Air Carrier	30
15. Profit by Air	64
16. Purolator	20
17. Sentry Air Freight	11
18. United Parcel Service	110
19. WITS	24
20. WTC	84
Total	1,502

Source: U.S. Civil Aeronautics Board.

economically viable freighter service in short- and medium-haul markets using existing aircraft, while the certificated route carriers have not been able to do this. The explanation is two-fold. First, the cost structure of the freight forwarders is quite different from the direct carriers; the aircraft are usually leased and only for the absolute minimum necessary time; if owned, the aircraft are almost invariably operated with nonunion crews. Second, because of the additional services provided, the nature of the traffic carried, their ability to unitize, the yield received by the freight forwarders is considerably higher than direct-route carriers.

In addition to freighter service offered by the freight forwarders, other developments since deregulation include: Seaboard's takeover by Flying Tiger, Airlift's withdrawal from the domestic markets, significant route expansion by Flying Tiger, substantial discounts for L-D containers, and the overwhelming entry into and growth of the small-package-by-air business. However, new entry on a large scale has not yet taken place. Acquisition of a fleet of appropriate aircraft and the necessary infrastructure, such as computers and terminal facilities, is a highly capital-intensive activity. And unlike passenger transportation, airfreight operators need to provide widespread geographic coverage, shipment size flexibility, and single-carrier responsibility. Therefore, in order to make strong competitive inroads, it is necessary to look beyond the number and size of packages. The potential entrant must be able to offer a wide spectrum of services and a full range of prices to go with each service. Such undertakings require large amounts of capital and, consequently, have discouraged newcomers to the marketplace.

One change that could take place within the industry is vertical integration. Since the airfreight business is bimodal, shipments must be picked up and delivered by a truck. Therefore, in the near future, it is conceivable that more airlines could operate their own trucks or trucking companies could operate their own fleet of aircraft. Such an operation could control a segment of the market for an organization by providing door-to-door shipper interface in an expanded market base. Federal Express is an example of this type of operation. This level of integration, combined with ownership of freight-forwarding businesses, could provide for a new dimension in the airfreight industry.

Airfreight Marketing

Although it is difficult to forecast breakthroughs in future airfreight growth and profitability, one cannot ignore the potential, given that airfreight accounts for such a small percent (by weight) of the total freight movements. Some industry experts believe that the often-predicted breakthrough will be achieved only through development of large dedicated freighters; others believe that the problem is one of lack of understanding of the airfreight market and its economics, and the lack of attention paid to airfreight by many of the combination carriers.[5] The differences between airfreight and air passengers are outlined in table 9-4.

Shipper Requirements

Surveys have consistently shown that service is the ranking shipper requirement. Although service means many things, a majority of shippers would include timeliness and completeness as the primary features of good service.[6]

Timeliness includes the following characteristics: arrival and departure times, on-time performance, and frequency. Many shippers, both direct and indirect (freight forwarders), require overnight delivery. But they are unable to tender their consignment until the close of the business day; the cutoff time is even more critical for the freight forwarders. Despite the availability of substantial rate incentives, these shippers find passenger flights (during daylight hours) to be inconvenient. For these shippers, the

Table 9-4
Airfreight versus Air Passenger

	Passenger	*Freight*
Market	Consumer	Industrial
Relative value	Highest	Highest
Relative price	Lowest	Highest
Market share	Dominant mode	Complementary mode
Services required	Homogeneous	Varied
	Round trip	One way
	Nonstop	Variable
	Daylight	Night
	Self-handling	Passive
Transactions		
Number of parties	Single party	Multi-party
Documentation	Simple	Complex
Rate structure	Complex	More complex

Source: W. Caldwell, "An Overview of Deregulation Impact on Strategic Cargo Planning."
Lecture given at the Air Transportation Planning Seminar at Stanford University. 18-22
August 1980.

jet aircraft has become an integral part of the design-production-distribution cycle. A number of combination carriers claim that the need for overnight delivery is exaggerated and that it is a syndrome created by the airfreight forwarder. These carriers would argue that there are many existing passenger flights that leave late in the evening. However, it should be noted that these flights may not leave late enough, or they do not have main-deck lift, or they are scheduled in passenger-oriented markets, or the turnaround time is so limited that freight cannot be boarded. The need for freighter service should not be underestimated since these aircraft provide greater dimensional and density capacity, more efficient container capacity, and the ability to accommodate hazardous materials. One should not overlook, however, the fact that passenger carriers offer a greater diversity of destinations, over-the-counter small package service, and a greater frequency of service.

Completeness has the following characteristics: broad geographic coverage, pick-up and delivery, good tracing capabilities, ability to handle special problems and consignments, adequate insurance, and efficient and adequate claims and security. Door-to-door service and broad coverage are, however, the most important characteristics of complete service. The latter implies not only the flexibility to handle any shipment size regardless of weight limitations but also a nationwide or even worldwide network. Since airfreight is bimodal and every carrier cannot offer worldwide service, it is necessary to have effective intramode and interline service. Shippers, however, do not like to deal with multiple parties and this leads to the requirement of single-carrier responsibility. Air carriers do participate in the

Air Cargo, Inc., program and they do have reasonable interline service. However, problems have arisen in at least two areas: the airline operating in the secondary market may not offer freighter service with main-deck lift available, or the airline may be unable to control the quality of service offered by the trucker.

Price

Although some shippers are more sensitive to service than to price, there are just as many who are more concerned with price than service (see figure 9-3). A sampling of thirty-eight U.S. shippers and consignees (with 65 percent of the companies having annual sales of over a billion dollars each), showed that 22 percent of the respondents weighed price and service equally; 41 percent valued service more than price, and 36 percent valued price more than service.[7] The survey included eighty-one commodities.

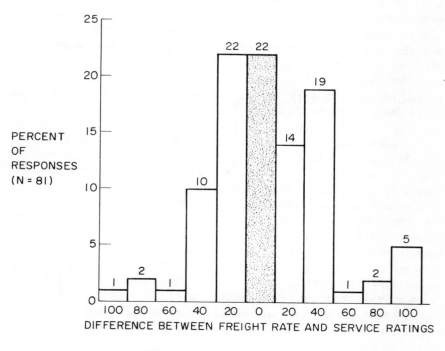

Source: Lockheed-Georgia Company, "Cargo/Logistics Airlift System Study," NASA Contractor Report 158915 (November 1978), 1:2-1.

Figure 9-3. Importance of Freight Rate versus Service

In a few cases daylight airfreight rates are competitive with surface modes, but in general they are substantially higher. For small shipments, truck is the least-cost mode for U.S. domestic operations, while for large shipments rail is the least-cost mode. However, lower surface rates usually imply lower service levels, particularly with respect to transit time and damages. Therefore, while low rates are always important, even more important are total cost to the shipper and the availability of alternative service and price options. A few such options have been offered in the past; for example priority, standard, and deferred types of service, and some combination of air and sea or rail service.

Given that freight is carried both in the belly as well as on freighters, pricing policy is a highly controversial issue in the industry. One combination carrier, for example, may favor implementation of low rates using marginal costs based on the by-product philosophy. Another combination carrier may prefer to base rates on fully allocated costs. Each philosophy will lead to a different policy on rates based on different costs and contribution to profitability. There are pros and cons for each method. From one point of view, by-product philosophy shows freight's real contribution to corporate profitability since the combination flight would operate even without cargo. Moreover, freight would normally be carried on a space-available basis, that is, after the needs of passengers and their baggage have been met. Such a philosophy, however, can lead to resistance on the part of the schedulers to make flight adjustments to meet the needs of the shipping public. While the use of fully allocated costs eliminates this problem, it can create other problems. Now there is a penalty for unused cargo space resulting from, for example, short ground times, frequent departures, aircraft upgrades, and weight-limited flights. Moreover, fully allocated costs can lead, in some cases, to significant accounting losses for some commodities and for some flights. Such a policy would take away the incentive to load freight on certain flights, resulting in a consquent loss of contribution.

Given the pros and cons of the two costing methodologies, some combination carriers are coming to the conclusion that there is a third alternative in which part of the total flight-capacity costs are allocated to freight operations on the basis of the revenue ton-miles used. Under this system, costs will not be assigned to freight if freight is not loaded on a given flight for any reason such as weight restriction or tight turnaround time. If freight is loaded, then the ground handling costs as well as a portion of the flight-capacity costs are allocated to freight. The portion allocated to freight is equal to the product of unit cost per ton-mile and the freight tons actually carried on the flight. The unit cost is obtained by dividing the total flight-capacity cost by the product of capacity (in tons), as if the aircraft were operated as a freighter, and the length of haul (in miles). Such a system would provide an incentive to promote freight operations since freight revenue can only be generated if freight is actually loaded, and the more freight loaded the lower are the costs allocated to passenger operations. Furthermore, this comprised costing methodology can produce rates that are a reasonable reflection of the service provided, and provide service that is warranted by the rate charged. As total costs increase, the question will be whether passenger or cargo has lower price elasticity.

Since there are many aspects of service and price to consider, and many carriers to choose from, how does a shipper make his choice? According to Flying Tiger's market research, a shipper may consider as many as thirty-five aspects of service in choosing a carrier (see table 9-5). Survey information was used to conduct factor analysis on these thirty-five characteristics. The most important factor was identified to be time sensitivity (weight 6.22) and contained, in that order, six benefits listed in table 9-5 (numbers 24, 23, 22, 10, 9, and 25). The second factor was price sensitivity (weight 2.04) and included four benefits (numbers 17, 7, 33, and 8). The third factor was information sensitivity (weight 1.67) and contained eight benefits (numbers 31, 32, 30, 33, 28, 29, 25, and 20). The fourth factor was pick-up sensitivity (weight 1.63) and included three benefits (numbers 34, 15, and 19).

Table 9-5
Service in Carrier Choice: Domestic Airfreight Benefits

1. Reliability	20. Salesman's knowledge
2. On-time performance	21. Container programs
3. Most professional	22. Good delivery service
4. Carrier's customer service	23. Handling of late-in-the-day shipments
5. Computer tracing system	24. Handling of emergencies
6. How often salesman calls	25. Assistance on special problems
7. Total cost considerations	26. Most cities served
8. Daylight rates	27. Frequency of service
9. Prime nighttime departures	28. Ability to trace
10. Door-to-door time	29. Accurate documentation service
11. Advertising	30. Freedom from worry
12. Carrier's knowledge of your problems	31. Keeping the shipper informed
13. Accurate billing	32. Honest and straightforward
14. Insurance and claim service	33. Best informed on new prices and schedules
15. Time between call and pick-up	34. Good pick-up service
16. Security	35. Size of carrier
17. Best price	
18. Size of shipment	
19. Truck driver's attitude	

Source: W. Caldwell, "An Overview of Deregulation Impact on Strategic Cargo Planning." Lecture given at the Air Transportation Planning Seminar at Stanford University. 18-22 August 1980.

From this analysis it is clear that time sensitivity is the most important common denominator.

Air Mode Eligibility Characteristics

Quantitative analyses of airfreight have shown that the market demand is a function of the state of the economy, rates (both air and other modes), and the level of service provided. Qualitative analyses have included many other variables, some of which are shown in figure 9-2. Under marketing, the identification and promotion of new commodities (identified through market research) will undoubtedly have a significant influence on the total demand for airfreight. Market research cannot only identify new air-mode eligible commodities, it can also provide valuable insight into the promotion aspects through identification of critical shipper needs and requirements. The identification of specific commodities most suitable for air transportation can hold the key to the future growth in airfreight.

The value of a commodity has always been considered a prime criterion for determining air eligibility; the higher the value, the greater the probability of shipment by air (see figure 9-4). This is a reasonable observation

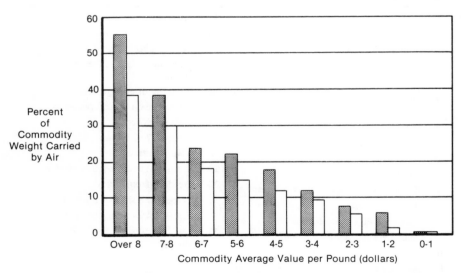

Source: P.B. Gibson, "Air Cargo Market Analysis Using International Trade Data," Presentation at the International Aviation Data Symposium, Transportation Systems Center (Cambridge, Mass.: 3-4 March 1980), p. 13.

▨▨▨▨   U.S. exports to world
☐☐☐☐   U.S. imports from world

Figure 9-4. 1978 Air Market Penetrations by Commodity Value per Pound Range

since not only do high-value commodities benefit more from reduced transit time, but they are more likely to absorb the higher cost of air transportation. However, commodity value is only one of the important factors in determining air eligibility. This hypothesis is reasonable and it can be substantiated by the scatter plot shown in figure 9-5. Although there is a tendency for air penetration to increase with the value of commodity, the extent of the scatter indicates the existence of other characteristics of air eligibility.

Many analysts have compiled a list of factors considered important in determining air eligibility. Boeing's list includes value, density, fragility, market-time sensitivity, and market growth rate.[8] Lockheed has produced a similar list which includes perishability and shipment size and weight.[9] A list compiled by Douglas contains similar variables, including transit environment, product range, and production process.[10] There is no real disagreement on the factors to be included in the list; disagreement arises

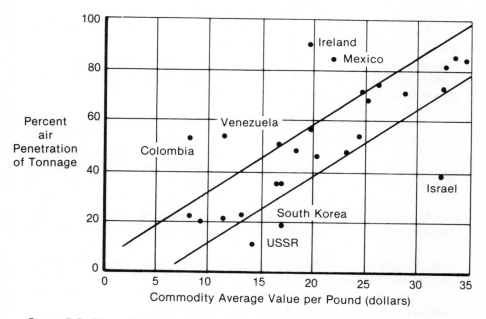

Source: P.B. Gibson, "Air Cargo Market Analysis Using International Travel Data," Presentation at the International Aviation Data Symposium, Transportation Systems Center (Cambridge, Mass.: 3-4 March 1980), p. 16.

• 27 largest air markets

• 86% of U.S. air exports of 874.6 to world

• Each dot represents one country market

Figure 9-5. Air Penetration versus Value per Pound: 1978 U.S. Exports of Measuring and Control Instruments (Schedule E Commodity Code 874.6)

on the methodology that will take into account each of these factors. Lockheed performed a multiple-regression analysis using supplementary information obtained from the Commodity Transportation Survey and the Commodity Attribute File.[11] The investigation did not provide definitive results due partly to the existence of disclosure and suppression problems inherent in the census data. Boeing, in its commodity analysis, assigned a factor score based on the five factors cited previously. Each factor could receive one of three scores: high (20 points), medium (10 points), and low (5 points). The maximum score possible for any commodity was 100 points. The higher the factor score assigned to a commodity, the greater is the probability that the commodity will be shipped by air. The procedure has been tested on historical data and produces plausible results.

Total distribution cost (TDC) analysis is an alternative method of evaluating the economics of airfreight versus surface transportation. Higher rates for air transportation can be justified if the use of air mode can produce sufficient offsetting advantages in physical distribution. The TDC concept takes into account all costs relating to the distribution system, including inventory-related and transportation-related costs. The basic premise is that the use of airfreight can reduce inventory costs sufficiently to pay for the higher transportation costs and still have funds left over for additional profit, possible price reductions, development of new products, or plant expansion. Moreover, it can be argued that the use of airfreight can broaden market horizons (market expansion), increase product-market life, reach premium-price markets fast, and capture impulse buyers at the peak time.

Despite the simplicity of the TDC concept, only a small percentage of the shipping public has made use of it. Yet it is the use of concepts such as this that could divert a substantial number of shippers using surface modes and achieve the often-predicted breakthrough in the airfreight industry. The hesitancy on the part of the shipper is a function of many variables: lack of knowledge of the potential benefits of airfreight; more interest in reducing transportation costs than in broadening the market horizon of the corporation; inability to change corporate policy; lack of qualified personel; lack of information on distribution costs; and lack of credibility in the empirical data.[12] While it is true that not every decision can be analyzed quantitatively (with respect to total distribution cost) in the framework of a shipper's total production system, sufficient research has been conducted to show that reasonable amounts of cost-benefit analysis can be performed at the level required for a decision.

Costs

The CAB undertook a comprehensive analysis of airfreight operations during its *Domestic Air Freight Rate Investigtion* (DAFRI) and produced a multielement rate formula taking into account capacity and noncapacity causative cost factors.[13] This formula, although no longer applicable in the deregulated marketplace, is informative with respect to the importance of various cost elements such as terminal and line-haul, and direct and indirect. The 1976 data showed, for example, that direct operating costs were closer to 40 percent. Another way to disaggregate costs is to separate flight, payload, investment, and management-related elements. Such a breakdown for scheduled operations provided the following information for 1976 data:[14]

Flight-related costs	49 percent
Payload-related costs	33 percent
Investment-related costs	13 percent
Management-related costs	5 percent
Total	100 percent

Given the increased price of fuel, the direct operating costs have increased substantially and will continue to increase in future years. Some industry analysts consider the development of advanced dedicated freighters to be the most viable solution for combating the impact of escalating flight- and payload-related costs. However, given the small projected production run for dedicated freighters, one should not underestimate the influence of aircraft price. An advanced freighter might provide a significant improvement in fuel efficiency relative to the current wide-body aircraft but its direct operating costs are likely to be much higher due to the higher price of the aircraft and related factors such as insurance. Reasonable direct operating costs can therefore be achieved by modifying existing and near-term versions of passenger aircraft such as the B-747, the DC-10, and the B-767. In addition, existing small freighters, such as Lockheed's L-100, can be stretched and made compatible with the larger wide-body aircraft such as the B-747. (Lockheed is currently proposing to stretch the original Hercules by 260 inches: the L-100-260.)

Indirect operating costs are a function of the size, type and degree of automation, degree of containerization, and the nature of ground-handling procedures. Terminal automation can increase productivity up to a point, depending on the type of terminal, the variations in size and type of freight handled, and the degree of containerization. Terminal operations are labor intensive, particularly given the peaking nature of the airfreight business. The real savings relating to terminal operation can be achieved only by providing incentives to shippers to load and unload their own containers and incentives to the smaller carriers to use joint terminals. The use of containers on a large scale does imply the need to improve compatibility not only with respect to containers but also modes and airport infrastructure.

Finally, a reduction in the tare weight of containers can save valuable fuel and provide revenue-generating opportunities.[15]

It is often claimed that the way to increase the air mode's share of total freight movements is to reduce the spread in the tariffs between air and sur-face modes. According to a recent Douglas Aircraft Company study, the cost of airfreight is 82 percent higher than truck (a single forty-foot trailer), 102 percent higher than a seventy-car mixed train, and 149 percent higher than a thirty-five-car through train.[16] The sample shipment weighed 2000 pounds, moved a distance of 1,230 statute miles, and intermodal ad-justments were made for shipment density and route circuity. These dif-ferences in the shipping cost are primarily the result of differences in three cost elements (line-haul, terminal, and pick-up and delivery) among the modes. Compared to other modes, line-haul costs (about 60 percent) are a lower percentage of total costs for the air mode. However, they are 42 percent higher than the truck, 66 percent higher than the seventy-car train, and 126 percent higher than the thirty-five car train. While the air mode benefits from the relative lower labor and maintenance costs, it suffers from the relatively higher capital and fuel costs. In the case of terminal opera-tions, the air-mode costs are 224 percent higher than the truck. Similarly, pick-up and delivery costs are 85 percent higher for air than for the truck mode.

For ocean transport, the Douglas study compared line-haul costs for air (DC-8-63F and B-747-100F) and container ship (1,250 and 2,500 twenty-foot equivalent units) on two routes (New York-United Kingdom and United Kingdom-Japan). Taking into consideration cargo density and route circuity, the cost of shipping 2,000 pounds varied between the modes by a factor of 2.1 to 2.7 for the U.S.-U.K. route and between 3.5 and 3.8 for the U.S.-Japan route. Fuel costs were high for the DC-8 and the 2,500 TEU, whereas capital costs were high for the B-747 and both sizes of container ships.

Competitiveness of the air mode is a function of technology as well as fuel, labor wages, and capital costs. Advanced technology will reduce some elements (such as fuel) and increase other elements (such as depreciation) of the direct operating costs. Increasing load factor, on the other hand, could provide the single most cost-effective improvement in direct operating costs. Although indirect operating costs can be lowered by some amount of automation and a change in handling procedure, the real potential lies in in-creasing the amount of shipper-loaded containers. An improvement in ter-minal costs will in turn make the air mode more competitive with the truck. It must be remembered, however, that cost, while important, is only one consideration. And from the point of view of about half of the shippers, cost is not the prime consideration; service often supercedes cost. The mode choice is therefore a function of rates as well as the total service offered.

Summary

Institutional road blocks have often been given as an excuse for the minute share of total freight market captured by the airlines. If this were true, then the industry has a very bright future (at least within the United States) now that the industry has been deregulated. The key to future development of the airfreight industry lies in the analysis, planning and control of the industry's marketing activities. If the industry wants to seriously expand its operations, beyond the captive emergency shipments, it must improve its marketing activities: establishment and fulfillment of shipper requirements; identification and promotion of air eligible commodities; comprehensive analysis of marketing-mix elements (service, price, distribution, promotion, and education of the shipping public in the use of total distribution cost analysis). The air mode will always be handicapped with total operating costs relative to other modes, given the influence of fuel and capital intensive nature of the industry. Some improvements in direct operating costs (through advanced technology and increased load factor) and indirect operating costs (increase in shipper-loaded containers and cost-effective automation) will increase the competitiveness of the air mode. However, the mode choice will continue to be made on the basis of total service offered and not just price.

Notes

1. Boeing Commercial Airplane Company, "International Traffic Assumptions and Scenario" (Presentation to IATA Traffic Forecasting Group, 29 January 1979).

2. _____ . "Dimensions of Airline Growth" (March 1980), p. 45.

3. W.M. Hoffman, "The Best May Yet Come," in *Corporate Planning Under Deregulation: The Case of the Airlines* (Northwestern University, 11-12 June 1979), p. 40.

4. J.H. Mahoney, "Domestic Airfreighter Operations by Airfreight Forwarders after Deregulation," Lecture given at M.I.T. on 30 October 1980.

5. T.E. Boullioun, "Equipment and Cargo are Not the Problem," Speech given to the Ninth International Forum for Air Cargo, Vancouver, British Columbia, 27 September 1978.

6. N.K. Taneja, *The U.S. Airfreight Industry* (Lexington, Mass.: Lexington Books, D.C. Heath and Company, 1979), p. 104.

7. Lockheed-Georgia Company, "Cargo/Logistics Airlift System Study," NASA Contractor Report 158915, vol. 1, (November 1978):2-17.

8. Boeing Commercial Airplane Company, "Potential Air Commodity Identification: A Suggested Methodology" (Cargo Analysis and Development Unit, March 1977).

9. Lockheed-Georgia Company, "Cargo/Logistics Airlift System Study," NASA Contractor Report 158915, vol. 1 (November 1978):1-60.

10. Douglas Aircraft Company, "Cargo/Logistics Airlift Systems Study (CLASS)," vol. 5 (Summary), NASA Contractor Report NASI-14948 (August 1979), pp. 8-10.

11. R.D. Samuelson, and P.O. Roberts, "A Commodity Attribute Data File for Use in Freight Transportation Studies," MIT-CTS Report Number 75-20, (Cambridge, Mass.: M.I.T., 1975).

12. N.K. Taneja, The U.S. Airfreight Industry, p. 120.

13. Ibid., p. 127

14. Douglas Aircraft Company, "Cargo/Logistics Airlift Systems," p. 60.

15. Douglas Aircraft Company, "World Freight Outlook," Report No. C1-800-6296 (Long Beach, Calif.: September 1980).

16. Douglas Aircraft Company, "Cargo/Logistics Airlift Systems," p. 18.

10 Concluding Comments

These are turbulent years in the airline industry. Not only has the industry been forced to deal with the new and changing regulatory policies, but it has had to cope with increasing levels of consumerism in an economic environment saddled with recession, inflation, and uncontrollable fuel prices. The free-market policies in the airline industry, led by the Carter administration in the United States and, more recently, the Thatcher administration in the United Kingdom, have produced total chaos on major high-density domestic and international routes. The entrance of new carriers has produced price wars at a time of rising costs, a substantial portion of which are outside the control of airline managements. The result is that the industry is experiencing one of the worst financial years in the history of aviation.

The worldwide regulatory changes have followed two different directions. For example, in the United States deregulation has relaxed capacity and price control whereas in other parts of the world capacity and price controls have been expanded. Both types of regulatory changes have allowed the introduction of deep discount fares to capture the price-sensitive market and increase productivity. The United States favors free determination of capacity while the majority of other nations support predetermination (or at least ex post facto review or a Bermuda Two type) of capacity. The United States supports double-disapproval or country-of-origin tariffs while others favor double-approval, third and fourth freedom, or multilaterally coordinated fares. The proponents of each type of policy consider their policy to be optimal for the consumer, airline, and government. The divergent policies are the result of how different nations view the function of their airlines and the roles these airlines play in national economies and political philosophies. The United States believes in competition and preservation of the free-market economy to the extent that it is possible. Other nations favor, in varying degrees, more direct government participation in the industrial sector of their economies.

In the United States the domestic airline industry has been deregulated for only two years and the jury is still out with respect to the net benefit of increased airline competition. On the positive side, the consumer has received a greater variety of discount fares on more carriers and increased service on dense and commuter airline routes. From the airline's point of view, management has received greater freedom in entry, exit, specialization, and pricing decisions. On the negative side, the consumer has experienced a sharp increase in the normal fares, a significant decrease in jet service to small communities, and an overall deterioration in the quality of service offered. Regulation has increased in certain areas, enormous financial losses have been experienced during the first recession since deregulation, and interlining problems have increased significantly.

Those who look only at the positive side, and even then at the short-term benefits exclusively, view deregulation as beneficial and wish the process to be speeded up both in the United States and abroad. Those who look at the negative side consider that the sooner we start the process of establishing enlightened regulation, the better would be the consumer, industry, and government. Melvin Brenner, an experienced airline executive, claims that while it is too late for the industry to return to its original structure, it is not too late for the government to take the necessary steps to "overcome the more glaring weaknesses of deregulation."[1] According to Brenner, the CAB is currently in a position to prove that the theory is not working. The CAB can collect, for example, detailed financial data to examine the profit mix of routes before and after deregulation. Such an analysis, according to Brenner, would show that free entry on more attractive routes has eliminated route cross-subsidization, an activity that is essential for the economic viability of an airline.

The attempt by the United States to deregulate the international airline industry also has had mixed results. Procompetitive agreements have produced lower fares and opened up new gateways for U.S. and foreign-flag carriers, but financial losses have increased, international markets have been fragmented, U.S.-flag share has further eroded, and the pursuit of U.S. international aviation policy has been accompanied by considerable anger from foreign states and consequent feelings of distrust within the worldwide aviation community.

At the global level, U.S. aviation policy has flung the international airline industry into turmoil. Free-for-all competition does have a certain theoretical appeal, creating an environment that could lead to innovation and low fares. However, air-transportation service has many of the characteristics associated with a public utility, and in many countries it is both an integral part of the economy and an instrument of foreign policy. As a result, the national carrier, the national traffic, and the coveted routes need to be protected. Each country sets different national objectives and establishes appropriate policies and plans to achieve these objectives. In the case of international airline operations, not only are national policies and plans coordinated to meet the requirements of other infrastructure elements (such as aircraft, airports, air-traffic-control systems, and tourist facilities), but they also attempt to balance competition, consumer benefit, and the economics of the airline industry.

Consider a developing region versus a developed region. In a developing nation the national-flag carrier often provides a vital and viable mode of communication, earns the critically needed foreign exchange, provides employment, and serves the (extremely limited) originating passenger traffic. In such a case, competition will undoubtedly be harmful. If a U.S. carrier is forced into bankruptcy or a merger, the consequences are not the same as if the flag carrier of a developing country were to go out of business or be forced to join the flag carrier of a neighboring state. Now consider the case of a developed region like Europe. An international airline faces a dilemma in such a market. No one can deny the attractiveness of low fares and high frequencies, but a given carrier serving both intra-European markets as well as providing service to, from, and via Europe, would need to maintain strong and stable feeder traffic through its network and gateway (usually the capital). Therefore, this carrier will need to protect from competition its feeder services to channel transit passengers to and from European points.

While each nation has the right to establish its own domestic and international policies, the acceptance of its international policies depends on other factors. The U.S. international aviation policy, except for about a dozen countries, is simply not acceptable to the rest of the world. Moreover, it is not clearly beneficial to the U.S. international carriers. These carriers, despite their efficiency, are being forced to retrench, given the nature of their foreign-flag competition. The latter are mostly government-owned carriers with access to government subsidy and ability (in some cases government support) to control the market. Such an assumption is clearly plausible given the recent experience of Pan American, TWA, and even more recently, Braniff.

For more than thirty years, the policy of the U.S. government was to trade, to the extent possible, traffic rights of equal benefit. Now the apparent policy is to relinquish traffic rights in exchange for the acceptance, and not necessarily implementation, of an ideology. Consider the impracticality of multiple designation. With the exception of a few major countries such as the United Kingodm, France, Canada, and Mexico, there is generally only one carrier authorized to provide international service. For most of these countries, because of insufficient market density and existing overcapacity, multiple international carriers have only been allowed to operate under different spheres of influence. Only in limited high-density markets and only by a few countries can multiple designation be considered feasible.

Current developments in the industry are leading to the establishment of a two-tier system of international aviation whereby some airlines (such as those from the United States) can operate in an unregulated environment while others (such as those from Africa, Australia, Italy, Japan, and Malaysia) can operate under a regulated environment. The two-tier system could eventually lead to polarization with one group advocating the aggressive policies of the new industrial countries (such as those in Southeast Asia), one group advocating the policies of the Arab world, and other groups for Africa and South America. Such groups will have bargaining power to protect the common interests of their members. For example, the implementation of its new policy by Australia led a group of Asian nations (Indonesia, Malaysia, the Philippines, Singapore, and Thailand) to band together to protest the substantial loss of stop-over traffic between Australia and Europe. Another example is the potential development of a consortium consisting of Alia, Gulf Air, Kuwait Airways, MEA, and Saudi Arabian Airlines to offer transatlantic service to the United States. The establishment of such groups would also improve the economies of the member carriers by pooling their resources and coordinating their activities to raise efficiency and productivity.

Turning to the economic environment, traffic growth during the sixties took place during a period of economic growth and low energy costs. World domestic gross product increased at an annual rate of 5.2 percent between 1960 and 1973. Jet fuel cost a typical U.S. airline a mere 10 cents per gallon between 1959 and 1973, representing a relatively unimportant factor in the operation of aircraft. Between 1973 and 1979, not only did the rate of growth of world gross domestic product decrease to 3.2 percent per year, but the price of fuel increased by an order of magnitude, making fuel consumption a prime operational consideration. The current and future aviation system is therefore being shaped as much by economic changes as by regulatory changes, if not more.

Future forecasts call for a lower rate of growth (lower than the 1960 to 1973 level) for the world gross domestic product and an increase in the price of fuel; the world gross domestic product is expected to increase at 1.8 percent between 1979 and 1980 and at an annual rate of 3.7 percent thereafter through 1990; the price of internationally traded oil (excluding trade within Soviet/Sino blocs, F.O.B. port of export) is expected to increase from $19.20 to $95.00 per barrel between 1979 and 1990.[2] While the airline industry cannot be expected to influence these economic trends, it will need to adapt to the changing trend as efficiently and as quickly as possible. In the United States, for example, airlines are modernizing their fleets, rationalizing their routes, and reducing their labor forces; in some instances actions on these three fronts have necessitated merger proceedings. In addition, some airlines are beginning to realize that they cannot be dependent on low-fare traffic since this traffic is more vulnerable to the downswings in the economy, inflation, and decreases in disposable income. As a result they are reviewing their discount-fare policy carefully to control its use in at least meeting costs.

Understanding and controlling costs, to the extent possible, is only one side of the coin; the other side is understanding and controlling the market, that is, the revenue. As mentioned in chapter 6, this aspect requires a thorough analysis of competition, customer, and environmental trends to assess market threats and opportunities.

Given that the marketplace has changed, the industry must change its mode of operation. However, within the industry, the required change has been perceived as a threat or opportunity, depending on the extent to which a given airline is able to adapt itself to new environment. Within the United States, the industry structure is likely to change drastically; some of the existing airlines will no longer be in business. The survivors will be those who are efficient, marketing-oriented strategic planners. Or, as Richard Ferris of United stated, the key to airline planning in the new environment is to "know your customers, know your competitors, know your costs."[3]

Notes

1. M.A. Brenner, "Is U.S. Deregulation a Failure? Here's How to Find Out," *Airline Executive* vol. 4, no. 9 (September 1980):22-23.

2. Lockheed-California Company, "World Air Traffic Forecast 1980," Report No. FEA/2968 (Burbank, Calif.: September 1980).

3. R.J. Ferris, "Know Your Customers, Know Your Competitors, Know Your Costs," in *Corporate Planning Under Deregulation: The Case of the Airlines* (Evanston, Ill.: Northwestern University, 11-12 June 1979).

Selected Bibliography

Abell, D.F., and Hammond, J.S. *Strategic Market Planning: Problems and Analytical Approaches.* Englewood Cliffs, N.J.: Prentice-Hall, 1979.

Air Transport Association of America. "The Significance of Airline Passenger Load Factors." Washington, D.C.: August 1980.

———. *Airline Capital Requirements in the 1980s: $90 Billion by '90.* Washington, D.C.: September 1979.

Alter, S.L. *Decision Support Systems: Current Practice and Continuing Challenges.* Reading, Mass.: Addison-Wesley, 1980.

Ausrotas, R.A.; Elias, A.; Simpson, R.; and Taneja, N. "The Shape of the Future." Paper delivered at the Honeywell Seminar on *New Directions in Airline Industry Automation.* Phoenix, Arizona: 21 January 1980.

Bakes, P.J., Jr. "As Fast as the Law Allows." In *Corporate Planning Under Deregulation: The Case of the Airlines.* Evanston, Ill.: Northwestern University, 11-12 June 1979.

Beane, J.L. "The Antitrust Implication of Airline Deregulation." *Journal of Air Law and Commerce* vol. 45, no. 4 (Summer 1980):1001-1026.

Boeing Commercial Airplane Company. "Dimensions of Airline Growth." March 1980.

———. "Current Market Outlook," Report no. Y9136. February 1980.

———. "Discount Fares and the Potential for Profit or Loss." Report no. W8868. October 1979.

———. "International Traffic Assumptions and Scenario." Presentation to IATA Traffic Forecasting Group, 29 January 1979.

———. "Potential Air Commodity Identification: A Suggested Methodology." Cargo Analysis and Development Unit, March 1977.

Boullioun, T.E. "Earnings and Quality of Service." In *Corporate Planning Under Deregulation: The Case of the Airlines.* Evanston, Ill.: Northwestern University, 11-12 June 1979.

———. "Equipment and Cargo are Not the Problem." Speech given to the Ninth International Forum for Air Cargo. Vancouver, British Columbia, 27 September 1978.

Brenner, M.A. "Is U.S. Deregulation a Failure? Here's How to Find Out." *Airline Executive* vol. 4, no. 9 (September 1980):22-23.

———. "Some Observations on the First Half Year of Passenger Deregulation," MIT-FTL Report no. R79-7. July 1979.

British Airways. "Appendices to Comments on British Airways in Response to Order 77-7-4." *North Atlantic Fares Investigation* (Docket 27918). 19 October 1977.

Brooks, M. "Clubs are Trumps." *Understanding More About the Passenger*. Air Transport Research Symposium organized by the IATA Industry Research Division and held in Dublin, 25-26 May 1978.

Callison, J.W. "Airline Deregulation—Only Partially a Hoax: The Current Status of the Airline Deregulation Movement." *Journal of Air Law and Commerce* vol. 45, no. 4 (Summer 1980):961-1001.

Carlton, D.W.; Landes, W.M.; and Posner, R.A. "Benefits and Costs of Airline Mergers: A Case Study." *The Bell Journal of Economics* vol. 11, no. 1 (Spring 1980):65-83.

Dhalla, N.K. "Assessing the Long-Term Value of Advertising." *Harvard Business Review* (January-February 1978):87-95.

Douglas Aircraft Company "World Freight Outlook." Report no. C1-800-6296. Long Beach, Calif.: September 1980.

―――. "Changing Patterns in European Vacation Travel," Report no. C1-804-6153. Long Beach, Calif.: June 1980.

―――. "Total Maintenance Cost Comparisons: DC-9-30/50, B727-200, B737-200," Report no. MDC 79-019. May 1980.

―――. "Total Maintenance Cost Comparisons: DC-10, B747, L1011," Report no. MDC 79-005. Long Beach, Calif.: 1980.

―――. "Cargo/Logistics Airlift Systems Study (CLASS)." vol. 5 (Summary). NASA Contractor Report NAS1-14948. August 1979.

Elias, A.L. "The Development of an Operational Game for the U.S. Domestic Airline Industry." M.I.T. FTL Report R78-5. February 1979.

Ferris, R.J. "Know Your Customers, Know Your Competitors, Know Your Costs." In *Corporate Planning Under Deregulation: The Case of the Airlines*. Evanston, Ill.: Northwestern University, 11-12 June 1979.

Flight Transportation Associates, Inc. "Competitive Airline Strategy Simulation: A Decision Support System for Airline Planning." Cambridge, Mass.: July 1980.

Friedman, J.J. *A New Air Transport Policy for the North Atlantic: Saving an Endangered System*. New York: Atheneum, 1976.

Garrett, W. "Management Confidence in Action-Oriented Research." In *Understanding More About the Passenger*. Air Transport Research Symposium organized by the IATA Industry Research Division and held in Dublin, 25-26 May 1978.

Gellman Research Associates. "Selected Factors Affecting the U.S. Flag Carriers' Share of the International Market." Report produced for the Air Transport Association, August 1980.

Gibson, P.B. "Air Cargo Market Analysis Using International Trade Data." Presentation at the International Aviation Data Symposium, Transportation Systems Center, Cambridge, Mass.: 3-4 March 1980.

Gidwitz, B. *The Politics of International Air Transport*. Lexington, Mass.: Lexington Books, D.C. Heath and Co., 1980.

Greenslet, E.S. "The Airline Profit Equation Revisited." *Aviation Log* vol. 2, no. 20 (17 December 1979).

Gritta, R.D. "The Significance of the Operating Ratio in Air Transportation." Proceedings of the Tenth Annual Meeting of the *Transportation Research Forum*. vol. 20, no. 1 (29-31 October 1979):177-179.

Grove, M.I. "The Growing Age of Specialization in Air Transportation." SAE Paper no. 800754. 20-22 May 1980.

Hoffman, W.M. "The Best May Yet Come." In *Corporate Planning Under Deregulation: The Case of the Airlines*. Evanston, Ill.: Northwestern University, 11-12 June 1979.

Hughes, G.D. *Marketing Management: A Planning Approach*. Reading, Mass.: Addison-Wesley, 1978.

International Air Transport Association. "The State of the Air Transport Industry: Annual Report." Montreal, 27-30 October 1980.

———. "Statement of Position of the International Air Transport Association." *Standard Foreign Fare Level Investigation* (Docket 37730). 30 May 1980.

———. "Mechanisms for Establishment of Scheduled Passenger Fares: The Currency Situation." Working Paper WP-21 presented at the ICAO's Second Air Transport Conference, Montreal, 14 February 1980.

———. "World Air Transport: 60th Anniversary 1919-1979." December 1979.

———. "The North Atlantic Air Travel Experiment. A Review of the 1979 Summer Season." Air Transport Research Symposium. London, 16 November 1979.

———. *Review* vol. 14, no. 3 (July-August 1979).

———. "The Airline Product in the 1980s—New Concepts of Service." Air Transport Research Symposium, Malta, 30 November-1 December 1978.

———. "Understanding More About the Passenger." Air Transport Research Symposium, Dublin, 25-26 May 1978.

International Civil Aviation Organization. "Tariff Enforcement." Circular 135-AT/41. September 1977.

———. "Policy Concerning International Non-Scheduled Air Transport. Circular 136AT/42. September 1977.

———. "Regulation of Capacity in International Air Transport Services." Circular 137-AT/42. September 1977.

———. *Bulletin*. July 1977.

_____ . "Panel of Experts on the Machinery for the Establishment of International Fares and Rates." Report of the First Meeting, 6-17 December 1976.

Institute of Air Transport. "Medium-Term Forecasts for Traffic at the Paris Airports." Bulletin no. 12 (Paris: 24 March 1980).

Karamoko, M. "International Nonscheduled Passenger Air Transport: Origins, Characteristics, Development, Issues." Master's thesis, M.I.T., June 1979.

Kotler, P. *Marketing Management: Analysis, Planning, and Control.* 4th ed. Englewood Cliffs, N.J.: Prentice-Hall, 1980.

Lauriac, J. "Air Transport Policies Regarding Public and Private Airlines." Report no. 2. Institut du Transport Aerien, 1979.

Lockheed-California Company. "World Air Traffic Forecast 1980." Report no. FEA/2968. Burbank, California, September 1980.

_____ . "Gateway Fragmentation Analysis: The Transatlantic Market." Report no. EATF 2975. September 1980.

Lockheed-Georgia Company. "Cargo/Logistics Airlift System Study." NASA Conractor Report 158915. November 1978.

Lorange, P., and Vancil, F.R. *Strategic Planning Systems.* Englewood Cliffs, N.J.: Prentice-Hall, 1977.

Magary, A.B. "What can Travel Research Do?" *Understanding More About the Passenger.* Air Transport Research Symposium organized by the IATA Industry Research Division and held in Dublin, 25-26, May 1978.

Mahoney, J.H. "Domestic Airfreighter Operations by Airfreight Forwarders after Deregulation." Lecture given at M.I.T. on 30 October 1980.

Mandell, R.W. *Financing the Capital Requirements of the U.S. Airline Industry in the 1980s.* Lexington, Mass.: Lexington Books, D.C. Heath and Co., 1979.

Mathaisel, D.F.X. "Air Transport Fleet Planning: Network Aggregation and Cell Theory." Ph.D. thesis, M.I.T., December 1980.

Maurer, R.S. "Deregulation—The Sword of Damocles or the Golden Fleece." Presentation made at the annual meeting of the Travel Research Association in Savannha, Georgia, 17 June 1980.

Meehan, J.C. *Observations on the Impact of Deregulation.* Report no. FEA/2946. Lockheed-California Company, August 1980.

Merrill Lynch, Pierce, Fenner and Smith, Inc. *Aviation Log* vol. 3, no. 15, (22 October 1980).

_____ . "U.S. Trunk Airlines: Converting Dollars Into Seats." Institution Report. Washington, D.C., August 1979.

Morrell, R.S., and Taneja, N.K. "Airline Productivity Redefined: An Analysis of U.S. and European Carriers." *Transportation* 8 (1979): 37-49.

Murphy, J.S. "How Airlines Advertise in 28 Magazines." *Airline Executive* vol. 4, no. 6 (June 1980).

Narodick, K.G. "The Travel Market of the 80s: How Will We Respond?" *A Decade of Achievement*. Proceedings of the Tenth Annual Conference of the Travel Research Association, University of Utah, October 1979.

O'Connor, W.E. *An Introduction to Airline Economics*. New York: Praeger Publishers, 1978.

Orient Airlines Association. "Statistical and Research Report." 1980.

Plaignand, J. et al. *Third Level Activities and Their Regulation*. Institut du Transport Aerien, Paris, 1979.

Pollack, M. "Some Elements of the Airline Fleet Planning Problem." *Transportation Research* 11 (1977):301-310.

Reschenthaler, G.B., and Roberts, B., eds. *Perspectives on Canadian Airline Regulation*. Montreal, Canada: Institute for Research on Public Policy, 1979.

Samuelson, R.D., and Roberts, P.O. "A Commodity Attribute Data File for Use in Freight Transportation Studies." MIT-CTS Report no. 75-20. Cambridge, Mass., 1975.

Shields Model Roland. "The Airline Industry—An Analysis of Asset and Investment Management 1959 to 1990." New York, 4 May 1977.

Simpson, R.W. *Scheduling and Routing Models for Airline Systems*, M.I.T. FTL Report R68-3. December 1969.

Speyer, J.J.W. "Planning Processes in U.S. Airlines." Master's thesis, M.I.T., September 1978.

Steiner, J.E. "Commercial Transport Aircraft Trends: Present and Future." Lecture given at M.I.T. on 10 October 1980.

Taneja, N.K. *U.S. International Aviation Policy*. Lexington, Mass.: Lexington Books, D.C. Heath and Co., 1980.

———— . *The U.S. Airfreight Industry*. Lexington, Mass.: Lexington Books, D.C. Heath and Co., 1979.

———— . *Airline Traffic Forecasting*. Lexington, Mass.: Lexington Books, D.C. Heath and Co., 1978.

———— . *The Commercial Airline Industry: Managerial Practices and Regulatory Policies*. Lexington, Mass.: Lexington Books, D.C. Heath and Co., 1976.

U.S. Civil Aeronautics Board. *Standard Foreign Fare Level Investigation*. Dockets 37730 and 37744. 12 August 1980.

———— . Testimony of Chairman Cohen before the Aviation Subcommittee of Committee on Commerce, Science, and Transportation on Fare Flexibility Regulation, May 20, 1980.

———— . "Part 399—Statement of General Policy." PSDR-66 (Docket 37982) Notice of Proposed Rulemaking. 3 April 1980.

———— . "Investigation into the Competitive Marketing of Air Transportation." Order no. 79-9-64 (Docket 36595). 13 September 1979.

_____ . "Part 399—Statements of General Policy." Regulation PS-80 (Dockets 31290 and 30891). 25 August 1978.

_____ . *Oakland Service Case*. Order 78-9-96. 1978.

Van Horne, J.S. *Financial Management and Policy*, 4th ed. Englewood Cliffs, N.J.: Prentice-Hall, 1977.

Walles, J.A. "Serving the Business Traveller." *The Airline Product in the 1980s—New Concepts of Service*. Air Transport Research Symposium organized by the IATA Industry Research Division and held in Malta, 30 November-1 December 1978.

Index

About the Author

Nawal K. Taneja is a lecturer in the Flight Transportation Laboratory of the Department of Aeronautics and Astronautics at the Massachusetts Institute of Technology. He is also president of Flight Transportation Associates, Inc., a research organization that provides consulting services to the aviation community. Prior to this he was a senior economic analyst with Trans World Airlines in New York City. At M.I.T. Dr. Taneja teaches and conducts research on airline analysis and planning. He is the author of four other books published by Lexington Books: *The Commercial Airline Industry: Managerial Practices and Regulatory Policies; Airline Traffic Forecasting: A Regression Analysis Approach; The U.S. Airfreight Industry*; and *U.S. International Aviation Policy*. Dr. Taneja has served as a consultant to major industrial and government organizations in the United States and abroad on subjects related to air-transportation planning.